Praise for *The Brand Bubble*

"The 21st century business will see two types of winners: the low-price/low-cost products and services, and strong brands. Today, margins, profits, and equities are driven by powerful brands. The grave danger is that brands are losing their way. *The Brand Bubble* explains the greatest risk to world business and how to avoid it. If you are in the brand business, only the intuitive geniuses should get dispensation from reading this brilliant, analytical, data-rich guide to sustained profitable growth in what will continue to be an extraordinarily competitive and challenging environment."

—**Peter Georgescu,** chairman emeritus, Young & Rubicam, and
   author, *The Source of Success*

"With a subject written about ad nauseam by both practitioners and academics, in *The Brand Bubble* John Gerzema and Ed Lebar have identified a significant trend that leaves most of the other theories in the dust. Building off the fifteen-year investment Young & Rubicam has made into the proprietary Brand Asset Valuator, John and Ed have captured the concept of *energized differentiation* in an easily understood and recognizable fashion. They have reinforced that although brands are 'owned' by the consumer, the financial rewards to the manufacturer or service provider are significantly greater when their brands are continually energized through creativity, innovation, and well-paced change. The book provides a well-thought-out approach to keeping brands vibrant and relevant in today's highly competitive environment."

—**Jim Murphy,** chairman and CEO, Murphy & Co., and retired
chief marketing and communications officer, Accenture

"After reading this book, you'll never think of brands the same way again. It will open your eyes to a new way of thinking and executing."
—**Dermot Boden,** chief marketing officer, LG

"This book is a must for anyone interested in the strategy and value of brands—a riveting read with serious implications for investors, corporate strategists, and brand managers. The intersection of brand strategy and shareholder value has been underserved by the literature, but these authors serve up something that is timely, big, and useful, with new thinking based on their research and real-world experience."
—**Justin Pettit,** partner, Booz & Company

"This book is a must-read for anyone who manages brands or invests in companies that manage brands. Through a brilliant analysis that charts shareholder value to brand value, Gerzema and Lebar identify a brand bubble that puts most companies at significant downside risk, and they then chart a path that the more savvy companies could follow to find their way through to the other side when the bubble almost inevitably bursts."
—**Mark Penn,** worldwide president and CEO, Burson-Marsteller, and president, Penn, Schoen & Berland

"This is a business book that happens to be about brands. Any manager in any line of business must learn how to protect and nurture their most cherished asset. Brands are under attack, and boardrooms need to pay attention."
—**John Rose,** senior vice president and managing director, the Boston Consulting Group

"Gerzema and Lebar propose a startling idea—that the value of a brand lies not in the stability and consistency of its promise, but in its constancy of motion. The implications are profound, and will keep even the most seasoned brand managers up late at night."
—**Chris Trimble,** coauthor, *Ten Rules for Strategic Innovators*

"This book is an indispensable tool for brand stewards who compete in today's dynamic, global, and digital marketplace, where the paths that lead to brand performance are ever more complex."

—**Chris Shimojima,** vice president, global digital commerce, Nike, Inc.

"*The Brand Bubble* will help companies navigate the complexity of driving consumer delight in an ever more complex and crowded world where media and messages can blur into a collage of confusion. Their insights provide a stimulating guide to building brand value through sound analysis and execution."

—**Michael Tatelman,** vice president and general manager, sales and marketing, Dell Consumer

"John Gerzema and Ed Lebar offer very creative and innovative insights about how to establish consistency between the financial market performance measure of a brand and the measure of the customers' esteem toward a brand, thus avoiding the fallout of a brand bubble. Empirical evidence provided for their concerns about current brand management and for their prescribed remedies is indeed impressive and well founded. It is an excellent book for brand managers to read and refer to for a successful brand management career."

—**C.W. Park,** professor of marketing, USC Marshall School of Business

"This book has been meticulously researched to provide a comprehensive yet accessible understanding into how great brands are built today to sustain competitive advantage and generate asset value."

—**Cammie Dunaway,** executive vice president, sales and marketing, Nintendo

"John Gerzema and Ed Lebar lay out a very dynamic way to think about brands and shareholder value. We are convinced that the Brand Asset Valuator is a valuable tool to assess the financial impact of your brand and the power of its marketing."

—**Joseph Plummer,** chief research officer, Advertising Research Foundation

"The Brand Bubble raises thought-provoking challenges and paradoxes. Can a company meet its demise through misguided efforts at brand building? Providing a compelling argument that long-term financial success is closely linked to what consumers truly perceive about your brand, the authors offer valuable insights on how to refocus brand building on fulfilling your brand promise to consumers."

—**Anne-Flore Goldsberry,** vice president of worldwide marketing, Logitech

THE BRAND BUBBLE

The Looming Crisis in Brand Value and How to Avoid It

John Gerzema

Ed Lebar

Foreword by Peter Stringham, CEO
Young & Rubicam Group

JOSSEY-BASS
A Wiley Imprint
www.josseybass.com

Published by Jossey-Bass
A Wiley Imprint
989 Market Street, San Francisco, CA 94103-1741—www.josseybass.com

Jossey-Bass books and products are available through most bookstores. To contact Jossey-Bass directly call our Customer Care Department within the U.S. at 800-956-7739, outside the U.S. at 317-572-3986, or fax 317-572-4002.

Jossey-Bass also publishes its books in a variety of electronic formats. Some content that appears in print may not be available in electronic books.

Library of Congress Cataloging-in-Publication Data

Gerzema, John.
    The brand bubble : the looming crisis in brand value and how to avoid it / John Gerzema, Ed Lebar ; foreword by Peter Stringham.
        p. cm.
    Includes bibliographical references and index.
    ISBN 978-0-470-18387-8 (cloth)
  1. Brand name products—Valuation. 2. Branding (Marketing) 3. Brand name products—Case studies. I. Lebar, Ed. II. Title.
    HD69.B7G43 2008
    658.8'27—dc22   2008027384

Printed in the United States of America
FIRST EDITION
HB Printing 10 9 8 7 6 5 4 3 2 1

CONTENTS

FOREWORD

This book has an important message—not just for marketers, but also for CEOs, financial analysts, and anyone who invests in consumer-facing companies. Every professional today must be acutely aware of the creative and management efforts required to launch a brand and sustain its profitability in the marketplace. We live and die on the strategic decisions that we must invent each day to ensure that our products capture not only dollars but also imaginations.

That's why the theories in this book are so critical. The message of *The Brand Bubble* will no doubt be as much of a shock to you as it was to me: that many, many brands are in serious trouble. I have no doubt that this bubble is already occurring, and it will probably continue. I applaud John and Ed for bringing this story out and making sense of it all. Their analysis of the problems devaluing brands today and their recommendations for possible solutions are insightful and worthy of attention.

Those who read this book will need to interpret its thesis in terms of the metrics they use to assess their own brand's performance. The same is true for the management and marketing recommendations presented in the second half of the book. No one knows for certain how to transform a brand caught in the brand bubble. While this book gives you some remedies, we are entering a whole new area of marketing thought. Discovering what solutions are right for you will require some testing and learning. Frankly, we do not have all the answers, but what we do have is the ability to assess how much individual brands are affected by this worrisome trend.

If there is one thing I can confirm, it is that this book is based on evidence from an amazingly accurate research tool that Y&R has maintained for more than fifteen years, BrandAsset® Valuator, (BAV). I can attest to the BAV's accuracy from personal experience as an agency executive and as a CMO.

I first learned of BAV in 1997 when Peter Georgescu and Alex Kroll, the original champions of BAV recruited me for a position at Y&R. I was, first of all, very impressed that an agency would invest tens of millions of its own dollars researching brands and consumer attitudes. But then I was even more impressed by the fact that it was the only analysis of how brands are built that had been tested against the financial metrics that create enterprise value. In the end, the BAV was one of the factors that led me to accept a job with Y&R as CEO of its North American operations.

Then, in 2001, I left to join HSBC in London as CMO, responsible for global marketing and brand development. Prior to my arrival, HSBC had been struggling to create a unified brand message in the minds of the millions of customers the company had picked up through dozens of acquisitions. Having originated as the Hong Kong and Shanghai Banking Corporation, HSBC was by this time the world's second-largest bank, composed of individual banks in dozens of countries around the world, all rebranded with the HSBC livery. To understand what the brand needed, I contacted one of my old colleagues at Y&R and asked him for the BAV profile on the banking industry.

The data and insights in that profile revealed what had to be done to make a world-class brand for HSBC. With the BAV data setting the guideposts, coupled with qualitative research that gave insight into what I call the DNA of HSBC, we created the positioning of "The world's local bank." The results were remarkable. In five years, HSBC went from a brand value of $100 million to $11 billion!

When I returned to Y&R in 2007 as its worldwide CEO, I discovered that in my absence, the company had discovered something new in the BAV data—the rumblings of the brand bubble described in this book. It proved to me that BAV is a living, evolving study. It constantly throws out new ways of looking at brands. It is a marvelous sieve that dredges up some amazing nuggets, if you have the right people to assay them and the determination to apply their advice. John and Ed lay out some very intriguing and challenging dilemmas in this book, which should occupy us all for some time. I hope you enjoy the challenge!

New York City   PETER STRINGHAM
July 2008   CEO, Young & Rubicam Group

THE BRAND BUBBLE

PART ONE

INTRODUCTION

Today, a dilemma faces marketing and the larger enterprise. The tried-and-true formulas to create sales and market share behind brands are becoming irrelevant and losing traction with consumers. We know this through extensive research we've been conducting through our BrandAsset® Valuator (BAV), an empirical model that, based on global consumer research, is designed to explain how brands grow, decline, and recover.

Between 1993 and today, BAV has grown into one of the most respected brand models based on its construction of the largest brand and financial databases in the world. In speaking at the Leaders in Dubai Business Forum in November 2007, professor Philip Kotler said, "There are few effective ways to measure the value of a brand, but one of the best is Y&R's Brand Asset Valuator." We've watched brands achieve popularity, blaze like comets, and come crashing to earth. We've seen brands build slowly from humble beginnings, and we've seen others that weakened, only to be resurrected. We've marveled as still others have changed the way consumers see in the world in which they live.

In the summer of 2004, we discovered several curious trends that took us by surprise. Our research clearly established that consumer attitudes about all sizes and segments of brands were severely declining. Across the board, we saw significant drops in consumer top-of-mind awareness, trust, regard, and admiration for not a few but thousands of brands. We found that most brands were not adding to intangible value of their enterprises. Instead, the majority of brands were stalled in the consumer marketplace, like cars on a Friday afternoon on the 405.

At the same time, however, brands were creating more and more value for their companies and shareholders. Our econometric models demonstrated this value creation was evident in increased share prices and significant bursts in intangible value. Because bullish investors believed that brands were growing, they expected future revenue growth and an increase in share prices, driving their value even higher. Why?

When all the facts were put together, we discovered that yes, there is an increasing expansion of intangible value, but this value is actually the by-product of *fewer and fewer brands*. The number of high-performance, value-creating brands is diminishing across the board. Sure you can say Google, Apple, and Nike and think all brands are financial juggernauts. But the reality is that while brand valuations on the whole keep appreciating, brand perceptions and actual value creation are crumbling.

This is a recipe for ruin.

This book lays out credible evidence that points to a developing problem that, if not corrected, could drive down valuation multiples and stock prices around the world. We've concluded from a detailed analysis of a decade's worth of brand and financial data that business is riding on yet another bubble: a *brand bubble*.

Why is this happening?

It's clear to us that the traditional business models and strategies marketers have used for generations no longer work. Their failure is not simply the result of living in a world of high technology, it stems from the birth of a fundamentally different consumer. Consumer behavior has changed so rapidly and so profoundly it requires an entirely new vision of brand management. While most managers still see metrics like trust and awareness as the backbone of how brands are built, our analysis shows they're dead wrong— these metrics do not add to increased asset value. In fact, the effort to follow them leads marketers astray, actually hastening the declining value of their brands.

The good news, however, is that our research also helped us identify the way to jump-start the power of branding again. Through our studies, we began noticing a new dimension coalescing around a few brands that were successfully performing. In BAV, we observed consumers being captivated by a certain property in successful brands—a quality that reflected a more exciting, dynamic, and creative experience. In essence, they're concentrating their passion, devotion, and purchasing power on an increasingly smaller portfolio of special brands—brands that keep exciting and evolving.

We now know the brands that are thriving already—and will succeed in the future—have an insatiable appetite for creativity and a questing spirit for change. What they have is a more powerful form of differentiation, one that is constantly evolving and leading consumers forward. It's something we call *Energized Differentiation*. Brands with this quality become irresistible to consumers by offering a palpable sense of movement and direction. We're now able to demonstrate the economic value of *irresistible brands* and explain how they break out to impact the future financial performance of their firms.

The implications are far-reaching: We're at the dawn of a new age in brand management and marketing. Both must undergo a great transformation in business today. Only in learning new rules of brand management will enterprises broaden the impact of their innovation and more closely align their brand and marketing efforts to desired outcomes in their overall business strategy.

We wrote this book to be valuable and practical for anyone involved in managing a company or a brand, or working in any capacity in product management, marketing, and sales. We are speaking to a wide assortment of people, from CEOs and chief marketing officers to brand managers to entrepreneurs and small company owners who may be launching brands of their own.

The literature on branding is extensive, but we promise you will find in this book significant new thinking to inspire your brand and, we hope, shift the foundation of your business and marketing models. Our analysis and recommendations pertain to companies of all sizes and degrees of reach. You can be a local grocer or a global conglomerate, it doesn't matter; if you have a brand, this book's for you. Cheers.

The Brand Bubble provides both analysis and prescription. The first half explains the research we performed at Y&R that caused us to recognize the existence of the brand bubble and to identify the attributes of energy infusing irresistibility into today's leading brands. We analyze the new consumer behaviors, expectations, and mind-set we call *ConsumerLand,* which demands that brands embrace speed, openness, and a commitment to constant change.

In the second half of the book, we guide you in detail through a five-stage model to show you how to develop an irresistible brand as well as how to completely alter your organization to become consumer-centric and embrace the brand as an organizing principle. These are the keys to ensure sustainable, profitable performance.

As you think about your brand management going through these stages, we offer a free invitation to assess your brand using our research. We have thousands of brands on hand, and chances are we have yours. Please visit www.thebrandbubble.com, where you can gather deeper, more comprehensive online data about your brand, along with reading additional information and updates to this book.

Our goal is to inspire you to find the energy in your brand and make it irresistible through new brand management rules that are in synch with today's world. Not only do we believe that you will find bigger profit and greater success following our principles, we also think that irresistible brands can help change the world to make life easier, more creative, and happier for people everywhere on this planet.

CHAPTER ONE

TULIPMANIA AND INFLATED BRANDS

*Men, it has been well said, think in herds; it will
be seen that they go mad in herds, while they only
recover their senses slowly, and one by one!*
— CHARLES MACKAY

In 1841, Charles Mackay wrote his famous book *Extraordinary Popular Delusions and the Madness of Crowds* to describe various marketing phenomena. Of special note was his passage on "Tulipmania," an occurrence that took place in Holland in the early decades of the 1600s. The madness began when tulip bulbs imported from Turkey were found to grow extremely well in Dutch soil. The Dutch aristocracy acquired an immense taste for their beauty, and seeing how much could be made from tulips, thousands of average citizens sold their assets and began buying the bulbs. People from all economic classes began trading in tulip bulbs at exorbitant prices. Speculators even took out futures contracts on unplanted bulbs, convinced that some varieties were slated to become the most expensive objects in the world. But at the height of the hysteria, which financial records trace to a few months between 1636 and 1637, the craze for tulips suddenly withered, leaving thousands of Holland's most successful businessmen holding worthless contracts while the less affluent who had invested in the flower lost entire life savings over a bunch of dried bulbs.

Tulipmania might have been no more than a footnote in Dutch history were it not such a clear example of something that has happened time and time again around the globe over the last several centuries. As recently as the past decade, modern business analysts using econometric models and computer algorithms acted as blind to irrational investing as their counterparts in seventeenth-century Holland. Financial busts stemming from the dot-coms, Internet equipment manufacturers, and subprime mortgages are but a few examples of recent market tumbles after which investors, like the Dutch and their shriveled bulbs, were left with inordinate losses. The bubbles of 1929, 2000, and most recently, Northern Rock, Countrywide, and the litany of credit-crunch-inducing banks, hedge funds, pension funds, and public trusts all over the world—continually prove that even the most intelligent analysts and savvy consumers can be every bit as susceptible to self-deception as giddy flower speculators in clogs.

A bubble is a curious thing. In hindsight, it seems so obvious and predictable, while anyone caught up in the middle of one is blind to its potential for disaster. In all bubbles, one constant always predicates a collapse. That is the optimistic assumption that someone else will always be willing to buy what you are selling, regardless of how irrationally high the price is relative to the bare facts of the product's underlying value.

THE IMPENDING BRAND BUBBLE

Now, another bubble is hiding in our economy. This bubble represents $4 trillion in S&P market capitalization alone. It's twice the size of the subprime mortgage market. And it accounts for over one-third of all shareholder value. Credible evidence suggests that *financial markets think brands are worth more than the consumers who buy them.* The constantly rising valuation of major brands is creating a brand bubble, one that could erase large portions of intangible value in firms and send a shockwave through the global economy.

Figure 1.1 illustrates the typical value exchange between brands and consumers. In essence, the multiples that markets place on brand value overstate actual consumer sentiment, so the

FIGURE 1.1. THE NATURE OF THE BRAND BUBBLE.

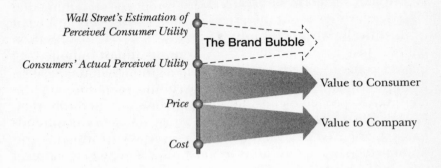

value creation that brands bring is greatly exaggerated. That is, Wall Street is long on brands; consumers are short on brands.

Fissures are forming in the pillars of brand equity. This conclusion is based on our research of fifteen years of brand and financial data from Y&R's BrandAsset Valuator (BAV), the world's largest study of consumer attitudes and perceptions on brands. Working with professors from several leading business schools, we've identified a growing divergence between brand valuation and brand speculation. Our data indicates that investors are irrationally overvaluing brands, and that if leading companies don't take steps to change their approach, more than a few of them might soon experience dramatic declines in market value.

Of course, this is not to suggest that some stellar brands are not genuinely outperforming the market and setting new standards in customer loyalty and financial performance. But in most cases, these are precisely the brands that serve as examples of what other companies must do to inject value back into their own brands. These are the brands consumers swoon over, tell their friends about, and buy time and time again. These are the brands that drive a company's stock beyond the estimates of financial experts. These are the brands that create surprise earnings quarter after quarter.

The problem is these stellar brands are becoming fewer in number. In today's changing consumer climate, exceptional brands are just that—exceptions. Most of the brands lining our supermarket shelves, hanging from department store racks, or touting their superiority on television are experiencing a rapid diminution of perceived value. Consumers are simply falling out of love with a majority of brands they buy.

This warning about the prices of assets such as brands being in decline is, without doubt, contrary to what most people believe. Just as with equities and property in past bubbles, the market values of brands have been consistently rising for decades. Even in today's recessionary climate, brand valuations reports continue to proclaim consistently rising brand values each year. How then is a brand value collapse possible? Thousands of brands have experienced large and long-term successes driving their corporate stock in a continuous upward pattern, enriching executives and investors alike. What exactly is the nature of this bubble? Are we talking about a simple market correction that will be forgotten in a few months or a year? And, if that is so, then why bother with it?

In reality, this is not a simple market correction. Our research foretells a significant loss of value for many brands that will jolt business and investors alike. Markets, being about expectations, have pushed brand values to unsustainable levels, where the earnings potential imputed to thousands of brands far outstrips their value to the consumer. These expected future cash flows that brands are expected to account for have grown to become a dominant force in driving total business value. But their future value is unsustainable when we uncover and analyze the true state of most brands today.

As CEOs search for future pathways to growth, their brands now account for a growing proportion of total enterprise value. This means their brands are making bigger promises of future earnings. Are those earnings going to be there in the future? Have most companies properly discounted the risk on their rising brand values?

When future earnings are in question, it's more than a brand problem; it's *a business problem*. Most of the discussion surrounding the tectonic shifts in the digital, consumer, and media landscape has been held at the marketing and brand level. By examining these phenomena through the lens of brand value, we can see how new consumer behaviors are causing widespread perceptual damage to the values of all but a handful of brands. Let's begin by examining the origins of the brand bubble. . . .

MEASURING THE WORTH OF AN ENTERPRISE IN INTANGIBLE VALUE

Every bubble presents an appearance of value that is eventually contradicted by reality. In the case of the brand bubble, it begins with the value business places on intangibles. Today, they are a significant driver of overall enterprise and market value of a firm, contributing far more than the value of sales and profits. It's an inexact science to pinpoint how much, because traditional accounting practices still don't have a precise method to estimate the contribution intangibles make to enterprise value. However, most accounting models recognize that brand names, logos, and other intellectual property are part of a company's overall intangible worth. The investor community has long acknowledged the market value of a company includes not just invested capital and tangible hard assets but also intangible soft assets.

Intangibles include the estimated value of effects like brands, market position, operational advantages, proprietary processes, franchise agreements, customer lists, patents, copyrights, and company reputation. Intangibles have no physical presence, but they are nonetheless powerful elements on the balance sheet. In this sense, "brand value" is one of four major elements of intangible value (Figure 1.2).

In the last five decades, the intangible value of firms has formed a larger and larger proportion of overall enterprise value. (Intangible value is estimated as the difference between enterprise

FIGURE 1.2. WHAT ARE INTANGIBLE ASSETS?

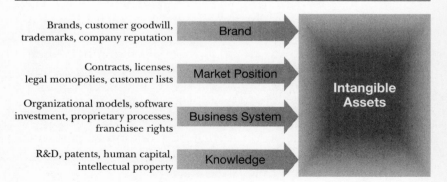

Brands, customer goodwill, trademarks, company reputation → Brand

Contracts, licenses, legal monopolies, customer lists → Market Position

Organizational models, software investment, proprietary processes, franchisee rights → Business System

R&D, patents, human capital, intellectual property → Knowledge

Intangible Assets

value and book value, the formula being "debt + market capitalization − book value = intangible value.") As we move further
into an ideas-driven economy, the measure of a firm's worth
revolves more and more around its inventiveness and intellectual
capabilities, and less around its hard assets.

In 2006, *Fortune* magazine conducted a survey indicating that
72 percent of the Dow Jones Market Cap is now intangible. Accenture estimated that intangibles accounted for almost 70 percent of
the value of the S&P 500 in 2007, up from 20 percent in 1980.
SAP reported intangibles to be as high as 80 percent prior to the
Internet bubble of 2000. Brand Finance plc stated that the market-
to-book ratio (market capitalization divided by book value) of
the S&P 500 grew from around 3 in the early 1990s to nearly
6.6 prior to the dot-com bust, dropping back to around 5+ today,
a growth indicative of a rise in intangible value. Our own estimates show intangibles playing a greater role in overall firm value.
(Figure 1.3.)

This rise in intangible value is also a worldwide phenomenon.
A twenty-year trend reveals the entire global economy is increasingly powered by imagination and ideas. Brand Finance recently
completed an extensive study of global intangible value, estimating
that the value of every quoted company among the world's twenty-
five leading stock markets reflected 99 percent of the world's

FIGURE 1.3. INTANGIBLE ASSETS ARE MAKING UP A LARGER
PROPORTION OF ENTERPRISE VALUE.

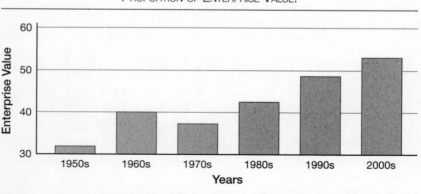

Source: BAV databases and Y&R historical research.

FIGURE 1.4. TWO-THIRDS OF THE GLOBAL ECONOMY IS NOW INTANGIBLE.

	Intangible Value of Businesses Internationally	
	Value of intangibles (billions)	% of enterprise value
India	$251	76%
Switzerland	$643	74%
France	$1,213	73%
Australia	$461	72%
USA	$9,201	71%
Canada	$795	68%
UK	$2,010	66%
Spain	$506	60%
Italy	$507	59%
South Africa	$217	60%
Brazil	$158	47%
Singapore	$92	45%
Total Global	**$19,500**	**62%**

Source: Brand Finance, 2007.

global GDP. This analysis demonstrated that 62 percent of the value of the world's business is now intangible, representing $19.5 trillion of the $31.6 trillion of global market value (Figure 1.4). When we look at fast-growing markets that have incredible growth rates, they especially exhibit an increasing proportion of their enterprise value largely due to intangibles. In India, for instance, where GDP growth rates approach 9.4 percent annually, intangible value represents a whopping 76 percent of enterprise value.

BRANDS AS DRIVERS OF INTANGIBLE VALUE

Brands have become an independent force in the modern economy. David Haigh, CEO of Brand Finance, told us in a phone interview, "The total worth of the 250 most valuable global brands is $2.197 trillion." To put this in perspective, these brands collectively exceed the GDP of France.[1] Even the value of the world's top ten most valuable brands exceeds the market capitalization of 70 percent of U.S. public companies, according to Booz & Company.

According to Joanna Seddon, EVP of Millward Brown Optimor, who oversees the *BrandZ* Top 100 Most Powerful Brands survey, "Brands account for approximately 30 percent of the market capitalization of the S&P 500. The S&P's market cap is about $12 trillion, meaning that brands represent about $4 trillion, on a pure stock market valuation basis." Joanna urges caution that this is not the total value of all brands in the world or even in the United States, only the brands owned by the five hundred companies included in the index. And while these companies are also U.S. based, they're often global as well. But regardless, the number is big—and growing: Brand values rose in their contribution to shareholder value from 5 to 30 percent over the past thirty years, as Figure 1.5 illustrates.

While estimates vary based on sector and company, David Haigh also found that in some cases, brand value constituted the bulk of enterprise value. Nike's brand value accounted for 84 percent of its total company value. Prada's brand represented 73 percent. In 2007 alone, the aggregate value of the brands in the

FIGURE 1.5. BRAND IS A CRITICAL AND GROWING DRIVER OF SHAREHOLDER VALUE.

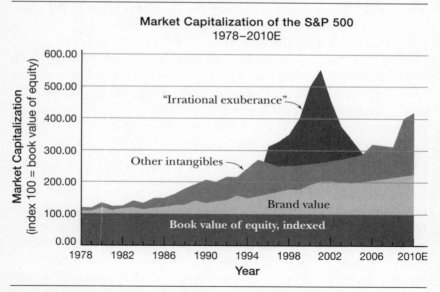

Source: Bloomberg, *BrandZ,* MB Optimor analysis, © Millward Brown Optimor, 2007.

BrandZ Top 100 report increased by 21 percent to $1.94 trillion, more than double the increase of the preceding year. A robust assessment of brands is also evident in many of the recent "big bang" deals, like News Corporation's acquisition of MySpace at a multiple of minus 514.5 times earnings, indicating that the brand and its potential to throw off future cash flows was the driving force in the deal. Google was running at a P/E ratio of fifty-four times earnings when we wrote this, and our Y&R BAV's last estimate of Google's brand value was 50 percent of its market capitalization. PepsiCo shows a tangible book value of $9.8 billion against a market value of $108 billion. Even if we include in PepsiCo's book value the intangible assets like goodwill that are actually quantified on its balance sheet, the Wall Street value is still more than $95 billion over the company's worth, indicating that investors are banking on the brand.

Based on careful scrutiny and analysis, it would be difficult not to conclude that sound brands are the single most valuable assets a company can possess. John Stuart, former chairman of Quaker Oats, put it well when he said, "If the businesses were split up, I would take the brands, trademarks, and goodwill, and you could have all the bricks and mortar—and I would fare better than you."

SNAP, CRACKLE, POP GOES BRAND VALUE

But as with Tulipmania, the belief that brands are worth so much is really only as sound as the credulity of the Wall Street investors, pundits, and executives who are driving up market prices. Beneath their belief is another story. While the last two decades have witnessed incredible intangible growth, the reality shows a precipitous decline in consumer respect and loyalty for brands. While brand value has been increasing, brand components that impact current performance have been decreasing. Lost in the discussion of new media, channel fragmentation, and the digitization of the world is the fact that the changing consumer landscape has hollowed out brand value.

To illustrate the basis for our prediction, we need to present the differences in brand metrics that drive intangible value and stock price versus those that drive current performance and sales. While these are both measures of the success of brands, they are based on different methods of assessment, which in turn leads to different results in evaluating a brand's future potential and sustainability. When the two measures correspondingly rise, a brand is achieving the results its management is working toward—growth in asset value and sales. But when the two measures don't jibe, there's something rotten in Brandville. . . .

The traditional goal of marketing is to create and capture consumer value. Marketers use brands to build consumer interest, esteem, and respect. Marketers know that when consumers stop respecting and trusting brands, their loyalty diminishes and they either stop buying or expect incentives such as price discounts to recapture their loyalty. Lost consumer interest can turn a brand into a commodity or destroy it completely. The time lag between a drop in consumer perceptions and lost market value will vary with the brand, but the correlation is undeniable.

Since 1993 we've conducted extensive statistical and attitudinal research through our proprietary research tool, BrandAsset® Valuator (BAV). Working with leading academics and undertaking enormous waves of consumer studies, we've produced one of the most stable financial models for valuing brands and branded businesses in the world. Y&R has invested more than $113 million to track forty thousand brands across forty-four countries on more than seventy-five brand metrics. With our headquarters in New York and key research centers in London, Sâo Paulo, Tokyo, Madrid, Shanghai, Mumbai, Singapore, Moscow, Milan, Paris, and Sydney, each year we interview almost 500,000 customers around the world with surveys in more than forty languages. From Arabic to Zulu, we ask consumers how they feel about local, regional, and multinational brands, media, and celebrities. We also measure the political status of countries as brands. In the United States, we assess brands and companies by talking to thirteen thousand customers quarterly. Collectively, the information we obtain forms the world's most comprehensive and longest-running global database on brands. To contextualize our data we conduct ethnographies, focus groups, consumer juries, and online panels in more than ninety countries each year. Because of its scale, longevity, and validation, BAV is recognized as a powerful diagnostic tool for understanding how successful brands are built and managed. BAV is constantly enriched with each new wave of research, and, as a result, has shifted over time to reflect the changing nature of consumers and their relationship to brands.

In 2004, we were examining the correlations between changes in various brand measures in BAV and changes in the future financial performance of companies. At the time, we were trying to measure how brands impact the current and future financial performance of their enterprises. We were studying a universe of nine hundred multinational "mono-brands," that is, companies that stake their market value on a single powerful brand and derive more than 80 percent of their annual revenue from that brand. This included firms like Intel, McDonald's, and Microsoft.

Much as meteorologists analyze the various forces of nature to assess which combination causes hurricanes, we began analyzing many consumer variables based on our years of BAV data to see if we could tell which group of brand attributes came closest to explaining unanticipated changes in stock price, especially upward valuations. Our emphasis was on unanticipated stock price changes, because market values already anticipate a wide range of corporate financial and performance factors. We mapped forty-eight different brand attribute scores in BAV against the brands' stock prices, trying to pinpoint which combination of attributes created the greatest market movement. We didn't doubt that brand values were rising, nor were we trying to prove they shouldn't. We were believers in brand value as a driver of intangible value—and we still are. But while doing that research, however, we discovered an enormous anomaly, a huge gap in valuations.

While Wall Street has been bidding brand values ever higher, consumer perceptions toward brands are substantially eroding. To our astonishment, as we were not even looking for it, we found that the consumer ratings on four key classic attitudes toward brands—awareness, trust, regard, and esteem—were tumbling!

These four measures are nothing more complicated than what is found in Marketing 101 textbooks. Generations of marketing professionals have long accepted them as the defining measures of brand health. These are the classic metrics that drive current brand performance and sales and account for brand equity. If the metrics of awareness, trust, regard, and esteem are high, it indicates a positive sign that consumers are likely to continue purchasing and remain loyal to their brands.

But according to the data, consumer attitudes toward brands were in double-digit decline. And this erosion did not pertain to just a few brands, but to thousands. We saw large numbers of well-respected brands that had, on average, lower scores on these metrics—results low enough that marketers would consider them indicative of "commoditized attitudinal patterns." These are numbers that basically say consumers know the brands well, but they are hardly inspired to buy them.

This discrepancy was enormously puzzling. We couldn't understand how brand values could be rising during this entire period when the data showed sharply falling consumer perceptions. If brand values were rising, why weren't the traditional metrics of brand equity as seen by consumers rising with them? The sane marketing professional would expect a positive correlation between brand value and the classic metrics of performance and sales. Instead, we found a significant negative correlation, as illustrated in Figure 1.6.

FIGURE 1.6. THE "VALUATION GAP" ACCORDING TO CONSUMERS.

Perception	*Reality*
If brand value is increasing, so should brand trust.	**Brands are less trusted than ever.** Trustworthy ratings dropped almost 50% over the last 9 years.
If brand value is increasing, brands should be more liked and admired.	**Brands are less liked and respected.** Esteem and regard for brands fell by 12% in 12 years, and very few brands are widely regarded across the general population.
If brand value is increasing, brands should be better known.	**But brands are less salient than ever.** Awareness of brands fell by 20% in 13 years.
If brand value is increasing, quality perceptions of brands should be increasing as well.	**Consumers feel brands are less quality.** Brand quality perceptions fell by 24% over the past 13 years.
If brand value is increasing, more brands should be clearly differentiated.	**Brand differentiation declined in 40 of 46 categories studied by Copernicus/ Market Facts.** And only 7% of prime time commercials were found to have a differentiating message.

Source: BAV 1993–2007 brand data. Copernicus, Jack Trout, and Kevin Clancy.

This inconsistency became a burning incentive for our analysts to look around to confirm if our measurements and conclusions were sound. Sure enough, we found other market researchers around the world noting some early signs of the same brand meltdown. The Henley Centre highlighted an erosion of big brands beginning in 1999 in the United Kingdom. In their annual study of the seventeen largest, most iconic British brands, sixteen showed a decline in consumer trust. Their research attributed this to the brands' inability to evolve their offerings to keep pace with public expectations. In successive studies between 2000 and 2007, the Carlson Marketing Group found a decline in consumer loyalty to brands. In 2000, four in ten consumers showed a genuine preference for or commitment to only one brand, but that dropped to one in three consumers in 2001, and crashed further in 2007 to less than one in ten consumers feeling committed to a single brand.

Since that original 2004 analysis, we have continued to witness erosion in traditional brand perceptions. Even as we write, the numbers persist in a downward spiral of declining awareness, trust, regard, and esteem among consumers. In July 2008, just as we were finishing this book, we found further evidence of the bubble when we examined the highest-performing brands in BAV on the basis of their contribution to intangible value creation. In that analysis, *we found an increasingly smaller number of brands accounting for a disproportionate share of the value being created.*[2] While the aggregate contribution of brands to intangible value creation was once distributed fairly evenly across our database, now it's becoming more like the 80/20 rule: Consumers are reserving their devotion and dollars for a basket of truly "irresistible" brands, leaving the rest to fight for existence on a hostile terrain of promotion and discounting. Fewer and fewer brands are actually creating the business value, leaving more brands on the bubble.

Meanwhile, markets trade on thousands of branded companies with inflated values relative to the future performance we predict them to have. While Wall Street is happily running away with the idea that all or most brands are increasingly valuable, the underlying facts show that most brands are simply riding along, relying on a dwindling number of exemplary brands to prop up their respective values. Yet cadres of business, finance, marketing, media, and advertising consultants seem to believe in a brand folly: that their brands are forever bankable and will continue rising. Their rosy forecasts sound like the makings of another Tulipmania.

These overstated assumptions of future brand earnings also lead us to wonder, Why has no one bothered to ask the consumer? Surely an asset as vital as a brand is best measured against the value attributed to it by the buyer, rather than by a speculator? It also begins to reveal how little the financial markets (and many businesses for that matter) really understand brands and brand building. This is something we explore in great detail in this book, in an effort to help you understand how consumers actually build desire in brands and how this passion creates future value.

MARKETING'S PERFECT STORM

We aren't Chicken Little saying, "The sky is falling," but there are macroeconomic implications when aggregate brand values, according to consumers, are overstated. Our extensively collected data is reliable cause for us to caution that the underlying infrastructure of most brands is weakening, portending potential damage to the enterprise values of many companies across various economies and regions of the world.

Thinking of brands collectively as an industry, such as real estate, is useful for underscoring our concerns. Residential real estate represents only 16 percent of the U.S. economy, but the ripple effect of the U.S. credit crunch has created widespread volatility in the global markets. Analysts at UBS now estimate the financial fallout from mortgage-backed securities to be nearly $600 billion. In the United States, the drop in home prices in the first quarter of 2008 was the largest in three decades. New home sales hit a record low, while mortgage foreclosures hit an all-time high in the fourth quarter of 2007. For the first time since 1945, the amount of debt tied up in American homes is now greater than the equity homeowners have built up. No wonder consumer confidence according to the Reuters and University of Michigan survey is at a sixteen-year low.[3]

We collected and analyzed this data for the years 1993–2007, a period of overall robust economic growth. But now we find ourselves in a value-driven economy. We expect further downward consumer sentiment in an environment where (as of this writing) commodity inflation is rampant: Wheat prices have doubled in the last year alone, global food prices have risen 77 percent since 2005, and oil edges to an all-time high of $140 a barrel, while the number of Americans who declared bankruptcy last year increased by 40 percent.[4] In previous recessions we had low energy and food prices. This time around we have the twin impacts of significantly higher costs and limited supply of both commodities affecting consumers' purchasing decisions, the implications of which few have inclination to grasp in their entirety. Brands will come under greater practical consumer scrutiny and the bubble is likely to envelop more and more brands.

The big question, of course, is what's behind this brand bubble? What explains why brands have lost consumers' trust and respect? What are brand marketers supposed to do about the falling metrics of performance and sales, the most meaningful signs that predict the future of their brands?

Needless to say, we have pondered these questions long and hard, seeking to identify causes. We have formulated many answers, most based on our BAV data (which we will be detailing throughout this book), but some are theoretical—though they reflect our substantive real-world marketing experience with thousands of brands. Clearly the issues are complex, with many diverse factors dragging down brand perceptions among consumers. These include a world of graying august products, whose marketability is running up against growing consumer boredom; the loss of consumer loyalty and emotional attachment to any one brand in increasingly competitive categories; dramatically changing consumer attitudes and purchasing patterns—which we are going to cover extensively in Chapters Three, Four, and Five.

For now, we distill our analysis to just three fundamental causes that we see as collectively diminishing consumer desire for brands. These causes are singular but interlocking, with each one intensifying the others, creating a bad cocktail that consumers are no longer interested in drinking. The question you may ask is, Why now? While none of these factors are entirely new, they've never before happened simultaneously, and against the dramatic backdrop of profound changes of a new digital, media, and consumer landscape. Collectively, as Figure 1.7 shows, they're taking a far greater toll on brands than anyone had previously thought.

FIGURE 1.7. THE TRIPLE THREAT.

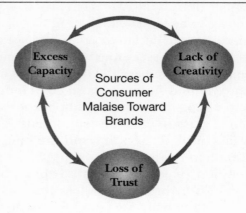

EXCESS CAPACITY

Every marketer is up against this new reality: the world is teeming with brands, and consumers are having a hard time assessing the differences among them. The average supermarket today holds 30,000 distinct items, almost three times as many as in 1991. In 2006, the U.S. Patent and Trademark Office issued 196,400 trademarks, almost 100,000 more than in 1990. And according to a Datamonitor report, 58,375 new products were introduced worldwide in 2006, more than double the number in 2002. This report points out that "despite the fact that advertising spending was up from $271 billion in 2005 to $285 billion in 2006, 81% of consumers could not name one of the top 50 new products launched in 2006, an all-time high for lack of recognition and a huge leap up from 57% in the previous year."[5]

Any way you view it, there's a glut of brands. *Paradox of Choice* author Barry Schwartz vividly demonstrated a shopping trip to the average supermarket where he found 285 varieties of cookies, 275 types of cereals, and 175 different salad dressings. (Fortunately he also found 80 different pain relievers.) In the "Decline of Brands" article for *Wired* back in 2004, *Wisdom of the Crowds* author James Surowiecki first reported a veritable dumping of brands on the market: "The average American sees 60% more ad messages per day than when the first President Bush left office. A handful of years ago, David Foster Wallace fantasized in *Infinite Jest* about an

America in which corporations sponsor entire years—the Year of the Whopper, the Year of the Depend Adult Undergarment. The fantasy seems more reasonable by the day."[6]

There are so many brands today that many companies have begun to rid themselves of poor performers and unnecessary line extensions. Unilever has cut almost four hundred brand SKUs from its holdings. Some companies are even divesting leading market position brands, succumbing to the pressure to drive growth, even if it has to be found in their lower-end brands. This is a growing problem for established brands in developed markets, where top-line growth can't keep pace with shareholders' expectations.

Consumers are not moving away from brands for want of choice; they have more choice than they could ever know what to do with. There's more of everything. More channels. More technology. More messages. More devices. More networks. The effect of excess capacity in media fragmentation, multi-channel distribution and ways to personalize content has resulted in more types of consumer behaviors, creating less differentiation among the waves of products on the market. Brands have blurred into a sea of sameness. A study by Copernicus and Market Facts reported that in more than fifty product and service categories, none became more differentiated over time and 90 percent declined in differentiation.[7] An Ernst & Young study of new brands showed over 80 percent failing due to lack of differentiation. Jack Trout and Kevin Clancy, writing for *Harvard Business Review*, said that only two categories of brands were becoming more distinct (soft drinks and soap), but forty other categories are homogenizing, as the brands within them become indistinguishable. They also found that "only 7 percent of ads out of a study of 340 prime-time commercials included a 'differentiating' message."[8]

This lack of brand difference ultimately leads to commoditization. Barring meaningful distinction, brands enter into a transactional relationship with consumers, letting price dictate the purchase decision. Whenever marketing turns on the price promotion faucet, consumers begin to commoditize products. And why wouldn't they? If price becomes all the marketer has to say about a brand, why wouldn't consumers come to expect more of it? After all, if brands descend into comparative advertising and everyday low prices, it only encourages consumers to play along and shop for deals. If no bargain arises, they are quite willing to switch to retailer brands with increasingly comparable quality.

Another study undertaken by Clancy found that brand name trumps price in importance only in the categories of automobiles, liquor, and beer. In twenty-eight of thirty-seven other categories, consumers buy on low price, not brand name.[9] In a 2006 *Harvard Business Review* article, Leonard Lodish and Carl Mella noted, "Price premiums have eroded, and margins are following suit. Consumers are 50% more price sensitive than they were 25 years ago. In recent surveys of consumer-goods managers, seven out of ten cited pricing pressure and shoppers' declining loyalty as their primary concerns."[10]

In the end, price promotions erode margins and profitable growth, inviting even faster commoditization. It's a bad cycle, especially for established brands. When a brand in this type of competitive position begins to say the same thing repeatedly (low price), consumers begin to think they already know everything there is to know about the brand, and it becomes even more challenging to build differentiation. As our BAV data demonstrates (Figure 1.8), consumers are largely sleepwalking through

FIGURE 1.8. THE MORE CONSUMERS KNOW A BRAND—THE LESS THEY FEEL IT'S DIFFERENT.

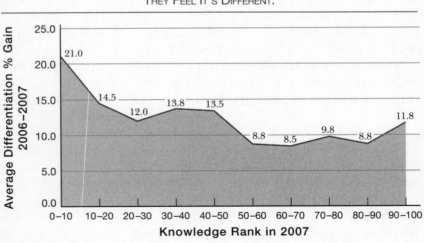

Source: BAV, 2006–2007; All Adults.

their relationships with familiar brands from too many rational appeals and too much repetitive marketing that shows up in all the same old familiar channels and doesn't say anything new or exciting.

Historically, preference for brands in BAV was always greater than usage. In 2000, on average, this preference was 25 percent greater than actual usage for any given brand. This reflected consumers' passion, interest, and even lust for brands, regardless of whether or not they currently used or purchased them. This desire to engage with a brand epitomized its potential beyond the product it offered.

Recently, something interesting has occurred. Brands are now used more than they are preferred. Functional benefits and relevance now outweigh the intangible and emotional allure of a brand. Today average usage of a brand is 8 percent greater than its preference. In a world where choices and distribution options are increasing dramatically, at a time where consumers are much more informed, the result is a more commoditized market. Ultimately, commoditization is the beginning of the end for a brand. As soon as a brand competes on price, consumer loyalty takes a walk. Citing retail industry tracking firm NPD Group, Surowiecki also noted, "Nearly half of those [consumers] who described themselves as highly loyal to a brand were no longer loyal a year later. Even seemingly strong names rarely translate into much power at the cash register." And, worse, he referenced another study that said, "just 4% of consumers would be willing to stick with a brand if its competitors offered better value for the same price." Did you hear that: just 4 percent. With numbers like that, there's not much of a brand left.

LACK OF CREATIVITY

Why do so many brands exist? One good reason is it doesn't take much today to launch a me-too brand. Technology has democratized industry, making it easy for anyone to imitate just about any product or service within weeks and market to millions. The Internet enables distribution costs to move toward zero. And many of the products being created today are more intellectual-capital-intensive than physical-capital-intensive. In some industries, so many copycat products have appeared that it takes an Excel spreadsheet to keep track of them all.

But it's not just a matter of more products—more of them are better made. Personal computing power is ten times faster in only five years. You can buy a $59 cocktail dress designed by Madonna at H&M. Muji can fill your apartment with incomparable style, at low prices. Mobile phones in Japan, Korea, and Scandinavia have so much functionality they practically make love to you. Even a $2 toy from China has a high-quality sound chip inside. Meanwhile, the shift in power over two decades to the retailer has eroded manufacturer margins and cut investments in innovation. Venerable brands are then forced to compete with these same retailer brands that are now anything but generic. As competition for available business intensifies and investors push companies to drive market performance beyond the organic levels of demand, quality levels continue to rise beyond the mean level of customer tolerance. Now even the lowest-priced goods exceed the average acceptable quality levels for most people. With high quality meeting surplus demand, consumers become more demanding while less willing to pay more, so highly innovative products tip faster into the mass market, whether it's a $.99 razor blade or a $29.99 Razr. When brands can't differentiate by simply being better and more affordable, the pressure to be more creative is even greater. Real creativity is the only way to break through the clutter.

Consumers are looking for highly creative brands to simplify choice. But much of what passes for creativity is imitative and incremental, and unduly rational. (Sometimes a brand can be downright unpleasant, like the flashing image of the 2012 London Olympics brand identity that turned out to induce epileptic seizures.) Back in the day when products were scarcer, a category might comprise just three brands, and marketing was a simpler, more linear process, it was easy to construct rational arguments and be top of mind. Production, distribution, and sales were more local, or regional at most. There was less media, channels, messaging, and competition for consumer eyeballs.

But today, escalating volumes of messaging compete for shorter and more distracted attention spans among consumers. As the 2006 *International Television and Video Almanac* points out,

"Americans are currently bombarded with an estimated 5,000 marketing messages each day, up from 3,000 in 1990 and only 1,500 in 1960."[11] As more and more information, brands, media, technology, and selling are squeezed into less space for consumers to make a decision, it gets increasingly unlikely an ordinary brand can consistently sit top of mind with a majority of people for very long.

Even brands that once enjoyed near-universal awareness now live in a world where consumers move quickly through consumption, chewing up brands and spitting them out when they no longer satisfy. Today's consumers are expedient, cycling through technology, information, products, media, and brands quickly. If a brand isn't heading somewhere with velocity and purpose, demonstrating creativity at every turn, it loses its distinction and place in the memory.

In the end, the lack of creativity shows up in a decline in brand awareness, differentiation, and saliency, the ironic consequence of giving consumers overwhelming choice. Sometimes people really can have too much of a good thing.

LOSS OF TRUST

Brands originated as trust marks during a time when quality, safety, and reliability were big issues. In this pre-regulatory world, brand name products offered assurance that they were better made and more durable. People needed to know things as fundamental as "eating this brand won't kill you."

Now it seems that while quality permeates many categories and price points, buyers are quickly losing expectations of having good product experiences. Indeed, we found through BAV that product quality ratings among many leading brands have declined 24 percent since 1993.

The facts show that the amount of trust resting on a brand today is a ghost of what it was ten years ago. In 1997, the majority of brands (52 percent) enjoyed exceedingly high levels of consumer trust. But society's faith in institutions, corporations, and leaders has been severely rocked with scandals and mistrust, from Mad Cow disease in our livestock to human growth hormones in our baseball players. One by one, scandal after scandal has

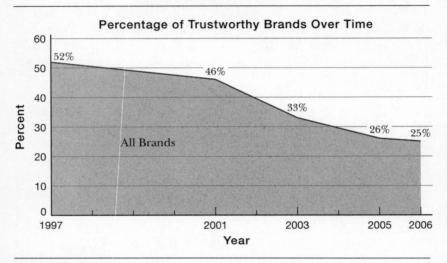

FIGURE 1.9. CONSUMER TRUST IN BRANDS HAS DECLINED
BY 50 PERCENT IN TEN YEARS.

* Defined as brands with >20 percent endorsement on Trustworthy attribute.

Base: BAV 1997, 2001, 2003, 2005, 2006; All Adults.

knocked corporate credibility, leaving few brands immune. By 2006, consumers voted only 25 percent of brands as trustworthy, halving the number of trusted brands in less than one decade (Figure 1.9).

In recent years, a variety of politically motivated movements have also begun to challenge the integrity of brands and consumerism. Naomi Klein's popular book *No Logo* explored the collateral damage of globalization in brands. One British man, Neil Boorman, attempted to live a year without brands and launched his campaign with a publicity stunt where he torched his Nike trainers and Gucci loafers. A year later, he wrote a book about his experiences, *Bonfire of the Brands: How I Learned to Live Without Labels,* which sought to denigrate brands and their value to commerce and society. His insurrection against brands continued with *Brand-aid* (brand-aid.info), which provides tips and guidance on de-branding your life, including how to "diagnose brand addiction and how best to beat it." There's also antiadvertisingagency.com, a blog devoted to attacking "out of home" advertising in order to "democratize the outdoors and return it to people, not corporations."

These anti-brand attitudes might be written off as fringe, but they are increasingly moving into the mainstream. Consider Facebook's beacon debacle, where fifty thousand members signed a petition on MoveOn.org within days to protest the company's controversial plan to track their movements. Even a cherished brand like Facebook is no longer immune from consumer backlash.

And when it comes to trust, most brands face a growing generation gap: In our discussions, Millennials soundly criticized marketers for being controlling and resisting change. We realized that like a wiki page, the concept of "what is the truth" is open to critique and always changing. Because Millennials live in an open source culture, they expect to co-create truths and accept they will evolve. They feel a brand's integrity is earned through openness and embracing flux, but since very few brands act this way, they have an even smaller repertoire of brands they truly respect.

Consumers also think brands are more disposable due to technology, mergers, and acquisitions. MindSpring was a beloved ISP of the late nineties; then EarthLink gobbled it up and retired the brand name. Cingular developed into a powerful brand, only to be reduced to the orange backdrop behind the blue AT&T logo. So many brand disappearances have occurred that consumers now actively contemplate the concept of "permanence" in a brand. Because without it, what's their reward? Why should they feel a brand is going to be there for them in the future, when corporations eradicate brands or change how they operate in the name of corporate synergies? Who wants to be loyal to a 128K modem or left waiting at the door for an undelivered movie from Kozmo.com?

The brand marketer's most cherished tool, advertising, has also taken a big hit in consumer trust. According to the Newspaper Advertising Bureau, 34 percent of American consumers in 1965 could name the brand of a commercial aired during a show. Thirty years later only 8 percent can do so.[12] A recent Forrester study also shows consumers find advertising less useful and influential, with significant drops in their assessment of advertising's ability to inform or persuade them, or to build respect for companies. Statements like "I buy products because of their ads" declined from 29 percent to 13 percent between 2002 and 2006. And "Companies generally tell the truth in ads" fell from 13 percent to a paltry 6 percent over the same period.[13]

This is because consumers are interrogating brands on their own, thank you very much. This behavioral shift from passive receiver to active investigator is growing. And it's remaking consumers as self-reliant, practical, and tribal. (See Figure 1.10.)

Instead of traditional advertising, consumers are increasingly turning to nontraditional sources of information such as search engines and peer-to-peer interactions. This information,

FIGURE 1.10. CONSUMERS ARE BECOMING HARDER TO SATISFY.

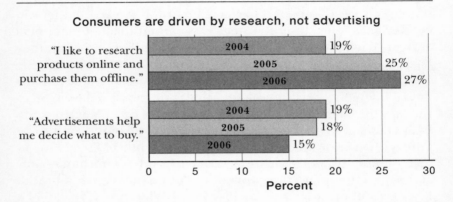

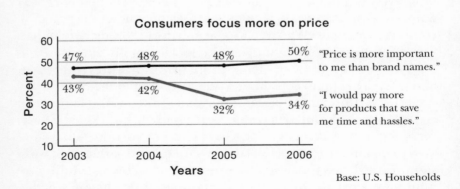

Source: "Topic Overview: Customer Experience," Forrester Research, September 2007.

collected from their social networks and ratings and reviews sites, is often more influential than the millions pumped into traditional marketing. Even though this is well known, a 2007 McKinsey survey found that over one-third of McKinsey clients still devoted less than 10 percent of their marketing budgets to nontraditional media.[14] Perhaps this explains why the ANA Marketing Accountability Study found that 42 percent of firms are dissatisfied with their ROI measurements: The world is dramatically changing and most companies aren't yet certain how to market to consumers and what criteria to use to measure marketing success.

NOT THE WAY TO ESCAPE THE BUBBLE

Now you know why we believe there's a bubble. On one hand, Wall Street, investors, and brand executives all believe that brands have limitless potential that will continue to drive already burgeoning enterprise and market values. On the other, consumers are sending out clear signals that they are no longer enamored of many of our brands and are not committed to future loyalty. Consumers are overwhelmed with undifferentiated brands and excessive choice; they are left uninspired by the lack of creativity in many brands, and they have lost their trust in brands to be unique and special enough to attract their emotional and financial commitment. The advent of social media and new communications technologies is dramatically empowering consumers, while upending the natural order of brand valuations at a terrifying rate of speed.

Where does this leave those of us who are responsible for marketing and managing brands? How can brands build sustainable long-term value to bring them back into alignment with Wall Street's expectations and valuations?

The answer is not found in simply redoubling efforts to win back consumer awareness, esteem, and respect. Too much has changed in the world to just return to the old methods of marketing and expect better results. As Einstein said, you can't get out of a problem using the same kind of thinking that created the problem.

A chess player who is suddenly confronted with a three-dimensional board will find the game disorienting. Even though the same basic rules still apply, the new dimension of play requires a quantum leap in conceptualization and strategy. Marketers and brand managers today are facing a similar challenge. New market realities require a fundamentally new approach to manage a brand as a moving target.

Yet much of conventional marketing continues to operate in a time warp. Most marketers keep striving to build consumer perceptions that only drive current sales today. They happily skip along, stressing reason over emotion and persuasion over inspiration, still believing that customers can be programmed to lifetime relationships, and that brands can forever maintain their intangible elixir of attraction and lasting cachet.

This manner of marketing pays too much deference to the brand's existing equities. Past as Prelude thinking in marketing and brand management has been the norm in many companies for decades. But the consumer is now clearly telling us a brand's reputation is only what it did yesterday. Brand equity is simply a reflection of *past accomplishments*. The images, emotions, and feelings form an accumulated impression of the brand right up to this moment in time. They can create a false sense of security, as though past recognition can continue to generate an endless stream of future profits. This creates a "brand as statue" mentality—and we know what pigeons do to statues!

The collapsing aggregate brand measures of awareness, trust, regard, and esteem reflect the complacent manner with which too many marketers are thinking about brand equity. With accountability for brand performance under increased scrutiny, working to improve metrics like trust, saliency, and regard is simply no longer enough to create lasting brand value. That old marketing paradigm has made us passive and unresponsive to the new world brands live in. Consumers no longer buy brands for the reasons marketers think are important. Marketers who continue to look at traditional metrics are missing what consumers are really after. Continuing the same marketing strategy will only further commoditize your brand.

Today, brands are in peril if they stand still. Currencies and market caps fluctuate constantly, and brand reputation is subject to the same market forces. Brand strategies have to evolve and adapt to meet the needs of consumers who care little for what the brand used to be. However much they knew it, liked it, or trusted it—that's all water under the bridge. Many famous brands are now in financial straits, and quite a few are even in Chapter 11. Look around at the airline and automotive industries—where brands regularly go belly up, despite 90 percent awareness.

Brand equity isn't the protective insulation it once was. Today, brands are decaying in compressed cycles of time. Every successful brand must be permanently leading, adapting, surprising, innovating, involving, and responding—behaving differently at different times with different customers, and collaborating, not just persuading. With limitless choice and expanding consumer power, nothing can stay the same, as consumer focus is now on what's moving and what comes next.

If marketing's role is to create value for the consumer, many marketers have forgotten the definition of marketing. They have replaced the word *value* with *sales*. Consumers then value brands less because business has forgotten what a brand really is. A brand is, after all, a promise. A brand offers a contract that's immensely emotional and personal. A brand reinforces our identity and self-worth. It offers a more opportunistic way to see our world. A brand makes us feel special and different. A brand makes our future more hopeful.

So we have in brands promises of future earnings to shareholders that now comprise a third of a company's value—but the promises brands make to consumers are now in doubt. Any bubble inevitably bursts. And all bubbles leave winners as well as losers. The next chapter holds the key to understanding how to be like those winning brands, those who are building true business value and making themselves irresistible to consumers.

CHAPTER TWO

CAN YOU SAY "IRRESISTIBLE"?

*Things in motion sooner catch the eye than
what not stirs.*
—SHAKESPEARE, *TROILUS AND CRESSIDA*, ACT III, SCENE III

Despite the presence of the bubble, $775 billion was invested in marketing communications across the globe in 2008. Companies are spending an astonishing $19 billion annually on market research, with very different results. There can hardly be six people in Uzbekistan who haven't met in a focus group for fruit yogurt. What are so many marketers missing? Why despite our best efforts are consumers falling out of love with so many brands?

FINDING LINKS BETWEEN BRAND PERFORMANCE AND STOCK RETURN

In the first chapter, we told you a portion of our story about the research we were performing in 2004. The rest of the story is even more fascinating, because it led us to identify the most important brand dimension, which has heretofore gone undetected in driving brand performance and sustainability.

As we said, we were scouring our BAV data in 2004, seeking to find the key correlation between various brand attributes and unanticipated stock market returns. In that process, we started working with a number of brilliant economists, academics, and brand strategists. Two of these people were professors Robert Jacobson and Natalie Mizik. Jacobson is the Evert McCabe Distinguished Professor of Marketing at the University of Washington, where he has been a faculty member since 1984. Mizik is Gantcher Associate Professor of Business at the Columbia University Graduate School of Business, where she has been on the faculty since 2002.[1] Both also did much of their early breakthrough brand equity research with branding guru David Aaker.

We need to retrace Jacobson's history as a professor and researcher to explain the origin of our work to correlate our BAV data with market values. In the early 1980s, he was studying how factors like market share and product quality influence accounting variables like ROI. In the course of his investigation, he uncovered that in certain cases, the financial markets anticipate the effects of these variables and react to them prior to the release of any accounting data.

"As it turns out," Jacobson told us, "a lot of things can explain changes in stock returns other than just accounting data. There's extensive information released by companies, voluntary and involuntary. A lot of that content is non-financial information, such as marketing and brand measures. But because this information has profit implications, if the market sees it changing, they realize it can have long-term impact on accounting measures. The markets then actually form their expectations of future performance from any type of *changing brand data,* ahead of when future profits are actually affected."

Translation: Brands signal important information, and investors and analysts look closely at this data for hints of performance and act on these expectations. The presumption of brand growth drives up current stock prices immediately.

Professor Jacobson then said, "We could also trace how changes in brands related to financial changes in the next two quarters. It seemed like, with the right research, we might be able to explain how financial markets react to changes in brand attitudes because, in fact, they do show a relationship with future long-term accounting variables. So while brand imagery changes have a current term influence, they also have a future influence in sales related dimensions."

Translation: Brand attitude changes are also valuable information about the future. Like the first winds of a distant typhoon, they can have a predictive value on future sales, earnings, and stock prices one or two quarters down the road.

As market researchers, we became very interested in his work and decided to test his hypothesis on several high-tech and Internet brands. Together we examined if changes in brand attitudes had early predictive effects on the market in explaining their stock returns, and, to our pleasant surprise, the findings were consistent with his hypothesis. For companies like Yahoo, Amazon, and eBay, in each case we found that attitude changes toward the brand were more predictive than other measures like brand awareness. In each case, we could actually see how attitude changes not only affected the current stock price but were predictive of a future upward swing.

Then, as we pondered over our weakening brand data in 2004 like doctors confounded by a mysterious illness, we formally teamed up with Jacobson and Mizik to perform the larger, more formal and comprehensive research project on those nine hundred multinational mono-brands we told you about. We created an analytic model using complex statistical regressions on more than ten years' worth of brand data from BAV, along with 1988–2003 financial data from Standard and Poor's COMPUTSTAT and the University of Chicago's Center for Research in Security Prices from 1993 through 2003. Using the BAV consumer attitude data we had gathered between 1993 and 2004, we began comparing brand attributes across forty-eight dimensions with the brand's market performance, seeking to identify which, if any, combination of variables best explained unanticipated changes in stock price.[2]

From this, we noticed that, in terms of driving financial value, not all brands performed equally. Some brands, it turned out, constantly created *exceptional attitude change* that kept driving their financial numbers upward. They pulsed with a kind of creative life force that pushed their values upward even in declining markets. They continued evolving over time, providing a steady forward-looking vision and continuous excitement among the customers they served. We realized they had something unique we had never detected before. We named this dimension *energy*.

ISOLATING THE NATURE OF ENERGY

Precisely what is energy? The simplest answer is that *energy is the consumer perception of motion and direction in a brand.* Energy can be found in any brand, large or small, new or old, in any category. And regardless of how much energy a brand has, a change in energy forecasts a change in financial performance of the firm.

Intuitively, we know that if something contains energy, it moves, or has the potential to move. It has power and motion. In people, energy makes them attractive, admirable, and worth following. Issues and causes that galvanize us to come together and act have an energy of their own. We get energized by ideas that reframe our view of the world, or help us reach deeper inside ourselves. Energy develops when there is conviction, creativity, inspiration, optimism, and hope. And just as in the human condition, there is energy in brands.

The fact is, isolating and identifying this brand dimension, which acts as a predictive force for unanticipated market value, required a sophisticated research process—and a fair amount of research dollars. Our intuition alone didn't detect this characteristic behind the reasons why certain brands were leaping ahead of so many others. We performed extensive computations to isolate the variables of energy from our enormous database of consumer attitudes.

Our BAV research showed us a set of upwardly moving attitudes that consumers ascribe to high-energy brands. These brands create a constant sense of interest and excitement. Consumers sense they move faster, see farther, and are highly experiential and more responsive to their future needs. In terms of our correlations, we saw a definite pattern: the more energy a brand has, the greater consideration, loyalty, elasticity, pricing power, and brand value (as a percentage of firm value) it commands. This unique measure establishes a direct link between brand momentum and creativity, financial earnings, and stock performance. We can explain, and even predict, the movement in their stock prices. The brands shown in the collage in Figure 2.1 are examples of some brands that currently have energy in vast quantities.

FIGURE 2.1. AN ASSORTMENT OF BRANDS WITH HIGH ENERGY
ACCORDING TO BAV.

ADD ENERGY, BECOME IRRESISTIBLE

As we kept poring over the data it began to dawn on us that the reason why brand valuations were askew from what consumers really think and feel is that consumers themselves simply refuse to be commoditized. Brands still mean things—sometimes great things—to the people who buy them. People continue to pay a premium for brands that offer more than their competitors. And they gravitate toward brands that, despite having little different to offer, seem to have a certain thing about them.

What is this thing? It's the ability of a brand to be "irresistible." The brands accountable for disproportionate value creation have a palpable and measurable energy that make them so compelling that they foster an irrational fidelity. Through our research we distilled our learning down to six key principles that identify the essential characteristics of an irresistible brand:

Principles of an Irresistible Brand:

- Irresistible brands are highly irrational and yet entirely irrefutable. They create lust, envy, and badge value. They are provocative and daring while pleasing and reassuring. They let people feel good about themselves (and good about paying more).
- Irresistible brands move with innate purpose and conviction. They convey the sense there's something more to them, which makes people join in, shape them, and share them with others. They create armies of evangelists.
- Irresistible brands constantly reinvent themselves; they have an insatiable appetite for change. They are restless and can't sit still. They despise idleness and fear getting stale. They see things from endlessly different and surprising new angles. They keep refreshing their meaning, bringing new innovation and surprise to the marketplace.
- Irresistible brands engage consumers on their own terms. They speak in a language all their own. They change how people see their world while hanging the rules around other brands, creating an unlevel playing field. They talk not of attribute but of ethos. They have a point of view on the world beyond profit making. These brands are often a category of one.

- Irresistible brands don't force devotion—they compel it. These brands have a magnetism that attracts without chasing. They are galvanizing, affecting, even moving. They create an imperative and an invitation to join. Their presence extends to a wider group of people without marketing. They have greater freedom to try new things and expand into new frontiers and reach places other brands can't.
- Irresistible brands move culture as well as categories. Often, these brands' actions have a disproportional impact on society. They act as a social catalyst, a spark of something that can be passed along. Their presence extends to a wider social radius, while often spending less on marketing.

It is not essential that consumers sense all six of these perceptions; one is sufficient, provided it is unique to the brand. But as with any recipe for success, the more energy consumers derive from a brand, the more irresistible it becomes and the more powerful it becomes as an agent of creating future value.

THE ROLE OF ENERGY IN CREATING IRRESISTIBLE BRANDS

Once we identified energy, we naturally asked, how does it make these brands more irresistible to consumers? What role does it play in keeping consumers fascinated with these brands? As a predictor of sales and sustainability, what function does energy serve to bolster brand value?

The answer: Energy boosts brand differentiation. In fact, its role is so critical that we have renamed this essential construct of marketing. Brands that keep moving, keep changing, keep innovating create an entirely new form of differentiation, which we call *Energized Differentiation*. We know Energized Differentiation isn't easy to say and doesn't sound very sexy, but understanding it is crucial to understanding why consumers feel some brands are irresistible, while others are merely acceptable or worse growing in discontent.

Every marketer knows that brand differentiation has always been pivotal to capturing consumer respect and loyalty and ensuring sustainability. All our original BAV studies bore this out. Differentiation is key to helping brands capture pricing power, remove excess capacity, and clear products off retail shelves. But like a fuse that ignites its charge, energy launches differentiation into new territory.

In Chapter One, we talked about the classic metrics of awareness, trust, regard, and esteem. These four metrics have long been the accepted measures of brand equity, contributing heavily to how marketers differentiate their brands one from another. Successful brands have long relied on a differentiated image to persuade their way into the consumer's consideration. These four measures came about over time, evolving naturally with the rise of brands.

In the early days of brands, simple *awareness* was sufficient to create product differentiation, especially when brands were small and regional. Back in the first decades of industrialized production, any enterprise that could invest in mass awareness could make itself stand out from the locals. We can still witness this dynamic playing out in many fast-growing markets, where competition is still limited and a simple mass awareness campaign can be effective to differentiate a brand. (But this is changing fast.)

However, in developed economies, simple awareness soon became insufficient to drive a brand's differentiation forward. With increasing competition came a greater need to differentiate because every brand in a category had to fight for the same awareness factor. If you're standing in a pack of penguins, it takes something more than a black-and-white suit and a two-step shuffle to get noticed. (Even penguin movies suffer from differentiation challenges: Do the kids watch *Surf's Up* or *Happy Feet?*)

Branding was forced to evolve, and companies began highlighting other qualities to differentiate themselves in the consumer mind. Two of these became *trust* and *regard*—indicators of superiority that leading brands tapped into to persuade consumers of their preferential value. Marketers sought to educate consumers that their products were consistently of high quality and would never disappoint (trust). Television ads highlighted the professional endorsements of doctors, dentists, hair stylists, or any other pertinent experts to build a brand's authority and credibility (regard). Some marketing measurement paradigms, including our own at Y&R, also measured a brand's *esteem,* that is, how the public thought about the brand in terms of its confidence and aura.

For years, the classic method of differentiation created from awareness, trust, regard, and esteem worked well enough. Nothing seemed to be able to budge this formula from its lofty pedestal. Brands could do well by following those simple principles. Despite frontal assaults and even guerilla attacks, the leading brands fought off loss of market share, and consumers seemed unwilling to change their attitude toward brands regardless of their experiences. Most leading brands were solidly impervious to attack.

But as we now know from our BAV research, that world is changing. Consumers are no longer buying brands based on these considerations alone, and that's partially why those metrics are tumbling. Numerous forces—such as the excess capacity, lack of creativity, and lack of trust that we discussed earlier—are reshaping brand marketing. All around us, established brands are losing ground to upstarts that are making inroads into conservative and stable categories, changing the rules and dynamics of consumer value as they go along. As we now see, at the head of the charge are these brands with energy. Consciously or unconsciously, they are defining themselves in a different way and building a new relationship with consumers that is more visionary, unconventional, and creative.

WHAT ENERGY ADDS TO BRANDS

In *Annie Hall* Woody Allen said, "A relationship, I think, is like a shark. It has to constantly move forward or it dies. And what I think what we got on our hands is a dead shark." This Woody-ism captures exactly what energy adds to brands.

Energy keeps brands constantly moving forward—and this prevents them from dying. It ensures that brands don't just sit still, resting on their past laurels and stagnating. While traditional marketing emphasizes building awareness, trust, regard, and esteem, those measures do not help brands keep pace with the ongoing future as it screams past. They help brands manage for today, but do little to prepare them for tomorrow. Energy keeps brands constantly evolving, refreshing, and staying in step with consumers. If you go back and review the five key characteristics of energy, you will see that they all relate to being future oriented and responsive to consumers.

Energy brands can escape the bubble because they know how to stand out in today's world—a world in which most brands perform identically, any product can be imitated within months or days, and your experienced staff could be working for your competitor in six months. Ordinary differentiation does little good when the slightest competitive advantage soon evaporates because everything can be reverse engineered and copied immediately.

Simply put, marketing based on "unique selling propositions"—USPs—no longer works. Other than an occasional fluke, parity in high-performance brands exists across the spectrum of price points. Six Sigma manufacturing reduces defects to less than one per million, while Wal-Mart drives prices lower and lower. Expert consultants and business schools disseminating leading-edge learning across the economy are duplicated as soon as the concepts have been defined. Disaggregated business models, offshoring, and lean management practices mean warp speed business. In a world where change is the only constant, the tried-and-true elements of brand differentiation along with two bucks won't buy you a nonfat latte at Starbucks.

The lesson for today's brand world is that *for a brand to sustain consumer interest, it can't just be different; it has to keep being different.* Today, consumers are constantly reevaluating their purchasing habits and choices, day by day, even moment by moment. Bombarded with waves of me-too choices, they are drawn toward that which is new and exciting. Consumers head for brands that are continuously innovating and reengaging them, because these brands help them live in a constantly changing and increasingly uncertain future. The brands that stand out are those that are moving, adapting, and leading the market.

Brands that stand the test of time are willing to battle time. They protect and nourish their differentiation by furiously redefining it, inventing new ways to give it meaning and keeping it vibrant. Jacobson concluded, "The one thing that keeps cropping up over and over and over [in our data] is that it's not awareness, it's not knowledge, it's not how much consumers know about a brand, it's what they believe. They want to believe a brand is different, and will keep being different. They want brands that will satisfy their needs in the future. They must have something in them that says we're going to be around and we're going to be good, not just now, but tomorrow. They're looking for a brand to have energy."

NOT JUST DIFFERENTIATION . . .
ENERGIZED DIFFERENTIATION

We then began tracking various success measures to determine what benefits energy brings to a brand. When we compared brands with merely strong differentiation to those with Energized Differentiation, we observed substantial differences in their ability to connect with consumers. The brands with Energized Differentiation commanded greater usage, consideration, loyalty, and pricing power, and they brought greater future value through growth in operating earnings and future stock performance (Figure 2.2).

The data also showed that energy is not a function of brand maturity. We found many established brands having as much energy as younger, flashier brands. Both Dr Pepper and Red Bull are highly energized. So are eBay and Zappos. The same goes for Bacardi and Svedka, as well as Dove and Method. We plotted the effects of Energized Differentiation across multiple categories and sectors and saw that it pertains equally.

FIGURE 2.2. ENERGY BOOSTS THE POWER OF DIFFERENTIATION.

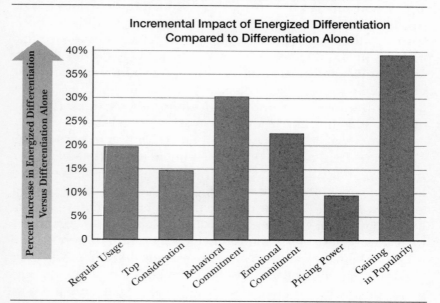

Source: BAV 2006 USA, Top 100 Differentiated Brands with Strong Energy Component vs. Top 100 Differentiated Brands with Weak Energy Component.

One result that struck us as especially interesting was how energy plays a powerful role in a commoditized arena where brands usually struggle to build loyalty, hampered by their lack of a meaningful point of difference. For example, in one of the most highly commoditized sectors, the airline industry, energized brands far surpass their peers. This is an industry that is driven predominantly by price, convenience, and availability, with customer satisfaction ratings so low you have to bend down to find them. So it's no surprise that airline travel would normally be seen as a low-energy category, with dismal levels of emotional and behavioral commitment from customers.

Yet our data indicated that a few airlines have established relatively high levels of energy compared to their competition. These included Virgin, JetBlue, and Southwest—each in its own way highly innovative and customer focused in its business model, product and service delivery, and marketing. We found that all had a level of Energized Differentiation that translated to loyalty almost twice as high as the rest of the airline category, helping them transcend the cycle of commoditization that continually plagues other airlines, as shown in Figure 2.3.

FIGURE 2.3. HIGH-ENERGY BRANDS HAVE GREATER LOYALTY.

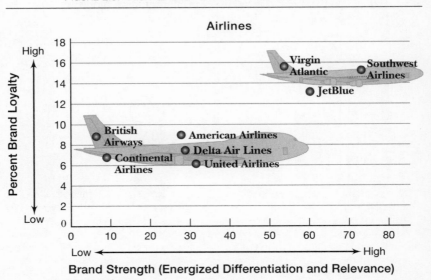

Base: BAV USA 2006 Full Year; All Adults.

THE PLOTTING THICKENS

Energy's role in keeping brands constantly forward thinking and evolving is critical to maintaining ongoing consumer appeal, loyalty, and enduring success. To understand this, you need some background on the methodology we use to measure brands. Our model has become well known in numerous marketing venues and is cited in many marketing textbooks. Many major marketers rely on the validity of our research methodology and its powers of measurement and prediction.

BAV is constructed around four "pillars" that help us identify the movement and success of a brand. These four pillars originally were Differentiation, Relevance, Esteem, and Knowledge. Needless to say, once we discovered the attributes of energy, we recognized those scores too, evolving our differentiation pillar into the more comprehensive measurement, Energized Differentiation. (See Figure 2.4.)

FIGURE 2.4. FOUR PILLARS ASSESS BRAND HEALTH, DEVELOPMENT, MOMENTUM, AND COMPETITIVE ADVANTAGE.

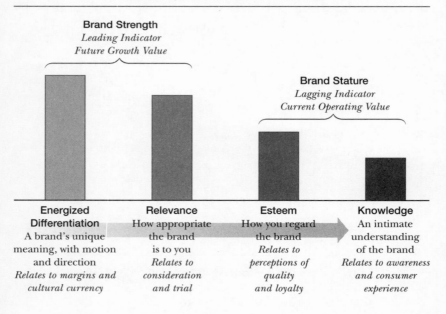

You'll notice in Figure 2.4 that the four pillars are paired in two categories: *Brand Strength,* composed of Energized Differentiation and Relevance, and *Brand Stature,* composed of Esteem and Knowledge. The logic of this reflects the significance that each pillar reveals about a brand's health, as follows:

• *Brand Strength, a leading indicator, predicts the future growth value of the brand.* Energized Differentiation reflects the brand's motion and direction in the marketplace. It impacts the brand's ability to capture loyalty and drive margins, both determinants of the brand's future. Relevance indicates how appropriate consumers perceive the brand to be. The greater the Relevance, the greater the potential market penetration. When combined, brands that excel on Energized Differentiation and Relevance have greater lasting Brand Strength and are more likely to differentiate themselves from the rest of the pack.

• *Brand Stature, a lagging indicator, shows the current operating value of the brand.* The measure of a brand's Esteem shows how consumers regard the brand. The greater the Esteem, the higher quality consumers perceive in the brand and the more they respect it. The measure of a brand's Knowledge indicates its degree of consumer awareness and understanding. The higher the Knowledge, the more consumers believe they know what the brand stands for. When combined, Esteem and Knowledge tend to reflect more how consumers feel about a brand today than what they may think about the brand tomorrow. For this reason, Brand Stature reflects a brand's current operating performance.

Before we go into the way Brand Strength and Stature help us form a comprehensive view of a brand's present and future health, it's worth noting that the way the four pillars interact with each other yields valuable information about a brand at any given moment. Figure 2.5 shows the various relationships that can exist between the pillars within each pair of measures.

More important, when we use and plot a brand's scores for measures of both Strength and Stature, we can paint a very accurate holistic picture of its status as a *forward-looking measure of performance.* We accomplish this by charting a PowerGrid of Brand Strength against Brand Stature. This can be done for a single brand at a time or even for thousands of global brands, creating a

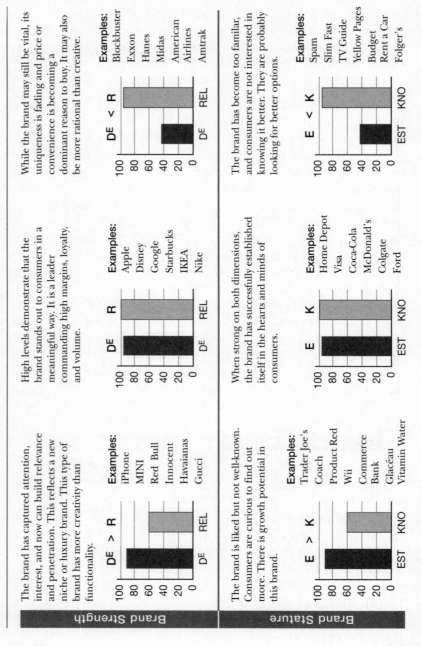

FIGURE 2.5. EACH PAIR OF PILLARS TELLS MANY STORIES.

Brand Strength

The brand has captured attention, interest, and now can build relevance and penetration. This reflects a new niche or luxury brand. This type of brand has more creativity than functionality.

DE > R

Examples:
iPhone
MINI
Red Bull
Innocent
Havaianas
Gucci

High levels demonstrate that the brand stands out to consumers in a meaningful way. It is a leader commanding high margins, loyalty, and volume.

DE ≈ R

Examples:
Apple
Disney
Google
Starbucks
IKEA
Nike

While the brand may still be vital, its uniqueness is fading and price or convenience is becoming a dominant reason to buy. It may also be more rational than creative.

DE < R

Examples:
Blockbuster
Exxon
Hanes
Midas
American Airlines
Amtrak

Brand Stature

The brand is liked but not well-known. Consumers are curious to find out more. There is growth potential in this brand.

E > K

Examples:
Trader Joe's
Coach
Product Red
Wii
Commerce Bank
Glacéau Vitamin Water

When strong on both dimensions, the brand has successfully established itself in the hearts and minds of consumers.

E ≈ K

Examples:
Home Depot
Visa
Coca-Cola
McDonald's
Colgate
Ford

The brand has become too familar, and consumers are not interested in knowing it better. They are probably looking for better options.

E < K

Examples:
Spam
Slim Fast
TV Guide
Yellow Pages
Budget Rent a Car
Folger's

FIGURE 2.6. THE BAV POWERGRID 2007.

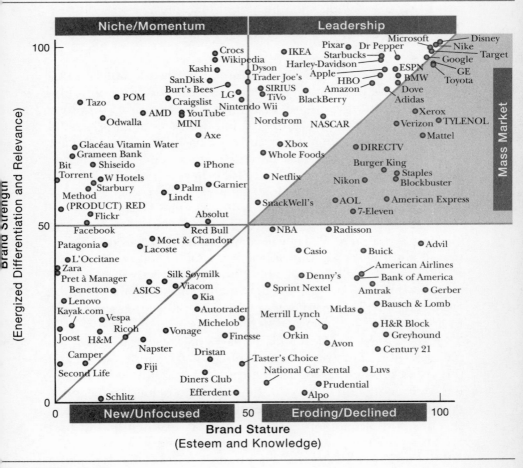

sort of "brand constellation," something that almost resembles a star-gazer map showing where all brands are at any given moment when compared to each other without regard to their category. This is because BAV is a category-agnostic study; it measures attributes on universal dimensions that apply to all brands, not just to brands within a given sector.

It is impossible to show all the brands we track, but Figure 2.6 presents a PowerGrid illustrating how a sampling of 125 brands from our study related one to another in 2007.

As Figure 2.6 illustrates, the PowerGrid naturally plots brand performance as falling into one of four quadrants, each indicative of a brand's status in a very specific and accurate way. Starting at the lower left and moving clockwise, we have:

- *The New and Unfocused Quadrant:* Brands that fall into this quadrant have little Brand Strength, with low scores in both Relevance and Energized Differentiation. This signifies that they haven't yet established meaningful knowledge among the general consumer population. Many brands falling into this quadrant are new entrants, trying to break into the market; others are lethargic brands that are being re-staged. Still others are poorly defined, middling brands that have lost their way. There is largely consumer misunderstanding or indifference to these brands.
- *The Niche/Momentum Quadrant:* These brands have low earnings but high potential. They have built some Energized Differentiation and Relevance, but only a small audience knows of them or considers them relevant. These brands are ready to pounce if they can build up their energy to launch into leadership positions. Here consumers are gravitating to these brands, expressing curiosity and interest. Their attraction is building.
- *The Leadership/Mass Market Quadrant:* These brands are simply irresistible. They have high earnings, high margin power, and the greatest potential to create future value. They've built both Brand Strength and Stature. If they slip down below the diagonal, their Stature has become greater than their Strength. Brands in this position often maintain their category leadership, but they are losing pricing power and future growth potential.
- *The Erosion Quadrant:* These brands are probably becoming commodities. Or they may be companies that do not rely on their brands as a driver of their growth, such as low-cost providers who create sales velocity at low margins. Consumers may know their brands well but regard them as less unique or relevant. These brands often struggle to overcome what consumers already know and expect from them. Attraction and irresistibility has turned into fatigue and discontent.

Most models explain how customers move from a state of awareness to the highest levels of commitment to a brand. They're often diagrammed as funnels or pyramids that portray a snapshot in time. In contrast, BAV is a fluid, developmental model, allowing us to identify clear patterns of growth, health, decay, or recovery over time. As we plot brand PowerGrids, we can literally study and track the evolution of brands through their movements as clearly as astronomers can learn from star and galaxy movement in the nighttime sky.

And like comets in their orbits, brands change in relative intensity through their life cycle, creating opportunities to maximize different financial metrics. In general, a brand that is niche, when brand strength is greater than stature, can maximize return on capital. As it develops into a leadership brand, managers can maximize margins and valuation multiples. And when the brand begins to decline and commoditize, managers can maximize its dividends and transactions. This points to the importance of matching brand development and business development strategies. When they're not aligned, bubbles happen.

IRRESISTIBLE BRANDS ELEVATE FROM THEIR CATEGORY

In regard to plotting movement, one revealing exercise is to plot high-energy brands against their category averages. Not surprisingly, some brands are so irresistible they transcend their categories and redefine their own market (Figure 2.7):

The BAV data driving this graph are related to the specific scores these brands received that attest to the multiples they have over their category averages. For example:

- Axe has 3.6 times the level of Energized Differentiation
- Dove has 1.6 times the pricing power
- eBay has 3.2 times the emotional commitment
- Geico has 2.8 times the momentum
- Google has 2 times the behavioral commitment
- iPod has 2.5 times the emotional commitment
- Orange has 1.6 times the usage and preference
- Starbucks has 2 times the pricing power
- Subway has 2.4 times the usage and preference
- Target has 2.3 times the emotional commitment

FIGURE 2.7. IRRESISTIBLE BRANDS BREAK OUT OF THEIR CATEGORIES.

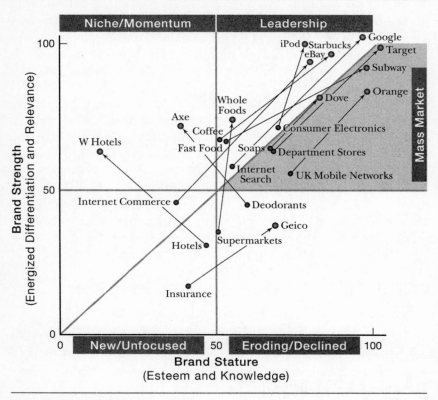

Base: BAV USA 2007 Q3; All Adults.

- W Hotels: 1.4 times the category pricing power
- Whole Foods: 2 times its category's pricing power (ah, but they're beautiful organic tomatoes!)

Irresistible brands are packed with energy. They become true leaders who set new expectations for the ways things should be. They don't hope for something as paltry as awareness. They upend ideologies and challenge convention. They market to value systems. They tap into mind-sets that source business from a broader cross-section of the marketplace, attracting new users and growing their categories. And they go where the money is, creating greater margin power and future value creation.

IRRESISTIBLE BRANDS ALSO
CREATE MAGNETISM

When a brand generates energy, it becomes more irresistible, which creates greater preference and usage, attracting new users. We analyzed over two thousand brands in BAV over a four-year period and found that brands with higher energy-to-equity ratios showed substantial growth in usage and preference over the following year. But those brands that had low ratios, or did not have the levels of energy to support the stature of their brand, suffered from virtually no growth in preference and usage over the following twelve months (Figure 2.8).

High energy-equity ratios demonstrate that passion can be rekindled in a well-established brand with a substantial near-term impact. This also means that consumers aren't closed off from hearing new ideas from a brand they may have once written off. In fact, they are willing to easily discard past brand impressions and open themselves up to seeing even a highly familiar brand in new ways. We see this in "Lazarus brands"

FIGURE 2.8. BRANDS WITH HIGH ENERGY-TO-EQUITY RATIOS DRIVE
INCREMENTAL BEHAVIOR AND ATTITUDES.

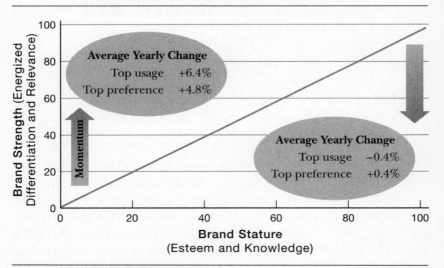

Source: BAV USA 2002–2008. Full Year; All Adults.

like Puma, Adidas, and Converse, as well as Gucci, Coach, and Burberry. Consumers also granted the resurrection of Marks & Spencer, IZOD, and Cadillac, which all came back as strong as John Travolta.

A prime example of a brand gaining energy and becoming irresistible once more is Dove. Like Southwest Airlines, Dove lives in one of the most established commoditized categories (soap), yet it has become one of the highest-energy brands. The brand elevated itself from a memorable product attribute focus ("one quarter cleansing cream") to engaging in a cultural conversation with consumers (reframing societal perceptions of beauty). In so doing, Dove proves that everything old can be new again, and the most ordinary of objects can again feel extraordinary.

STAGNANT BRANDS: PROOF OF THE BRAND BUBBLE

Now let's examine further proof of a brand bubble. Recall that a brand's position on our PowerGrid actually relates to level of intangible value. We measure this as "intangible value as per dollar of sales." (The circle in each quadrant shows the multiple factor analyzed across ten years of data and a thousand brands.) So only the brands that are moving toward greater Brand Strength (future value creation) and Brand Stature (current performance measures) are significantly performing for their companies. But movements of more than 2,500 brands across the PowerGrid found that *most brands showed little movement in Brand Strength between 2001 and 2006.* In Figure 2.9, the top number in each quadrant shows the percentage of brands that remained in the same quadrant after one year. The bottom number shows the percentage after three years. The overwhelming majority of brands in our study are standing still—or declining.

Despite Wall Street's ever-rising brand valuations, less than one brand in ten showed any positive movement over three years. After three years, 77 percent of brands were essentially motionless. Even after five years, 74 percent of all brands showed no sign of development. While brand valuations keep rising, the BAV brandscape looks like a parking lot of idling brands.

FIGURE 2.9. THE BRAND "PARKING LOT."

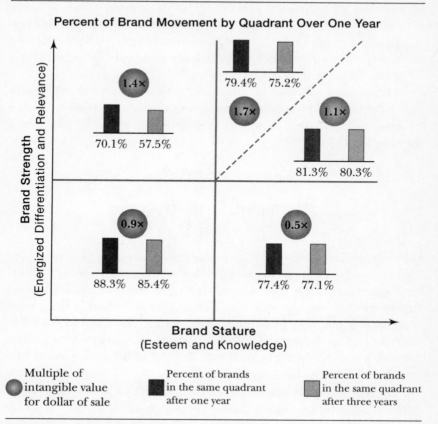

Percent of Brand Movement by Quadrant Over One Year

Base: BAV USA 2001–2006 Full Year; All Adults.

And of the few brands that did move, they were as likely to decline as to grow. Among brands in the niche/momentum quadrant, they were twice as likely to decline as become leadership brands. Let's call this the "Von Dutch" effect: Emerging brands more frequently emerge, only to disappear before they take hold in the culture. The patterns averaged out across all quadrants to suggest brand decay was occurring in those rare instances where brand attitudes were changing at all.

Once again, the data forces us to ask how it is possible that, with so few brands actually growing, the financial value of brands continues to experience such precipitous growth? Brands are accounting for a growing percentage of intangible value creation. Yet, from a consumer perspective, most brands are not delivering against expectations. A brand must be constantly evolving to increase in real value, but most have reached a plateau, if not stepped onto a steep slope.

This analysis should be a wake-up call. Why are we disregarding the realities of what consumers perceive and experience? Are brands really worth that much? Consumers seem to be offering a different opinion.

PUTTING OUR MONEY WHERE OUR DATA IS

Why are brands stalling? Why is energy important? A brand with higher levels of energy creates greater shareholder value. In 2004 we started an energy index fund that allowed us to track whether the markets actually pick up on nonfinancial attitudinal data concerning changes in brands. We created this fund in order to validate exactly how much higher consumer expectations for the greatest energy-gaining brands translated into actual financial performance over the long term.

Deciding to play our own "what-if" game, we invested a hypothetical $10,000 in the top fifty energy-gaining brands.[3] We compared our investment against an equal one in the S&P 500 index fund between December 31, 2001, and June 30, 2007. This time frame encompassed varying market conditions, including high, modest, and low growth periods in the S&P 500. We spread our $10,000 investment in each portfolio on a semi-annual basis, allowing six months for the energy to work its way through the price of the stock.

Since the second half of 2002, we have regularly compared our fund results with the performance of the S&P 500—and over the five-year period, our energy portfolio cumulatively beat the S&P 500 by 30 percent. On an annualized basis, the S&P 500 gained 5.02 percent, while the energy fund gained 10.15 percent (Figure 2.10).

FIGURE 2.10. IRRESISTIBLE BRANDS OUTPERFORM THE S&P 500.

The BAV fund of the top fifty energy-gaining brands netted $17,014 (+70%), versus S&P 500 $13,094 (+30%) on $10,000 investment made in 2001.

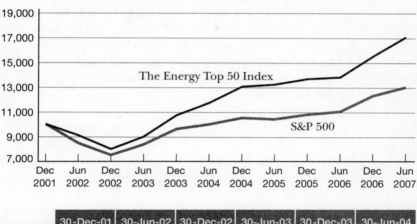

	30-Dec-01	30-Jun-02	30-Dec-02	30-Jun-03	30-Dec-03	30-Jun-04
S&P 500	$10,000.00	$8,621.52	$7,663.40	$8,488.08	$9,685.04	$9,936.94
BAV Top 50 Index	$10,000.00	$9,103.06	$7,951.63	$9,181.12	$10,857.64	$11,857.18

	30-Dec-04	30-Jun-05	30-Dec-05	30-Jun-06	30-Dec-06	30-Jun-07
S&P 500	$10,556.06	$10,376.72	$10,872.85	$11,063.69	$12,353.67	$13,094.47
BAV Top 50 Index	$13,034.74	$13,142.69	$13,709.51	$13,847.13	$15,574.70	$17,014.23

Source: Top fifty energy gainers (in a six-month period) identified from Y&R BAV (December 2001—June 2007); financial metrics from Yahoo Finance.

THE KEY TO DIFFERENTIATION: KEEP BEING DIFFERENT

Management gurus constantly assert that innovation resides at the heart of successful companies (although their starting point is often operational innovation, not consumer-side innovation). Michael E. Porter, perhaps the seminal thinker in innovation theory and author of *Competitive Advantage: Creating and Sustaining Superior Performance,* probably said it best when he argued that to have sustainable competitive advantage, you have to go way beyond operations (total quality management) to develop a competitive strategy difficult to imitate. This is how value is created, he insisted.

We agree. Porter puts his finger on why energy must be added to brand differentiation. In today's fast-changing world, *brands do not have lasting differentiation unless they have Energized Differentiation.* Real brand innovation and real brand value are driven by energy. Today, a brand must be constantly moving and shaped by the accelerated pace of marketplace and consumer change.

Since our discovery of energy and building our theory of an irresistible brand, we've spent many hours fleshing out our understanding of its nature and role, gathering insights into how energy is built and how it emanates from the brand into the marketplace. We're going to take the rest of the book to elaborate on the concepts and principles we've developed and teach you how to infuse energy into your brand and extend it through the value chain into your entire enterprise. We've created very precise steps, processes, and laws that can be applied to any product or service.

Before we get to that, however, the remainder of Part One delves further into the forces driving the necessity for Energized Differentiation. These forces are deeply embedded in the new world in which we live, a world that redefines consumer behavior and the business models brands must follow. We call this new world "ConsumerLand," and it's a place where consumers act like investors, crave creative products, and hold power over brands. The analysis presented in the next three chapters will nourish a more contemporary understanding of how consumers feel and experience brands—and of why your brand needs to infuse itself with energy.

CHAPTER THREE

WALL STREET, MEET MAIN STREET

*Consumers always choose to move forward,
rewarding the companies that anticipate their
demands and punishing those that don't.*
—STEVE HUGHES, DIRECTOR, CAMBRIDGE GROUP[1]

Each year since 1985, tens of thousands of Apple devotees flock to Macworld, eager to learn more about the company's present and future products. For attendees, the event is inspiring and exciting. As Macworld's Web site proclaims, "Macworld isn't just a hall full of exhibitors or rooms of conference sessions; it's a series of calibrations of the world as you know it. Your perspective will be jolted. Your creativity will be ramped up. You will walk away realizing it's not just the world that's changed. It's you, too."

Macworld's success and popularity provide insight into a new truth about consumers today: they don't just buy brands—they invest in them. Faced with so much choice in the marketplace, *consumers now select brands based on the same principles investors use to select stocks.* In choosing a brand, consumers now seek to maximize the return on their investment, whether that return comes to them in enjoyment, knowledge, security, appearance, or social currency. And in doing so, they project out to imagine a brand's potential usefulness. They want to invest in a brand with a plan, one that brings them benefits tomorrow, not just today.

This is a familiar concept to marketers, who think of the "lifetime value of a customer." Only now the tables have turned. Instead, consumers think of *the lifetime value of a brand*. To even contemplate a future relationship, a brand must have built-in expectations that entice customers to come back again and again. Most firms don't recognize this new "consumer as investor" behavior. Instead they focus the majority of their time and effort on managing their shareholders, whose needs are more immediate, tangible, and demanding. Consumers, by contrast, are fickle, ever changing, and their motivations are often unclear. The result often becomes that consumers are viewed with the purpose of stimulating the immediate bottom line through hard-nosed, persuasive sales appeals.

But what business has not realized is that consumers and investors are more alike than not. The qualities consumers look for in a brand are increasingly similar to what investors seek in a company. Just as enterprise value reflects investor confidence in the company's ability to deliver future earnings, brand value reflects consumer confidence in a brand's ability to deliver future enjoyment and utility. This explains the disparity between business and consumers when it comes to perceived brand value: Consumers are no longer confident in the future performance of most brands they buy.

FIVE PARALLEL BEHAVIORS OF CONSUMERS AND INVESTORS

We observed that consumers apply five of the same thought processes in choosing what brands to buy as investors use to choose what assets they hold. Like stock buyers, consumers evaluate a brand based on the utility they expect to receive today, as well as in the future. Figure 3.1 lays out the five core traits that align consumer and investor behavior.

Let's examine in detail the similarities between investor and consumer behaviors you'll need to begin understanding in order to build energy into your brand. Being marketers, not psychologists, we are making some generalizations in describing these behaviors, but we're confident you will find them more accurate about consumers than most mutual fund managers are about your investments.

FIGURE 3.1. INVESTORS AND CONSUMERS THINK ALIKE.

Behavior	Investors	Consumers
1. Seek future benefit	Investors evaluate an asset based on the cash flows they expect to receive in the future.	Consumers assess brands based on benefits they expect to receive in the future.
2. Maximize current return	Investors aim to maximize current earnings. They discount cash flows, placing a higher value on cash today.	Consumers have greater expectations for brands to instantly gratify, surprise, and delight.
3. Accumulate information and knowledge before investing	Investors rely on a variety of information and market indicators.	Consumers are now expert interrogators of company and brand intentions.
4. Seek movement and innovation to simplify choice	Investors follow the movements of innovative and visionary companies to inform their investment decision making.	Consumers examine brand movement and creativity as a way to decide which brands to hold in their portfolio.
5. Demand transparency and accountability	Investors demand ever more transparency in all aspects of a company's performance.	Consumers make brands and companies accountable for their actions, not just their words.

PARALLEL #1: CONSUMERS AND INVESTORS SEEK FUTURE BENEFITS

Today's consumers are voracious planners. Almost nothing they touch goes unplanned. The planning craze is equally characteristic of Baby Boomers, Gen Xers, and Millennials.

Throughout the country, parents anxiously configure their children's lives as soon as the tykes can walk. They choose homes based on school district, or they evaluate private elementary schools as if they were sending their five-year-old to Harvard. The *New York Times* reported "fierce competition for private preschool in New York City has been propelled to such frenzy . . . by the increased numbers of children vying for scarce slots that it could be mistaken for a kiddie version of 'The Apprentice.'"[2] College consultants, SAT prep classes, and internships have all become big business in preparing kids to get out of the gate early and stay ahead. And minors pick majors in Florida, Mississippi, and New York by committing to career paths in coursework as early as the sixth grade.

Futurist thinking sometimes goes to wacky extremes. BioEden is a company that extracts and preserves baby teeth for parents who bank on potential stem cell therapies for their kids. Other companies store everything from umbilical cord blood to the head of baseball great Ted Williams. Kids and adults alike purchased 1.5 million copies of *Harry Potter and the Deathly Hallows* from Amazon before it hit the shelves. Wine lovers buy Bordeaux, Rhone, and Italian futures to plan dinner parties ten years hence.

The point is, today's consumers decide their future *now,* and this extends to their brand choices. They contemplate their brand choices with a keen eye to long-term horizons, and they evaluate products and services based on the future benefits they might derive. They project onto brands their expectations and hopes about tomorrow's performance. Like investors picking blue-chip stocks, consumers select brands that will be around for years. If they are going to affiliate with a brand, they have to believe it will produce more value for them beyond today.

Consumers especially want to feel a sense that a brand has more to come down the line. They look for a "Version 2.0" for virtually every aspect of life, a perpetual hunt for the next upgrade. This behavior does not derive from a concern about depreciation or product failure. Today's products are actually built to last longer than they were ten years ago, but consumers replace them more quickly. From laptops to cell phones and car leases to adjustable-rate mortgages, consumers cycle through consumption faster than ever before. This means that brands must be forward thinking and innovative, not only in their offerings but in their conversations with consumers.

Think back to professor Jacobson's research about consumer attitudes having a future impact on brands. Like investors, consumers have no desire to buy a company with flat earnings and poor prospects. They want brands that demonstrate staying power by creating anticipation for the future.

PARALLEL #2: CONSUMERS AND INVESTORS WANT TO MAXIMIZE CURRENT RETURNS

While one eye is on the future, the other is on the here and now. Like investors, today's consumers also want as much immediate return as they can get. We're talking impulsive, live-in-the-moment behavior and instant gratification. That's why, according to Paco

Underhill in *The Science of Shopping,* two-thirds of all purchases are unplanned.

Anyone who minored in psychology understands why consumers behave this way. At least 95 percent of all cognition occurs in the subconscious. People subconsciously filter and rationalize in order to justify their behaviors. Scientists have identified at least sixty-seven cognitive biases in the human brain. These biases distort the way people perceive reality, which, in turn, affects the formation of beliefs and decisions. Many cognitive biases are coping strategies that help maximize current happiness:

- *Confirmation bias* supports our tendency to search for or interpret information in a way that confirms our current preoccupations.
- *Self-serving bias* supports our tendency to claim more responsibility for our successes than our failures, and to evaluate ambiguous information in a way beneficial to our interests.
- *Choice-supportive bias* supports our tendency to remember our choices as being better and wiser than they actually were.

Our subconscious wills us to constantly crave and live in the moment, so our coping strategies are structured to reaffirm our happiness and keep us believing we're making the right decisions. Buying for the moment follows the same psychology as investors. You have to believe what you're investing in is a good choice that will pay off big, hopefully both now and later. Think back again to Figure 1.1 (The Nature of the Brand Bubble). Consumers will select brands with the most "added value," but their expectations increasingly aren't being met by most brands. So when it comes to long-term brand loyalty, consumers are nearsighted.

PARALLEL #3: CONSUMERS AND INVESTORS ACCUMULATE INFORMATION AND KNOWLEDGE BEFORE INVESTING

Today's consumers behave like analysts: they have an endless appetite for information, and now they have access to it. They pre-search their product purchases, evaluating in-depth product innovation and collecting brand feedback from ratings and consumer review sites, trying to spot its growing or weakening potential. They judge customer experience and the retail environment where transactions occur. And they will gladly share their knowledge with others.

One of the forces behind this new appetite for information is simply that people are savvier today and can absorb more data. A higher level of education in most of the Western world and Asia has produced hundreds of millions of literate, discerning, intelligent consumers who are hungry to understand their surroundings. In *The Average American,* Kevin O'Keefe points to the GI bill after World War II, which enabled millions of returning soldiers to go to college.[3] That generation then encouraged their Baby Boomer children to reach ever higher for more degrees, and Boomers are now doing the same with their kids. In 2006, 85 percent of the U.S. population over age twenty-five had a high school diploma, while 27 percent had a bachelor's degree (Figure 3.2).

Through education, people have developed intellectual capabilities, becoming more conceptual and able to juggle more data. Our perpetual multitasking trains us to store and process vast amounts of information at once. Today 70 percent of media users consume more than one medium at a time.[4] Millennials, in

FIGURE 3.2. PERCENTAGE OF POPULATION TWENTY-FIVE YEARS OLD AND OLDER, BY HIGHEST LEVEL OF EDUCATIONAL ATTAINMENT—1940–2006.

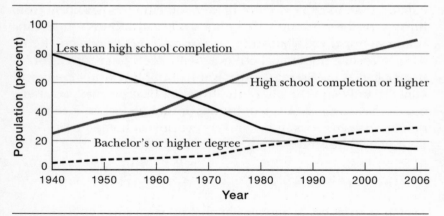

Source: U.S. Department of Commerce, Census Bureau, "U.S. Census of Population," 1960, Vol. 1, Part 1. Current Population Reports, Series P-Z0: "Current Population Survey (CPS)," March 1961 through March 2006. "Education of the American Population," 1960 Census Monograph, John K. Folger.

particular, are the first generation to grow up with multitasking as a dominant form of behavior and communication. Many popular television shows feed into this newly developed tolerance for multiplicity, packing a dozen storylines and scores of characters into complex "procedural dramas" that demand a level of intelligence and cognitive engagement never asked of TV viewers before. When *CSI* was presented for review to ABC in 1999, it was dismissed as too confusing for the average viewer. Hit movies like *Memento* and *The Da Vinci Code* prove the more complexity, the better.

The rise of video gaming equally speaks to a growing fascination for rigorous mental workouts. In *Everything Bad Is Good for You: How Today's Popular Culture Is Actually Making Us Smarter,* author Steven Johnson explains, "The first and last thing that should be said about the experience of playing today's video games, the thing you almost never hear in mainstream coverage, is that games are fiendishly, sometimes maddeningly, hard."[5] And as games get harder and harder, more people, not fewer, want to get involved. Nearly 60 percent of households with adults age eighteen to forty-four now own a video game system. When Halo 3 came out, it significantly disrupted summer movie box office receipts.

Like today's investors, today's consumers have a growing aptitude for organizing and reducing complex information, and that has increased the amount of data storage they can handle from brands. As a result, providing open and ready access to information is now one of the most important aspects of brand building. This "information democracy" is equally likely to grow a brand— or to kill it. We've returned to a John Stuart Mill world of perfectly competitive markets, where the Internet blasts apart traditional barriers, giving unprecedented opportunities for brands to develop in new markets around the world—across political barriers, and with less investment and scale required to compete. People can help a new brand or a new idea find millions of new consumers with little or no media investment. Today, new brands have just as much chance of being discovered as established brands have of being maimed.

Perhaps brands are becoming overvalued because a lot of big businesses still believe they have barriers to competitive entry in their markets. In fact, such barriers no longer exist, courtesy of digitization, media fragmentation, and globalization. In the past, media costs were the biggest barrier to entry in most markets. In most cases, the only organization with significant customer impact was the brand leader. All the others had the same media costs but much lower sales to pay for them. Therefore number two, three, four brands either lost money or died off altogether. But today this is no longer true. Now the interrupt-and-repeat model is gone. And big brands are increasingly vulnerable to attack from niche brands that weren't profitable yesterday—but today can be very profitable indeed.

The brand that satisfies the growing consumer thirst for information is exploring new technologies such as smart bar codes, click-and-know, point-and-know, text-and-know, video billboards, talking house-for-sale signs—anything with potential educational value.

PARALLEL #4: CONSUMERS AND INVESTORS WATCH FOR MOVEMENT TO SIMPLIFY CHOICE

With more than fifty thousand public companies traded on stock exchanges around the world, investors need reliable methods of sifting out the leaders from the laggards. One of the key techniques they employ is watching for movement. They notice hot stocks based on how many others are buying or selling them, how fast the stock is rising or falling, and which stocks lead their industry pack. The Internet and newspapers have responded with daily, hourly, and minute-by-minute lists of the most active stocks, the biggest gainers and biggest losers, the biggest percentage winners and losers, and so on. Meanwhile TV screens feature the ubiquitous bottom scroll banner as a constant reminder that the market moves.

Today's consumers do exactly the same thing to select brands and form a portfolio of winners. Like investors, they constantly track brands, share information and ask each other, "Is this a hot brand?" "Where is this brand heading?" "Is it worth sticking with?" With so many brands roaming the landscape, they are swayed by the motion of brands that change, create, and innovate. The products, services, and ideas that thrive are the ones that catch the eye.

The search for motion explains why consumers love blogs, dashboards, and widgets—tools that help them track movement and spot winners. They help each other find the leaders through Web sites like Tripadvisor, where 6 million consumers post travel reviews. Epinions.com hosts more than 2 million reviews from

400,000-plus members, while FlyerTalk posts 4.5 million reviews that report on the airline industry.

It's not just consumers watching brands for movement; brands watch each other for movement, too. Pricenoia monitors the best prices across the various international Amazon.com Web sites. Scanbuy will return to your phone the best price on any given brand when you send a photo of its barcode.

Given the speed at which things change, today's consumers believe they cannot sit back and miss out on something new. They constantly debate and revise their choices in an effort to stay on top of the brand world. Their selection radar is always turned on, assessing the brand horizon, then adopting and adapting as needed—to stay ahead and in control.

Marketers often talk like they can hunt consumers, using terms like *targeting, captive audience,* and so on, but the deer now have the rifles. Consumers act as their own V-Chips. Around 160 million phone numbers in the U.S. are on the "do not call" list, 43.6 million U.S. households have some form of DVR, and 73 percent of online consumers use spam blockers. Brands simply no longer dictate the terms of the relationship. Consumers constantly assess a brand's motion, momentum, and direction as a prerequisite to future consideration.

PARALLEL #5: CONSUMERS AND INVESTORS DEMAND TRANSPARENCY AND ACCOUNTABILITY

Since the Enron debacle and the parade of corporate scandals that followed it, investors have little tolerance for executive chicanery. The Sarbanes-Oxley Act and the Federal Sentencing Guidelines hold corporations and their directors responsible for truthful and timely accounting practices, implementing a corporate code of conduct, and overseeing ethical employee behavior at every level.

The same corporate scrutiny has worked its way into the consumer mind-set. A brand's integrity is emerging as a critical purchasing factor for consumers. Evidence of ethical behavior, social responsibility, and concern for sustainability now weigh heavily on consumer choices. The Conference Board conducted a poll of twenty-five thousand people in twenty-three countries, and two-thirds agreed that they want business to "expand beyond the traditional emphasis on profits and contribute to broader social objectives."[6] In the United States, 81 percent of consumers say they are likely to switch brands to support a cause if price and quality are equal.

Corporate and brand responsibility are so intertwined with brand image now that when consumers feel an incongruity, they react swiftly. Best Buy came under scrutiny for hosting a secret employee intranet site that blocked customers from getting the best prices advertised on their regular site. Sure enough, a retaliatory Web site called "Goodbyebestbuy.com" enlisted individuals to boycott the brand. *Ghetto Big Mac* was a popular video on YouTube that attacked McDonald's nutritional and social values. Just typing the word *scandal* retrieves more than thirty thousand videos on YouTube.

Today's consumer is armed with technological advances that allow no misinformation or scandal to remain hidden for long. Anyone can instantly find and expose almost any brand or company secret. It's pointless to think otherwise. As consumers increasingly look for a commitment to ethics, transparency, and accountability, brands need to practice complete disclosure with consumers. That's why many companies now act swiftly by voluntarily announcing problems to their customers and offering apologies or product rebates. JetBlue apologized to customers caught in the winter storm fiasco and Apple made good to the early adopters of iPhones after it dropped its original $599 price tag. To be a high-energy brand today, you have to be open, helpful, and compliant—because your actions speak louder than your words.

A HISTORICAL PERSPECTIVE

When you put all these behaviors together, the result is a consumer who bases decisions on a psychology not all that different from the savvy investor's. This behavior is relatively new, a reflection of the increasing sophistication today's consumers bring to the buying process. Historically, consumers based their purchasing choices on which price segment best fit their earnings. Lower-income households purchased entry- or economy-level goods and services, while middle-class households traded up to mainstream goods, and the upper class exclusively bought luxury.

This made sense in a *Jeffersons* kind of world. In that era, companies created an offering for every income and a purchase path for those who were "moving on up." Different brand segments functioned to simplify choice, guarantee quality (reduce risk), and create aspiration for people to climb from their current station in the world.

That model has changed. Consumers routinely break through the old brand management caste system. The performance and styling of products has flattened, and democratization of quality now permeates fashion, retail, hotels, automotive, and most consumer goods. Traditional mass brands are left struggling to maintain existing levels of market share as consumers buy brands based on their passions, rather than simply price.

And if a consumer can now buy a brand with the necessary features and benefits (utility) in the lower or even lowest price tier—and if these goods meet or exceed quality expectations—then utility and risk are no longer points on which brands can sustain competitive advantage. Brands that stand only for trust, reassurance, and simplification of choice are no longer positioned for long-term success. This too begins to explain the declining brand measures from Chapter One. Consumers are looking for something more.

THE RATIONAL CONSUMER: MAXIMIZING VALUE

When we put together the five behavior parallels, today's "irrational consumer" is better understood by examining the mind-set of a "rational investor."

We know that investors base their purchasing decisions on three steps: assessing the net present value of the company, evaluating its option value, and considering the risk factors. Investors seek to maximize total potential value while minimizing risk. In the end, the financial asset with greater net present value, most option value, and least risk is usually the most desirable.

Today, consumers implicitly evaluate brands by the same formula. They estimate which brands will return the greatest value for the least risk both today *and* tomorrow. The "net present value" equals the expected functional and emotional enjoyment from usage. The "option value" equals the potential future meaning of choosing this brand today. And the "risk adjustment" is the brand's perceived level of quality, its innovation, and in essence its permanence. The brand with the greatest net present value, most option value, and least risk is usually the most desirable.

The option value of an investment is higher when it offers greater future potential. An asset with higher option value will have a higher net present value and can sell for a higher price today. The same is true for brands. Even if the product is consumed or disposed of, a brand has option value if consumers believe it brings future benefits to them, is planning new innovations, and will take them to new places. *The perception of option value is what consumers feel in an irresistible brand.*

An irresistible brand is worth more today because it has greater potential to do more tomorrow. Consumers can envision greater options by selecting it. They can imagine future experiences and possibilities that are more expansive and exciting than those offered by other brands. Here's a short quiz to prove this point. In each pair, which brand has more option value in your mind?

- Toyota or GM?
- Netflix or Blockbuster?
- Wikipedia or Britannica?
- Google or AOL?
- Puma or Reebok?
- Whole Foods or Safeway?
- Virgin Atlantic or Delta Air Lines?
- Craigslist or Yellow Pages?
- Geico or State Farm?
- Best Buy or Circuit City?

Just as investors choose financial assets that give them the greatest upside with the most flexibility, consumers will search for high-energy, irresistible brands because they seem to assure the greatest long-term upside. Consumers—time-pressed and inundated from all sides—are searching for beacons that provide order and direction. Their loss of trust, coupled with the urgency of adjusting to a rapidly changing world, creates the need for that scarce signal of certainty and help that is found in an irresistible brand. As the future looks even more uncertain to navigate, these special brands create an irresistible force of gravity and grounding.

This need for managing the future translates into a new consumer purchasing behavior. Even when today's consumers can get "good enough" and "works fine" for less money—and where risk has been largely removed from most transactions—they are willing to spend more on a brand that promises more down the road. They want brands that come with compliments, envy, and desire; brands that point the way to a more hopeful future; brands that are so creative—so full of possibilities—have such momentum—feel so in the moment—they attract a following. These brands bring badge value, narcissism, social currency, belongingness, aesthetic beauty, and other dynamic, fulfilling, positive feelings. They're irresistible.

And herein lies another discovery: *Consumers have already figured out the brand bubble.* As we've seen with past bubbles, ordinarily rational investors can turn a blind eye to risk if they see enormous returns on the horizon. But in this instance, even when risk has been nullified, consumers see fewer rainbows in the brands they buy today. They've concluded that brands in their repertoire have various levels of emotional and financial investment, with most of them not worth the effort. Across the myriad purchases they make in their daily lives, consumers are pruning their portfolio to a special set of brands that help them feel they are moving forward and offering new ideas, hope, and optimism. These are brands with an abundance of energy. These are the ones we've found that are driving disproportionate future value in the BAV index fund.

How is this future value created? Let's reveal another interesting dynamic we found in consumer behavior.

THE DELAYED IMPACT OF ENERGY ON SALES

Remember that one of the key tip-offs about energy found in Jacobson's research related to how brand attitude changes were predictive of unanticipated market changes one or two quarters later. We've talked about how the classic marketing methods of building trust, awareness, regard, and esteem are insufficient in today's world because they deal only with today, while Energized Differentiation helps brands build for tomorrow. And we've emphasized how energy functions to keep brands moving forward and in step with consumers.

This future-orientation is a constant theme about Energized Differentiation, and we can see it play out in the marketplace in a pattern that reinforces the insight that consumers act like investors. We found that when a brand asset improves, indicated by rising Brand Strength and Stature, one-third of the effect is directly recognized in the current period as sales increases. This indicates that some number of customers perceive the brand momentum and go out and buy the brand right away.[7] But there is also a lag effect; two-thirds of the effects of the brand improvement appear in future sales, often two to three quarters later. For example, if thirty people feel more favorably toward Puma today, ten of them will go out and buy new sneakers, while twenty will buy Pumas in the not-so-distant future. Both groups feel the brand has improved in their estimation, they just behave differently: twenty more pairs of sneakers will ring up in cash registers one to two quarters hence. Figure 3.3 illustrates the timing on returns.

Both these effects reinforce the point that Energized Differentiation not only has a predictive value in the market, it inspires additional future performance.

This also means that the intangible brand can be made more tangible. Our composite measure of Brand Strength (Energized Differentiation plus Relevance) reflects an impressive level of explanatory power relative to future earnings. We determined that it is 81 percent as effective as sales growth and 53 percent as powerful as earnings-to-assets ratios in explaining changes in a brand's market value. It also adds an incremental 64 percent to sales growth and 61 percent to earnings-to-assets in explanatory power in understanding future financial performance. We're able to quantify a brand's impact in creating both current and future

FIGURE 3.3. WHEN A BRAND IMPROVES ITS ENERGY, TWO-THIRDS OF THE VALUE IS CREATED IN THE FUTURE.

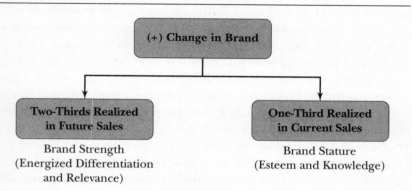

financial value for a firm. Our measure explains more than 16 percent of enterprise value movement across almost a thousand brands. We're beginning to establish a statistically valid bridge between brand momentum and financial success metrics.

Overall, there's an important lesson here. Given the tendency to measure marketing's effectiveness in the current period for quarterly sales, firms are erroneously missing two-thirds of the value they are creating from successful brand building. It's necessary to look further ahead to see what value the brand asset changes will bring beyond today. Today's brand decisions actually have twice the impact on the future as on the present. You can build future value by creating Energized Differentiation today.

TYSON FOODS DISCOVERS BRAND IMMORTALITY

To demonstrate just how much future value creation is possible, we turned to Justin Pettit, a partner at Booz & Company, to study the effects further. Pettit works with businesses of all kinds who are seeking growth strategies through acquisitions, new products, M&As, and the like. Often these firms are capital constrained, credit ratings are tight, and margins are slipping, and that comes through in their evaluation. Pettit is looking for something he calls "brand immortality," where multiple layers in the revenue line exist in a business, and to achieve this, Justin is bullish on brands. He told us, "Often the biggest asset a company has is right under its nose." Witness his investigation of Tyson.

In 2002, Tyson Foods (trading at about six times EBITDA) began a journey that would eventually lead to a dramatic revaluation of the company, manifesting in a much higher multiple—about thirteen times EBITDA. The company signaled its new strategy with the announcement to extend its well-known poultry brand into other proteins. This was followed by actions over the next five years that also added meal kits, prepared meals, and canned chicken, beef, and pork to the Tyson brand. Pettit says, "This new strategy required analysts to view the stock in a whole new light. Rather than a single stream of revenue, with an outlook, and ultimately a finite life, the brand represented a portfolio of multiple streams of cash flow of varying size, outlook, and life span, such that in aggregate the franchise represented something with no obvious endpoint—an infinite stream of cash flows and a much greater proportion of the enterprise value now attributable to growth." Tyson's brand had achieved a greater degree of immortality and the stock's valuation reflected this. (See Figure 3.4.)

FIGURE 3.4. MARKET REWARDS FOR BRAND IMMORTALITY STRATEGY.

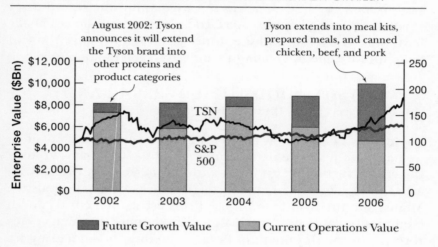

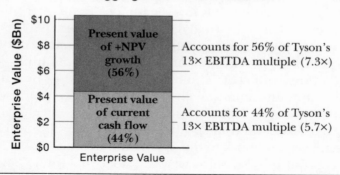

Note: Share price adjusted to include dividends.

Source: CapitalIQ, Booz & Company analysis; peer group includes Pilgrim's Pride, Smithfield, Hormel, and ConAgra.

POWER OF BRANDS TO CHANGE INDUSTRY VALUATION MULTIPLES

The success of our index fund and Tyson's expanding value creation actually underscores the exceptional predictive market powers of a high-energy, irresistible brand. In a recent exploration of data, we found that Energized Differentiation plays a powerful role in driving up the multiple between sales and market value in industry valuations. The multiple is defined in this case as "the log of enterprise value over sales."

Given that every industry follows a different multiple, we examined a wide range of industries, looking at dozens of brands within each industry to assess which factors most strongly affect the industry multiple. In common thinking, it is usually perceived that financial results are the driver of an industry's multiple, but our data showed that the Energized Differentiation can change the multiple significantly:

- *Financial and insurance industry:* The Energized Differentiation of a brand had 40 percent of the power of financial results to increase the multiple.
- *Manufacturing industry:* The Energized Differentiation of a brand had 27 percent of the power of financial results to increase the multiple.
- *Travel industry:* The Energized Differentiation of a brand had 43 percent of the power of financial results to increase the multiple.
- *Technology and Internet industry:* The overall Brand Stature (including Energized Differentiation and Relevance) of a brand had 27 percent of the power of financial results to increase the multiple.

In all these industries, data like this provides weighty support that *brands can protect their future earnings by constantly reinventing themselves.* What are the consequences of resting? If we think back to ten years ago, was there a brand bubble in Sony? As they were enjoying the vaunted "Sony premium," did they properly discount the risk of their enormous brand value? Now they exist in a world where LG, Samsung, and Apple are equally dominant forces in consumer electronics. Consumers are investors looking forward, and your future earnings rely on servicing their future expectations of your brand.

IMPACTING PRICING POWER AND VOLUME, TODAY

What we also saw from the Tyson example is that well-disciplined and carefully managed brands can travel across categories and create future value, often far more efficiently than speculative mergers, acquisitions, and other growth strategies. And for the C-suite that is focused on putting energy into the brand to energize business valuations, there's also this good news: *Energy drives margins and volume simultaneously.*

Whenever an overflow of consumer choice and ease of imitation meet technology and globalization, there's a tendency for brands, products, and services to commoditize. As that happens, managers face a choice between *differentiation* (be special and cling to a niche to hold up pricing power) and *relevance* (have mass appeal to drive volume generation through lower pricing). It's usually a no-win trade-off: go for the volume with lower pricing, or take the higher price point position at the expense of market share.

An energized brand is able to bridge this chasm. Energy drives both margin and volume. It can boost market share with profitable growth.

How is this possible, especially when (according to Economics 101) the volume of goods sold increases only as the price of a product decreases? It's usually a negative pricing relationship from niche to commodity. The answer: While a brand's differentiation traditionally stimulates pricing power, and its relevance impacts potential units sold, energy has an uncanny ability to boost both. Energy creates greater net present value, so its pricing power remains strong in the present. But in addition, its option value, derived from its Energized Differentiation, also creates greater pricing power at each level of quantity demanded. The net effect is that a brand with energy shifts the demand curve outward, improving pricing power for each incremental unit of product sold without diluting the quantity of units sold (Figure 3.5.)

FIGURE 3.5. ENERGY SHIFTS THE DEMAND CURVE OUTWARD.

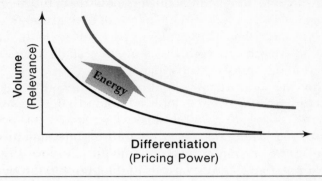

Note: Across the U.S. brandscape, energy significantly drives relevant differentiation, $r = .59$.

Source: BAV, 2007. All adults 18 and over.

Compare this behavior to that of a hot stock whose price and demand both rise. With energized brands, the same phenomenon happens: as demand increases, the brand's pricing power also rises. Its greater energy means greater option value, so more consumers are willing to pay more for the brand. (This means these brands fight the forces of today's commoditization by driving margin power today, while stimulating demand and expectations for tomorrow.) Even small increments of Energized Differentiation can enhance market share and margin in any category and in any type of brand. Look at Herman Miller's Aeron chairs, which have become the default choice in corporations today, even at the hefty price of $750 (and even though they bombed in focus groups). The option value of these chairs is clearly a lesson to sit on.

BUILDING FUTURE VALUE

There's simply no doubt that the market value of a brand is influenced by its energy, which raises its irresistible quotient, which affects its future earnings and creates its future value today. Consumers react to this energy well in advance of actual sales. When Apple announced the iPhone, its shares shot up $7.10 in one day on the NASDAQ, adding over $6 billion to its market capitalization. Meanwhile, shares of RIM (BlackBerry) lost $11.16, and Palm, Nokia, and Motorola slipped as well. Apple's energy clearly signified future value in the minds of both investors and consumers. Not surprisingly, this brings us back full circle to Macworld, as Apple is certainly one company that treats all its stakeholders—consumers and investors—with equal regard.

By showing your organization how consumers think like investors, you can urge everyone to look at brand management through a familiar lens—creating shareholder value. Since basic principles of investor management now apply to brand management, customer relations become remarkably similar to investor relations, making it possible to unify various ideologies about how brands and companies should be managed.

Ultimately, investors in a brand must now be managed with the same emphasis as investors in the company. We can no longer afford to ignore consumers or exclude them from the boardroom. If anything, the strong link between changing consumer sentiments toward a brand and that brand's stock price demands we see consumers' opinion of our brands as being at least as important as that of shareholders' impressions of our stocks. Brands with energy have the greatest chance to turn their investors into consumers—and their consumers into investors.

CHAPTER FOUR

THE POSTMODERN CRAVING FOR CREATIVITY

Happiness is not in the mere possession of money; it lies in the joy of achievement, in the thrill of creative effort.

— FRANKLIN D. ROOSEVELT

Anyone with children of middle school age or younger will know that Radiator Springs is the fictional town just off Route 66 featured in the animated movie *Cars*. It's the place where rookie race car "Lightning" McQueen works out his community service, while falling in love with the tired old town and its big-hearted inhabitants. This pixilated dot on the map sprang from the imagination of those clever people at Pixar—the animation house that's given traditional studios a stop-frame lesson in entertaining the American public. Pixar achieved its dominance by making astonishing shifts in what was thought possible in animated filmmaking. And in Radiator Springs, we see pure creativity exemplified in reviving the fortunes of a small town by finding new creative avenues to lure people and businesses back to what had become a ghost town.

Two hundred years ago, creativity, art, and culture were considered diversions for those engaged in industrial activity: unproductive recreations offering no more value than a little R&R. We can't blame people for seeing things that way. The Victorian Age was all about moving physical objects around in the physical world, of natural resources mechanically hewn from the earth, converted into goods, and transported to the consumer's door. After all that activity, people needed to relax in front of the latest Renoir or Rodin: the LCD TVs of their day.

Today there's growing recognition that creativity, art, and culture are far more than just decorative. Creativity is now an economic force, reshaping the work world, putting the Industrial Age to bed. Creative invention and creative work are now understood to be essential drivers of jobs and wealth. Richard Florida argues in *The Creative Class* that those cities that cater to creative individuals working in high technology, education, publishing, medicine, law, and artistic endeavors will be the ones to succeed in the future. Like Radiator Springs, old factory cities like White River Junction, Vermont, and Pittsfield, Massachusetts, once thought dead and depopulated, have started a revival process based on bringing in creative industries.

The U.S. economy is changing so radically that the Bureau of Labor Statistics estimates that workers employed in industry now make up less than 10 percent of the workforce, the lowest level since 1850. Similarly, the United Kingdom has shifted its focus away from manufacturing and now proclaims itself the world leader in creative services. The British estimate their creative and cultural industries such as architecture, filmmaking, and advertising account for 7.1 percent of their overall economy, employing almost 2 million and placing this type of work on a par with the financial industry. The creative edge is now where competitive advantage is achieved through startling innovation and paradigm-shifting thought.

It's only reasonable to wonder, What is making creativity the driving force of the modern world? Why has it become so crucial, not just to our economy and social structure but to our well-being as well? And what role does creativity play in energy brands and how does it drive consumers to gravitate toward them?

The growing societal attraction to creativity has its roots in the postmodern world's existential angst and our need to realize the human search for meaning. Modernism romanced us with the idea that things can only get better. Modernism promised our whites can be whiter, our cars can be faster, and our houses can be bigger. It perpetuated the idea that progress is our birthright and that we can buy improvement through material acquisition.

So what about postmodernism? It happens when someone points out that modernism can no longer conceal the truths made all too apparent by contemporary life. After all these years, maybe "progress" isn't all that it'd been made out to be? Since World War II, the dawn of the postmodern era, Western culture has been roiling with the loss of a centralized organizing principle (for example, God). The simplicity and the natural cycles of life that formerly brought stability and reassured people have been replaced with complex systems, cynicism, and doubt. Intellectually and spiritually, we no longer feel we understand the human purpose; deriving meaning out of life eludes many of us day by day. Blind consumerism is hollow, and material possessions seem to provide little help in knowing why we exist on this planet.

Like nine-year-olds wrestling with the question of Santa Claus, we believe, consumers are torn between wanting to believe modernist promises and being too savvy to suspend disbelief. As witness, note how consumers have grown less fascinated by marketing and have begun to shift their relationship to it. Marketing can no longer fool consumers—but who wants to buy a straightforward, albeit honest product? It's a conflict that few marketers can recognize. Yet we've found that creative brands transcend their skepticism of marketing, allowing them to believe with no sense of hypocrisy, thus resolving the conflict.

At its most primal level, creativity promises *happiness, honesty, and hope*. Creativity counteracts the lack of meaning. Creativity promises guidance. Creative people and innovative ideas are inspirational. Creativity subliminally signals numerous benefits to our well-being, qualities like youthfulness, immortality, confidence, truth, freedom, and self-determination. We admire creative people, companies, brands, products, and services because they produce a positive and often unfiltered vision of human existence, which brings added meaning in small or even large ways to our lives. Creativity is embedded in the spirit of irresistible brands.

In this chapter, we provide a brief analysis of how creativity functions to provoke these feelings in consumers and drive people to invest in a select portfolio of brands. These high-energy brands now account for the majority of the value creation for consumers and business. Our intent is not to present a formal treatise linking creativity with marketing strategy, but rather to paint in broad strokes how consumers feel about and interpret creativity and why they constantly crave innovation and uniqueness as elements of energy found in the world's most admired brands.

FOUNTAIN OF YOUTH

You've no doubt noticed that when you're in a creative mood you're apt to be feeling happy and engaged. Equally, when you're happy, you'll find creativity flows more easily; it's easier to day-dream and play. Young children prove this. Creativity is part of how they learn and grow; they are inquisitive, playful, experi-mental, and always willing to try new things. These qualities are expressed in lots of different ways: singing, drawing, dancing, skipping, acting silly, dressing up, improvising, and playing make-believe.

As we grew older, that youthful creativity gets beaten out of us, replaced by pragmatic behaviors we must emulate to assume the mantle of adulthood. By the time we are working adults, most peo-ple lose most of their natural tendency to be creative and playful.

But something intriguing about creative brands can make us feel like kids again. When we encounter creative brands, they seem to have simplicity and playfulness that we find refreshing or even liberating. They have a kind of magic, and this creates a desire to reclaim both our buried creativity and perhaps our own happiness. Just watch adults loitering around an Apple store, get-ting their hair cut in the Virgin Atlantic Clubhouse, or imperson-ating Axl Rose in a game of Rock Band, and you will witness signs of playfulness, joy, and wonder. Encountering brands with energy, consumers resonate to a creative pulse emanating from within, and that rekindles a desire to reclaim just a little bit of lost youth.

The word *creative* comes from the Latin *creare,* to make or pro-duce, and is related to *crescere,* to grow. This seems appropriate, given that consumers are seeking brands that seem birthed out of brilliance and likely to grow into experiences that surprise and delight. It's this quality of being reborn into a new life that con-sumers are drawn to when they see brands swathed in creativity. It's no coincidence that purchasers of goods are called *consumers.* When we buy brands with energy, it may be that we are looking to consume the creativity they possess to have it inside ourselves.

Creativity: Elixir of Happiness

In our postmodern era of amazing technology and knowledge-based progress, there is nevertheless a significant negative correlation between happiness and wealth. Many studies have shown that the world's richest countries contain the unhappiest people, while poor countries tend to have the happiest. Economists and government policymakers are beginning to understand that material possessions are no guarantee of a smooth-functioning, nonviolent, happy society. The Japanese are much better off now than in 1950, but the proportion of citizens who say they are "very happy" has not budged. Americans have remained much as Alexis de Tocqueville found them in the nineteenth century: "So many lucky men, restless in the midst of abundance." Researchers for World Values Survey even go so far as to describe the desire for material goods as "a happiness suppressant"!

As the road to happiness, material wealth is starting to look more like a cul-de-sac. Pondering that potential dead end forces us to question the role of brands and what they contribute to our lives. Brands have always reflected the times in which they've operated, and the issues they reflect today are nothing new—they're just different. In today's world, it seems that energy brands feel irresistible—and we only want more of them. Energy brands draw people in, make them smile with delight, and renew the feeling that life is good. They inspire, uplift, encourage, and entertain. The creativity in energy brands may not have the answers to the world's problems, but it at least brings consumers a sense of well-being and a brighter future ahead.

Recent research in psychology and neuroscience shows a close link between creativity and happiness. Mihaly Csikszentmihalyi, a professor of psychology at Claremont Graduate University and author of the book *Flow,* studied high-performance workers and determined that when people are fully involved in tasks they find engaging and challenging, they enter into a "flow" state of mind that results in higher levels of creative thinking, productivity, and emotional happiness.

Perhaps an energized brand induces the same state of flow in people. It offers a sort of elixir—a potion that keeps people going forward, even in bad times. Within these brands is the subtle promise of personal growth, of solutions to current problems, of overcoming life's difficulties through new ideas. In some fashion, creativity acts as a quality or ingredient that, when sprinkled over life, inexplicably makes it more joyous.

THE WOW FACTOR

Buckminster Fuller once said: "You never change things by fighting the existing reality. To change something, build a new model that makes the existing model obsolete." That's what energized brands do. They don't take their reference from the past; they take it from the future, where anything is possible. Their creativity produces innovations that surprise, delight, and produce squeals of "Wow" from consumers.

Arthur Koestler offered what is widely considered to be the best definition of creativity, giving us insight into where the Wow comes from. He introduced the concept of "bisociation," which posits that creativity arises as a result of bringing two previously unrelated frames of reference together to create a third, new one. When done right, the resulting innovation is far greater than the two inputs alone. Something truly creative proposes new solutions that were previously unimaginable. You know you have innovation when you can look at something and feel a sense that 1 plus 1 equals 3. That's the Wow factor.

The world is full of examples of bisociation as the origin of creative innovation. Perhaps the most profitable in recent times is Apple's bringing together two previously unrelated frames of reference—an MP3 Player and an online music store—resulting in the iPod. David Byrne from the Talking Heads demonstrates the remarkable creative potential of PowerPoint. Or more crucially, when American soldiers in Iraq wrote home asking for Silly String. As it turns out, this staple of fourth-grade birthday parties can reveal bomb trip wires in a dark room. If the soldiers spray Silly String and it hangs in the air, there's nothing silly about the situation. That's bisociation putting together a toy and the reality of warfare to save lives.

Consumers love the Wow factor they find in creative brands. Innovation experts like Michael Porter and Gary Hamel have long beat the drum that innovation must drive corporations of the future. What's important is that the Wow factor is not just some peripheral added advantage, and it almost never emerges without big thinking and even bigger collaboration. David Aaker put it best: "The difference between an incremental and exponential idea lies in the ability of the organization to break down the barriers that hinder creative thinking."

To the consumer who's thinking like an investor, creativity offers people the perception of a more interesting future. If we had to live in a world populated exclusively by products lacking differentiation, offering little creativity, and instilling no enthusiasm, we'd be living in a dingy, gray world. Creativity calls out to people everywhere to follow the allure of energy brands.

It's also not surprising that these brands seem to cause people to become more active in their involvement as consumers. *Our research shows that people actually become smarter curators of their own consumption.* They play a more active role in making brand choices and they seek out deeper, more meaningful brand relationships. Brand loyalty moves from a passive to active state. Consumers place greater emphasis on selecting brands that continuously surprise, inspire, and lead them forward.

IRRESISTIBLE BRANDS TELL THE TRUTH

One of the hallmarks of superior creative works is that they ring true to audiences. Great creative work has an authenticity and honesty that resonates with the public and gives off a feeling that it couldn't have been otherwise. Pablo Picasso's "Art is a lie that tells the truth" equally says a lot about creative brands—they don't lie; people feel that they can't resist the truth shown before their eyes. Despite creative brands' being, in part, exercises in marketing, they provide an insight into a truth we all want to believe. These brands give consumers a window into the meaning they ultimately want to find.

As any kid who wrote away for Sea-Monkeys from *Boy's Life* knows, consumerism and marketing have not always been about truth. The history of selling brands to consumers is peppered with white lies, falsehoods, and generous doses of manipulation. One can trace it back to the early 1800s, as formal brands began emerging in the days when mass consumerism originated and populations demanded a guarantee of consistent product quality. In the next century, brands began to differentiate themselves, and companies discovered that, by suggesting psychological superiority such as status or prestige, they could command significant premiums. In the coming decades, marketers made ever more elaborate claims about brands, and many crossed the line beyond truthful. It was an evolution of marketing that went virtually unchecked throughout most of the twentieth century.

It was not really until the early 1990s that consumers started to question the claims marketers were making. Seriously, was the Subaru Impreza really like punk rock? Consumers could no longer be cajoled by marketing; they organized to strike back, even soliciting attorneys general to quash false advertising. They wanted honest brands, stripped of hype. We see this in the success of several new brands like Starbury, NBA star Stephan Marbury's sneaker that sells for just $14.98—one-tenth the cost of Nike Air Zoom. Tesco's baby club acts more like an au pair for new moms than a supermarket. In these types of brands, consumers feel they are buying authenticity.

The revolt in consumer tolerance for marketing results in large part from the "perfect information" that has become available in the fragmenting media landscape. This term comes out of game theory and refers to the state of being when an opponent has complete knowledge about other players, such that competitive information is instantly updated as it arises. In terms of marketing and advertising, the sudden availability of perfect information evened the score and provided consumers the wherewithal to disprove inflated product claims. The rise of the Internet, in particular, has given consumers opportunities to blast through the hype using their own research and by sharing data.

One of the most important by-products of perfect information has been a confirmation of the postmodernist perspective that no amount of spin and CGI can mask the fact that no one really knows where we are heading. Consumers began to see that the institutions they once placed so much faith in were far less in control than they thought. Increasing numbers of insoluble issues presented themselves, from ideological conflict to climate change, from global migration to the depletion of natural resources. No truth seemed to last long. People bought shares in Enron, which

Fortune named "America's Most Innovative Company" six years running, only to discover accounting fraud. People thought food and cars were safe, only to learn about deadly strains of *E. coli* and submit to auto recall after recall. Parents discovered they couldn't even trust Thomas the Tank Engine, or other toys made in China.

This has been the state of marketing up till today. But the fact is, whether consumers know it or not, *postmodernism is now mainstream.* Pretty much everyone everywhere accepts as a given that politicians lie, business is greedy, and science fails regularly. When it comes to marketing and brands, consumers are left feeling vulnerable, cynical, and detached.

Marketers conducting research receive constant confirmation of this when consumers tell them that they want X but they also want its opposite Y. Consumers don't want inauthentic, overdone products sold through inflated, hyped-out advertising. But at the same time they don't want unexciting, generic products that strip out all emotion and passion.

But there seems to be a growing willingness to concede that some brands deserve respect. We believe that *with creativity, brand integrity becomes believable.* Consumers are attracted to brands they see making the effort to transcend the mundane as being more earnest, straightforward, and authentic. These brands transcend consumer skepticism of marketing, allowing consumers to believe without feeling a sense of hypocrisy. They resolve the consumer conflict because they deliver on what they promise. They add quality, esteem, improvement, and hope to a future otherwise filled with cynicism and doubt.

CREATIVITY AND IRRESISTIBLE BRANDS

When taken together, the role that creativity plays in the brand bubble is becoming clearer. Consumers are short of expectations in most brands. Creativity of thought offers hope in a way that's never been more important. As consumers move past adjusting to exploiting the radical changes of a very young century, the thirst for creativity is growing in their everyday lives. In a world of limitless broadband, virtually any idea is within a keystroke's reach, fueling an explosion of entertainment and self-expression, most brands look incredibly literal and uninteresting. They are unable to keep up with the creative IQ of their customer.

Suffice it to say, for now, creativity is the new must-have of the marketplace because it offers honesty, progress, and a place to turn to find answers to life's uncertainties. Innovation and new ideas, whether in media, consumer content, products, architecture, design, or science—or other pursuits—is in such demand because it comforts like never before. Consumers are on a continuous journey, seeking new ideas, innovation, and a direction in which to go. It's creativity that encourages people to dream about tomorrow and nurtures their efforts to do so. It's a kind of magic.

But in focusing on the present, most brands aren't painting a canvas of hope and new ideas. They don't have time to consider their future promises, and as a result, consumers (as investors) are discarding them in droves, accounting for declining brand perceptions and stagnation, fueling the bubble. In contrast, brands that are constantly thinking about tomorrow—that believe in creativity and inspiration in everything they do—are capable of being an integral part of people's lives for years to come.

CHAPTER FIVE

WELCOME TO CONSUMERLAND

Moore's Law is a violation of Murphy's Law.
Everything gets better and better.
— *THE ECONOMIST*, MARCH 2003

Meet Alex Tew, a nineteen-year-old in Wiltshire, England, who harnessed the power of blogs to scale a business quickly. Beset by tuition expenses, Alex came up with an idea to sell ads on a Web site he created called the "Million Dollar Homepage." His site is the equivalent of a billboard made up of 1,000,000 pixels, each costing $1. Initially he asked his friends and family to buy space, but he also spread the word over blogs. He began receiving press requests, and a whirlwind media tour in Britain, Europe, and the United States ensued. Traffic to the site skyrocketed, and his home page now looks like an online Times Square. Within a matter of months, he sold all 1 million pixels, culminating with an auction of the last thousand pixels on eBay.

Who is Alex?

a. A consumer?
b. An advertiser?
c. A media entrepreneur?
d. An Internet destination?
e. All of the above?

The correct answer is "e"—and that's the crux of this chapter. In many ways, Alex personifies other important characteristics of the new world we call "ConsumerLand," a magical place where fantasy meets reality, creativity meets commerce, and technology meets passion. This is a land where consumers have unprecedented technology at their fingertips to envision more ambitious dreams and express themselves more vividly, which in turn gives them unprecedented power to alter their relationship with brands. The broadband world has amplified consumer behavior as critics, creators, parents, buyers, and citizens. And it has heightened their expectations of brands and putting air into the brand bubble.

Only a radical consumer metamorphosis can explain statistics like these: *All in the Family* had a 34.0 household rating in 1972 compared to 14.6 for *American Idol* in 2008. Crazy Frog, a ring tone, became a U.K. top ten single. China's version of *Idol,* called *Super Girl,* attracted one-third of the country's population for the season finale and 8 million people texted in a vote. A study by the Fortino Group predicts that current ten- to seventeen-year-olds will spend one-third of their lives (twenty-three years) on the Internet. According to Nielsen's SoundScan, CD sales declined by 19 percent in 2007. The global PC market will double by 2010. More than 17 billion devices will be connected to the Internet by 2012.

In ConsumerLand, people may behave differently, but they're still pursuing timeless human wants and needs. We've always had friends; now we log on to Facebook and MySpace. We've always let our fingers do the walking; now we use Google and craigslist. We've always shared memories; now we have Flickr and Shutterfly. We've always kept lists, now we use del.icio.us. We've always phoned our kids; now we text. And we've always watched movies from Hollywood; now we stream them direct from studios on sites like ABC On Demand.

The problem is, many companies still operate their marketing departments according to the old thinking of persuasion, metrics, and an "us-them" landscape. They're blind to the behavioral shifts transforming customers right in front of their eyes. As a result, consumers drift further away, and we continue to see brand measures decay and crack. It's those enterprises that can't see the brand bubble blowing up around them.

Our goal in this chapter is to describe this new terrain wherein consumers have co-opted the brand government. We suspect you're not only familiar with the media and digital trends we cite, you're dealing with their impacts on your marketing strategies. But change is happening so fast that most of us are struggling to understand the overall impact, to see the forest through the gigabytes, so to speak. You may have specific thoughts but no unified theory regarding how to market to this new ConsumerLand. Fixing that is our intention here.

OF COMPUTER MICE AND MEN: INNOVATION AND HUMAN NATURE

When we first began writing this chapter, it was going to be about the speed of innovation and brands needing to keep up. We planned to cite the now well-known prescient prediction of Intel co-founder Gordon E. Moore, who back in 1965 predicted that the number of transistors on a silicon chip would probably double every two years or so, a geometric growth pattern that has largely proven true. Moore's Law became the metaphor epitomizing the accelerated rate of change in this increasingly fast world. The same nonlinear speed explains why, while it took radio thirty-eight years to reach an audience of 50 million people, TV took only thirteen years—and the Internet just four years. And why the work that took Britannica almost two hundred years, Wikipedia accomplished in six.

However, due to the very speed of change, even that topic fell by the wayside. Speed was no longer the issue. The more salient distinction about today's ConsumerLand is that *the nature of change itself has changed*. Change is no longer linear or geometric: it's gone holographic. One change impacts all others. Everything is now so tightly interconnected, it's hard to put your arms around what a single individual change means. Each alteration reverberates through the cosmos and later you are perplexed when some distant, unconnected mechanism also changes. How did that happen?

Go back in your mind to the consumer marketplace just five years ago, in the period of the dial-up modem. In those early Internet years, sending e-mail and browsing static text Web pages was the marketing equivalent of the discovery of copper. It allowed brand managers to create some new tools, but we were still doing our work according to largely the same old paradigms for creating our messages and using the media to talk to consumers. The Internet added some excitement to our marketing, but it wasn't a fundamental revolution.

Then broadband came along, and it was like inventing the wheel. Big pipes opened the flow of vast potential. Broadband brought storage, transportation, and communication. Suddenly content was essentially free and readily available. In simple economic terms, this development placed content in servitude to the market. Now, if content isn't instantly engaging, creative, and differentiated, it's worthless.

These three factors have had a critical transformative effect, heightening how people experience and use the Web, how people go about communicating and entertaining themselves, and how companies market and bring their brands to life. The very same forces that forever altered our experience of the Web created a catalyst for the powerful social change among consumers that the rest of this chapter will cover. Broadband connected the world, not just with speed, but also with a bigger capacity to carry the lifeblood of the human race: energy in the form of ideas and expression.

One of the outcomes of this change is that innovation becomes unpredictable in its effects. Today we can't even imagine what further innovations might appear and what effect they may have on society. We usually don't even know we need an innovation until its benefits are demonstrated in our own lives. The German physicist Max Planck once said: "A new truth does not triumph by convincing its opponents and making them see the light, but rather because its opponents eventually die, and a new generation grows up that is familiar with it." That's probably how most of us feel these days about the flood of innovations we've had to contend with in just five years.

Even when we try to imagine innovation using the best tools and knowledge we can put our hands on, we are as likely to be wrong as right. If you're a Baby Boomer, think back on what you might have said if you'd been asked in the 1960s how we might be traveling to work in the year 2000. You might reasonably have suggested the personal jet pack (or a similar sort of *Jetsons* fantasy). You were wrong, but at least you were close, given that the gizmos have been invented and tested. But ask yourself the same question now: How do you think we'll be traveling to work in 2050? There's no way to know this time around; anything is plausible, including the possibility that we won't go to work at all, it will come to us, or that we'll be working on the moon.

Innovation today makes an ass of us all. It used to be that innovation went just a teeny baby step beyond whatever had gone before, but now innovation tends to take huge leaps, making it impossible to predict the future based on past experience. If you think you understand how things are going to change, you really are in trouble, because now things change in ways you don't recognize, let alone understand.

The lesson for brands is that the "what's" of innovation are no longer predictable or constant. You can't prepare for innovation anymore, you can only be flexible and loose, and try to dance around it. And be aware that every generation has its own reference point of what's normal. Twittering is endemic among fifteen-year-olds, but forty-somethings would probably wonder why we're saying kids act like birds. (Feed "Twitter" to a search engine if you're wondering.) This points out the lesson "Don't follow the technology, follow the behavior."

While some have suggested that innovation drives the advancement of human nature, we suggest that more often, it's the other way around—technology advances largely in response to human desire. The Wright brothers would not have invented the airplane if humans had not wanted to travel faster and further. Wozniak and Jobs would not have created the first Apple if humans didn't seek to have personal computing power at their fingertips. Tim Berners-Lee and others would not have developed the World Wide Web if people hadn't wanted faster ways to share information.

We emphasize this point because the remainder of the chapter is devoted to describing numerous newfound consumer powers and attitudes that require brands to alter how they engage with customers. It's important to keep in mind that although broadband and mobile technology enable consumers to grab onto these powers, it was human nature that drove innovators to create that technology.

So if you were still resisting and fuming that brands wouldn't be in this pickle if technology hadn't come along, you're dead wrong. Consumers are simply following their nature and that will constantly drive more innovation to help them.

CONSUMERS AS PRODUCERS OF CONTENT

One of the most fundamental changes in the new ConsumerLand is the incessant consumer desire to be heard and to participate. People are no longer willing to sit back and consume the content brands feed them. They blog, vlog, tag, mebo, podcast, twitter, wiki, and ning to make their voices known about everything. They spend hours gardening their MySpace, Bebo, and Facebook pages to define themselves and make statements about life, the world, or your brand. They legally or illegally "borrow" content from thousands of professional and nonprofessional sources, including your brand's Web site, to create mashups, music videos, or movie takeovers of their MySpace page. If you need proof the old world of media has been turned upside down, note a recent survey of users of Bolt Media, a youth networking site, which found that only one out of three users were able to name even one of the four American TV networks.

Blogging and mobile chatter have eliminated the distance between an individual and a mass audience. Today, a laptop and a cell phone are the equivalent of a printing press. Blogs are nothing more than a timeless expression of diaries; a need to express oneself, even if no one is listening—but now, people may be listening. Consumers have become citizen journalists, media channels, brand creators, and entrepreneurs. The growth of blogging surely reflects an enormous consumer desire to speak up and be heard. Today, 26 million "active" blogs are read by 57 million people in the United States. The greatest impact of blogs occurs in Asia, where China leads the way in creating and sharing content with 42 million bloggers.[1]

While most of the 110 million blogs worldwide don't offer much more than innocuous content for friends and relatives, thousands of bloggers attract wider audiences, and a small cadre like Gawker, Engadget, Perez Hilton, Apartment Therapy, and Huffington Post have built genuine mass readership. Bloggers have (for the time being) become the new opinion makers, the advance guard of truth that consumers are increasingly trusting to report honestly, without spin.

Blogging suggests a content meritocracy. Whereas before, content needed to find its structure, be it advertisers or network executives, now people decide what rises to the top. Blogging has grown credible enough that it is no longer ignored as a communications strategy for brands. Category blogs like Gizmodo and Engadget are increasingly vital to the success of consumer electronics. The British comedian Stephen Fry dresses up in drag and blogs about the latest gadgets. Companies everywhere are launching blogs of their own, written by CEOs or corporate thought leaders. The most forward-thinking brands are designing strategies to tap into the opinion-making power of popular bloggers, seeding them with advance information or product samples to create buzz in the marketplace.

Meanwhile, when blogging met its cousin, vlogging (video blogging), it took only a short step to invent YouTube, adding another new tool to consumers' power to participate. With its library of over 78 million videos, and over 150,000,000 new ones uploaded each day, YouTube quickly became the third-most-recognized digital brand, after Apple and Google, and the fastest-growing Web site in the history of the Internet. YouTube's popularity attracts a major share of the estimated $36 billion online ad market, which itself is growing fast within the overall $446 billion global ad market. But we felt this way about Yahoo and Netscape. It's likely way too early for the digital fat lady to sing.

Consumers are also airing their voices via podcasting. People are programming their own talk radio with commentary, product reviews, music, and news . . . without being subject to the same regulations as terrestrial radio. Companies are no longer overlooking the utility and ease of pod and v casting. Microsoft discovered a groundswell of interest in its developer forum "Channel 9," which connects the Microsoft community. Ford uses podcasting to sell quality, and Vanguard disseminates a popular series called "plain talk on investing."

Consumer-generated media (CGM) has become a nonstop, multifarious, and multimedia channel of consumer communication over which brands have no control. Video streaming, music and photo sharing, real simple syndication (RSS), personal enriched content, collaborative searching, product reviewing, and social networking are all technologies that give consumers tools to route around brands. CGM gives consumers a pass around the traditional business models to talk back to brands—or, like Alex, to create their own enterprise.

Examples of successful CGM-originated business models are growing. The pioneers in music were British pop star Lily Allen and The Arctic Monkeys, who built followings and sold albums through their MySpace pages. Newer artists like Kate Nash and Jamie T. are using the same model and gaining acclaim. Gnarls Barkley's single "Crazy" was the first song to reach the U.K. charts based on downloads, 20 percent of the audience accessing it via mobile cell phones. Radiohead offered its new album online with no list price, asking consumers instead to set their own price for what they think the music is worth. (Brands, are you listening?)

The significance of CGM is more than its effect on changing business models; it is altering the "trust equation" for brands. The reality is, *consumers now trust each other more than they trust brands.* Mediaedge:CIA found that 76 percent of people rely on what others say versus 15 percent on advertising. Ninety-two percent of consumers now cite word of mouth as the best source for product and brand information, up from 67 percent in 1977. Also, nearly 80 percent of people surveyed in AOL's Brand New World research reported they would think twice about buying a product or brand if they saw a negative review about it on the Internet. And they're likely to find a lot of brand chatter: 74 percent of all global Internet users have reported writing a review online.[2] Another e-commerce study found that 75 percent of people consult blogs before they buy, and consumer-generated reviews resulted in a 77 percent increase in reported traffic, 56 percent improved conversion rates, with 42 percent having higher dollar values in their purchase basket.[3] No wonder reviews sites, such as Digg and Reddit, have become the third-most-common use of the Internet after e-mail and search.

Retailers are responding fast to the trend. The survey firms E-consultancy and Bazaarvoice researched the effect of customer-generated ratings and reviews among online retailers in the

United Kingdom, the United States, and Europe in June and July 2007 and found that nearly eight in ten online sellers agree that consumer-generated reviews increase site traffic, while 56 percent saw improved conversion rates and 42 percent higher average order values.

As unbelievable as it is, the high level of faith people put in what complete strangers think explains why a single negative review from a guy in Texas named Jack S. can sit on a retail Web site like an eight-hundred-pound gorilla, carrying an enormous chilling effect on a product. But is CGM incorruptible? Could its credibility withstand a Jack S. who is really an advertising copy-writer working for a competing brand? Ultimately CGM will need the same filters as every other trust-based institution.

As we've said, our research indicates that trust in brands is declining; now there's no doubt that CGM is filling the vacuum. With tools like search, collaborative filtering, blogs, podcasting, YouTube, and epinions abounding, consumers are redefining where they will go to find the truth. CGM is the ultimate mega-phone, proving that one person can make or break a reputation by videotaping or writing about a single blemish in a brand and letting it reverberate in waves to ever-larger audiences.

A good example of CGM affecting a brand's reputation is the unfortunate fate of Kryptonite bike locks in 2004. For years, Kryptonite rode along with an invincible reputation for the most secure locks in the world, until a blogger showed up in an online bike forum with a video showing the new Kryptonite Evolution 2000 lock being picked with a Bic ballpoint pen. For the next six days, the behind-the-story meta-dialogue between Kryptonite executives and the bike blogging world went something like this:

Day 1

Kryptonite: Our bike locks are the best.
The Market: Yes, your bike locks are the best.

Day 2

Kryptonite: Our bike locks are the best.
The Market: Yes, your bike locks are still the best.

Day 3

Kryptonite: Our bike locks are the best.
The Market: Ummm . . . yeah I'm sure they are, but what's all this about some recent video on the net that's supposed to show how you can crack your locks in ten seconds using a Bic pen?

Day 4

Kryptonite: Our bike locks are the best.
The Market: Hey, I just saw that video on a friend's Web site. And I'm kinda ticked off because I just paid $60 for one of your new locks three weeks ago, and I'm wondering if a Bic pen can crack my lock or not . . . does the pen crack all Kryptonite locks or just one or two models?

Day 5

Kryptonite: Our bike locks are the best.
The Market: Hey, I just visited your Web site and saw no mention of the Bic pen problem. What are you doing about it? Are you going to fix the locks? Are you going to give me a refund?

Day 6

Kryptonite: Our bike locks are the best.
The Market: No, they're not. My bike just got stolen! A whole bunch of my friends are going to hear about this.

Kryptonite executives claimed they were listening, but the damage was done when it took them eight days to respond; that's dog years in ConsumerLand. Marketers are in effect now like the World War II code breakers. They must constantly monitor conversations and chatter, looking for traffic levels and patterns in chatter in order to decipher insights from the general noise in the marketplace. And if you don't track conversations and respond swiftly, the community will do it for you.

The sheer force of CGM means brands have to invent their own new business models that marry CGM with brand content, or even to completely hand over some aspect of it to consumers, as now happens with viral content. Brands can benefit by harnessing the wisdom of crowds, by giving consumers applications and opportunities to rank, rate, vote, tag, review, comment, detract, and support the brand. They must allow consumers to meet others and have "experiences" through their brands.

An inspiring example of the successful merger of CGM with brand strategy is the campaign Doritos conducted for the 2007 Super Bowl. Doritos invited consumers to submit their own video spots highlighting the brand, with the grand prize being an airing of the spot on the Super Bowl broadcast. Contestants were invited to post their videos on Yahoo, the others voted on their favorites. Doritos was not involved in the selection.

The company received more than a thousand spots, producing hundreds of thousands of pre-game impressions plus huge amounts of publicity both on- and offline. The five top winners each received $10,000, and two top spots aired during the Super Bowl. The first spot ranked fourth among all spots in a *USA Today* poll following the game. In 2008, they extended the competition to consumer-generated music with the prize being a recording contract and a sixty-second music video during the Super Bowl.

Numerous other brands are inviting consumers to produce video spots in favor of their brands. Some praise, while others attack. Yet many brands are learning to help consumers, giving them partial content to integrate into their videos or letting people borrow brand and product hero pages to integrate into their Facebook aps. As long as it's good content, consumers will pinch it.

WE DON'T WANT TO BE "HERD," JUST PERSONALLY SEEN

Picture a herd of zebras, roaming the plains of Africa. A lion approaches, and together—as one massive group—all the zebras flee, swerving to the left, then to the right, in lockstep unison to protect each other and save themselves from certain destruction. But despite their behavior as a herd, each zebra is unique, with its own pattern of stripes. If you were to zoom in closely with your digital camera, you could actually tell one zebra from another because each is different, as different as . . . well, you and me.

While mass marketing will always have some level of appeal, many consumers also want brands to see their individual stripes, not their "herdiness." This shows up in many different ways.

First, micro-addressability and mass customization is building in appeal. What started out three decades ago at Burger King as "Have it your way" has transformed into a massive movement to personalize. Starbucks is perhaps the leader here, offering more than 87,000 combinations of drinks (and thus requiring baristas to get Ph.D.'s at Starbucks University). Other companies are moving fast to accommodate this trend. At Nike ID.com, our digital chief strategist at VML, Mike Lundgren, was able to design his own shoes with the logo "Nike" turned into "Mike." Such build-your-own sites are both e-commerce and brand engagement.

Wunderman CEO Daniel Morel says marketing must now make "Unique Selling Propositions" truly unique. He says, "Today, no one message can have ubiquitous appeal. Consumers need to be able to view a brand from the lens of their own wants and needs. Think of Georges Seurat's painting 'A Sunday on La Grande Jatte.' That work of art is a composite of miniature little dots of various color and emphasis. A brand today can be looked at in a multitude of personal ways. The more intimate and customized a message is, the more relevant and differentiating your brand experience is to each individual level. And each customer builds part of the canvas that is your brand."

What's interesting about micro-addressability is that more consumers are willing to give out information to get it. Eighty percent of people want meaningful personalized content, and up to 58 percent will pay more to get it, according to ChoiceStream. The same study found that 57 percent of U.S. adults over the age of eighteen are willing to share their demographic data and 47 percent will actually let you track them.[4] With greater consumer willingness to reveal personal habits, along with more advanced tracking technology, brands will increasingly be able to do narrowcast ads based on highly individualized factors such as hobbies, size of backyard, or type of blender in the kitchen. The question is, When is too much choice debilitating?

Not in music, it seems. The online radio station Pandora exemplifies how a brand can even be built from the ground up to appeal to personalization. We sat down with founder and CEO

Tim Westergen and learned that the company originated when he and his partners sought to discover the "genome" in songs. They painstakingly analyzed and "deconstructed" songs to find their musical DNA, which allowed them to classify music according to deep inner similarities and differences. A listener who goes to Pandora.com enters a single artist or a song; Pandora then plays a stream of highly related songs that contain the same genome. Consumers effectively end up with a totally personalized radio station that airs only the types of songs they like, while introducing them to new artists they may not have known.

In many ways, the rise of innovations that allow consumers to watch TV on their own schedule or location also reflects the demand for personalized control over brands. Mimicking the software *PC Anywhere* that lets people use their office computer from home, a whole slew of "shifting" technologies now exists to put consumers in the driver's seat. Chief among these is time shifting, which is done using digital video recorders (DVRs) that let people become their own program directors, determining their own lineup of shows and viewing schedules. Then there's platform shifting, which takes content originally intended for one medium such as television and plays it on another such as the Internet. All the networks now run episodes on the Internet for download. And finally, there's place shifting, such as Slingbox, which lets consumers launch their home cable signal or satellite set box or personal video recorder programming over a broadband connection to another location so they can watch their TV subscription elsewhere. And soon you'll be able to program your DVR from your cell phone.

What is radically different about all these shifting technologies is that viewers have the power to create their own channel, allowing them to watch whatever and whenever they please. This has forced the media and advertisers to rethink the entire medium of television, and recognize that *TV is just another form of video*. Programs are just digital entities that exist in time and space, each one ready to be viewed only when the consumer wants, not when the networks choose to show it. The myriads of media options suggest "the message is now the medium." President and chief strategist Ernest Simon at MindShare says, "Media is dissolving to the point where the boundaries are so vague, they're essentially worthless.

What does 'TV' really mean? Is it an appliance? A program to watch on your iPod? A Web site where you can interact with the characters from *Grey's Anatomy*? Today we can place messages into virtually just about any medium."

Rob Norman from Mediaedge:CIA says we're at the beginning of the "post-broadcast age": "Media will be more addressable to households or individuals, resulting in better targeting and requiring far more specific messaging. Media will also be more portable across time, device, and place, leaving events like the Super Bowl and The Academy Awards among the few known time and place audience aggregators." Consumers are increasingly drawn to these changes. A 2007 survey by the Conference Board and TNS Media Intelligence indicated that 16 percent of consumers now view entire television episodes on the Internet, double the number from 2006. Online viewers cite convenience and the lack of commercials as their top reasons for watching TV on the Internet according to the "Consumer Internet Barometer" survey, conducted in the third quarter of 2007. As Max Planck suggested, what's changing is the generational comfort level with technology solutions. It's just how life is.

Researchers are also exploring the implications of platform shifting for brands. In one study from Millward Brown's Futures Group, researchers tracked how consumers reacted to a thirty-second ad from a leading brand in each of the quick service restaurant, consumer packaged goods, and financial services categories. The ads were viewed across three platforms: a prime-time network TV show viewed at air time, the same episode time-shifted via DVR, and the same show aired at the network's Web sites. The study found that the advertising performed positively across all three platforms, but the results attested to a higher level of engagement among online viewers, who showed increased awareness, brand favorability, and consideration. Overall, the online viewers were 53 percent more likely to pay attention to the ads during commercial breaks than the live TV viewers were. The time-shifted viewers were the worst prospects, being 30 percent less likely to pay attention to the ads than even live TV viewers.

The online viewers also had the greatest ad recall, four times higher compared to the live and time-shifted viewers. In large part, though, the online success may be skewed, given that only that single ad aired three to six times during the online program. In contrast, ads on a network TV are shown once within a pod of several commercials, and several commercial pods interrupt a single program.

Despite the uncertainty about which format is best for brands, the research confirms that personalization is vital for consumers. Even the viewers who watched the repetitive ads online stated that the advertising needed to be made more relevant to them and that it was boring to watch the same ad over and over again. That's a bit of a reminder that too much knowledge begins to erode differentiation.

SEEKING COMMUNITY AND EXPERIENCES AMONG FRIENDS

In 1623, the English poet John Donne wrote, "No man is an island." Little did he realize how apt his phrase would be nearly four centuries later. Consumers are more attached to each other than ever before.

While consumers crave micro-addressability and personalization, the desire to be part of a community is not going away—in fact, it is growing. This yearning may derive from that postmodernist existential angst we talked about earlier, from which people try to take solace by having close friends with whom they can talk and share. Modern people have become unhinged by dissolution of community. Over several decades subtle shifts began to isolate society. In the 1960s and 1970s, houses were designed with the porch in the back rather than on the front. Urban planning eliminated sidewalks and malls replaced main streets. Automobiles, suburbs, shifts in economic bases across the United States all impacted families, communities, and social structures.

Today, this duality in the consumer mind creates a two-headed beast—one head seeks belonging, the other uniqueness—causing people to perform funny, antithetical behaviors, like buying the exact same brand of jeans all their friends have, but then inking or drawing on them to personalize them and leave their own mark.

Of course, people have always been social creatures. Consumers' gathering, sharing, and talking about products and services is not new. They did it in Colonial times, meeting at the supply store.

They did it throughout the twentieth century, using the telephone and the shopping mall. What's different about socializing now is the wealth of broadband-related innovations like IMs, social networks, and alternative worlds that give people tools and unprecedented immediacy to connect and share. People can contact in real time almost anyone anywhere in the world, across political and cultural boundaries, while forming widely diversified networks that have clout.

Social networking creates a newfound power in numbers. Originally designed for people to meet each other and just have fun, social networking sites have blossomed into vast communities whose sharing of knowledge and opinions can alter the fortunes of political candidates, companies, and brands. These online communities have the capacity to change the future of a brand faster, more effectively, and with less bloodshed than any revolution ever did.

Consider MySpace. Were it a country, it would be the eleventh largest in the world. And it's not just for kids; nearly half of its users are over thirty-five and one in three is over forty-five. More than 85 percent of its members are of voting age and 42 percent of them listen to online political messages. The company receives more than 36 billion page views per year, more than Google and eBay combined, making it the most popular site in the United States.

Coming up fast behind MySpace is Facebook. Scores of social networking sites exist outside the United States, such as Cyworld in South Korea, Mop.com in China, and Habbo Hotel in Finland, all of which are expanding throughout Europe, South and Central America, and Asia.

Part of what makes social networks so inviting to consumers is that search for purpose discussed earlier. People seek to create meaning for themselves, and what better way to do it than to join an online community that lets you define yourself to the world, write and blog your thoughts, link up with friends, and decorate the walls of your profile page with the artifacts of your existence. These are ways to build a community and enrich life, which instills the sense of purpose people seek.

But the other aspect is that popular culture is increasingly influenced by the behavior of the Millennial Generation. Jack

MacKenzie of Frank N. Magid Associates, who runs the Millennial Strategy Program, told us, "MySpace exists in part because of Gymboree. Thirty years ago parents flocked to these play centers to nurture interaction among their kids. This generation has been so socialized, they don't just want contact—they need it." Their research found Millennials work together to dismantle the edifice of any institution, be it a politician, company, or brand. Jack says, "Millennials believe that there isn't a 'truth,' only a series of facts that can be spun in different ways. They find the concept of an anchorman to be ridiculous: one person who holds all the information? Forget it. The voice of the community *is* the community."

And because Millennials have always been encouraged to believe that they are right, that there are no bad questions, and that everything matters—they're bred to sculpt the truth and press their positions, especially on parents. According to MacKenzie's research, 29 percent of twenty-three- to twenty-eight-year-olds live with a parent, which is reshaping Gen-Xer and Boomer attitudes toward technology, and often their own opinions. Witness Caroline Kennedy, who said her kids convinced her to back Barack Obama. This generation is closer to their parents as well as their friends, creating a social network with vast power and many strands of influence.

But the most successful social networks give consumers not just the ease of uploading photos and videos or blogging capability; they give them a powerful creative opportunity to define themselves as a unique entity in the world. One might view social networking sites as lowering the barrier for every individual to become a personal brand. Consumer demand for connection, conversation, and experience also helps explain the proliferation of alternative reality sites, such as Second Life, a virtual community in which real people go online as avatars to imitate real life online. Players convert real dollars into Linden Dollars to buy and sell virtual property, conduct virtual businesses, and eventually exchange back for U.S. dollars. With its economy growing by a red-hot 10–15 percent a month, Second Life is keen to avoid the hyperinflation that can taint both real economies and their virtual one. The company keeps an especially close eye on the Lindex, the booming currency exchange, where U.S. dollars and Linden dollars are bought and sold. Second Life, however, has proven corruptible. Are the marketers driving down real estate values? Increasingly this virtual world looks more like a virtual mall.

Gaming is another story entirely. Ninety percent of teens play online games, yet adults outnumber them by more than 6:1. According to the Yankee Group, 130 million gamers are in the U.S. alone, and 38 percent of them are women. The average age of a gamer is thirty-three. Video game revenues grew 19 percent (to $125 billion) in 2007, and are expected to double every few years.

With numbers and demographics like these, brands need to begin eyeing opportunities in gaming, ranging from advertising around the games, contests and promotions, in-game advertising, product placement, and the new hybrid, advergaming. One of the most fascinating aspects about gaming as a medium is the proliferation of MMOs, or Massively Multiplayer Online Games, that host up to hundreds of thousands of gamers simultaneously. These are intensely competitive and highly social online global communities in their own right.

So far, we've looked at social networking and alternative reality sites, but the "killer AP" of consumer interest is the *mobile phone*. Without question mobility is becoming the most far-reaching technological innovation ever. Research in mobile phones always highlights that more people around the world have access to a hand phone than to any other medium. Today, there are twice as many mobile phones as Internet connections—around 2.3 billion versus 1.2 billion, and by 2011, analysts expect about 3.3 billion mobile subscribers. In many countries, cell phones are the only way people can connect to the Internet because there is no infrastructure for cable or DSL.

The key to future growth in mobile technology exists in the adoption rate of cell phones for data exchange beyond simple text messaging (SMS), such as multimedia messages (MMS) and video reception. Mobile subscribers in Europe and Asia are far ahead of U.S. subscribers, but 4G is ushering in a new marketing galaxy for brands. The bright stars include incredible opportunities like text and video message campaigns delivering special alerts, contest offers, interactive voting, and links to Web sites; specially designed mobile phone Web pages called WAP (wireless application platform) that can be viewed in the phone's online browser; specially made-for-mobile videos and brand-sponsored "mobisodes," short videos with advertising or that include product placements; Quick Response (QR) code reading and receiving back data (video, info, coupons) directly to the handset; applications that cell phone users can download and install directly on their phone without having to go online; and location-based services using mini-GPS devices, allowing marketers to know who the consumer is, where that consumer is, and what help is needed, like OnStar for your cell phone.

SEEKING CONVERSATION AND DIALOGUE

Yet another characteristic of ConsumerLand is that consumers now insist on being part of the marketing conversation with their brands. Brands have always lived or died by the way people were talking about them. But consumers have never before had the ease of conversation nor the reach of connection they have now through e-mail, blogs, videos, social networks, and cell phones. Old-fashioned referral marketing had just two basic precepts: if people talked about a product, it was word of mouth; if a company talked about a product, it was advertising.

Today's word of mouth (WOM) is far more sophisticated and richer, which makes it more important to know how to use. Consumers are driven by a fascination for interacting with their brands; they use their social networks, blogs, and message boards to share information vociferously. Ninety-two percent of people cite WOM as the best source of product purchase information, up from 67 percent in 1977.

Another dynamic of today's WOM is that consumers are increasingly bored with the ordinary. Just as people made eye candy a requirement on early Web sites, they equally crave "experiences" when it comes to making WOM stick. They want brands to help them discover chatter that is fun, exciting, interesting, and different to talk about. Such as when George Lucas released 250 video clips from *Star Wars* to eager fans to create their own mashups with no fee.

The essential difference in twenty-first-century WOM versus the old stuff is that modern consumers are highly motivated to positively represent the things they love. When there's something they've experienced or content they value, they will voluntarily spend hours blogging, vlogging, chatting, e-mailing, posting, sharing, ranking, and rating their brands. The brands that help consumers start conversations will be the winners. One caveat about today's sophisticated, super-fast WOM world is that, in exchange for their contribution, consumers also expect brands to make them look good. Most brands don't get this; their first impulse is to make themselves look good.

ConsumerLand is a nasty world when a brand fails at facilitating good WOM. If a consumer has a bad experience with your brand, technology has exponentially increased the number of people who will soon know about it. Research shows that following a single negative shopping experience, 6 percent of consumers tell the retailer, but 31 percent tell friends, family, and colleagues. And worse, 8 percent tell one person, 8 percent tell two people, and 6 percent tell six or more people. Putting those numbers together, it means that if a hundred people have a bad experience at a retailer, the shop has a chance to lose between thirty-two and thirty-six current or potential customers. (Think *Snakes on a Plane*.)

Most important, brands are a belief system. All belief is based on trust, honesty, and transparency. Brands must also avoid all appearances of falsifying or faking WOM, which only angers consumers and makes them flee. Out with stealth marketing, shilling, infiltration, and comment spam—*be honest with your consumer.*

Paraphrasing what Mao Tse-Tung said in *Strategies and Convictions,* the best defense is to be consistent and stand for something, whereas the best offense is to find contradictions and exploit them. Words to think about when you practice your own guerilla marketing warfare. As illustrated by the rising criticism of "anonymous blogging," the terrain is very dangerous for an insincere or scheming brand.

WANTING INFORMATION AND A SENSE OF DISCOVERY

By now, you are developing a good picture of why brands are living in a different ConsumerLand today, but here's another important characteristic: Today's consumers have morphed into information-hungry machines. While humans have always pursued knowledge, now innovation and technology have put enormous amounts of data instantly at everyone's fingertips. Numerous research studies have attempted to calculate how much information the average person can get access to today, but there's only one word to express it: mind-boggling.

If one company personifies the human quest for information in the modern era, it's Google. The importance of comprehensive, searchable information that Google imparted to the world is as critical to brands today as the old one-sheet flier was to brands fifty years ago. Over 80 percent of all consumer Web sessions start at a search engine; 85 percent of all visits to Web sites originate at the major search engines, and 91 percent of Internet users report conducting searches daily.[5] And the future is likely to boost those percentages, because increased broadband usage will only drive greater search activity.

One could assert that search engines have created another communications medium. Brands now have to think as strategically about optimizing their online presence for search engines as they do about their television spots, radio ads, and press advertising. Successful searches contribute to a brand's visibility to in-market consumers; they improve or maintain brand positioning; they drive self-qualified traffic to the Web site, capture responses to offline advertising, and help brands acquire new leads and customers. The value of search engine optimization is so significant to brands that companies will probably soon be insisting that universities offer Ph.D.'s in SEO and SEM. What we have today is the equivalent of the Library of Congress and no librarian!

We believe the fascination for search engines has to do with the aura that has always surrounded human discovery. Finding a fact hidden amid a sea of information billions of documents deep is a little like Magellan discovering. . . . (Wait a minute, we have to Google this. . . .) Like Magellan discovering All Saint's Channel to get around the tip of South America (now renamed the Strait of Magellan, of course). It's a natural human desire to discover, but curiosity can be a benefit or a curse to brands. It's a benefit when consumers seek something very specific and your brand has put in place the online architecture that allows them to easily find the data. Look at the great results brands like Dell, eBay, and Geico achieved because they built info-rich Web sites providing consumers with extensive searchable product knowledge.

But today's easy search and discovery can also be a curse when brands try to hide bad news or a major screw-up. Given the omnipotence of search engines today, a single consumer acting alone can usually find the necessary information to expose any deception. The search engines are forcing honesty on you.

Consumers are no longer willing to sit back and passively absorb information companies feed them. Their natural curiosity will always take over when they are seeking product information, criticism, reviews, and ancillary facts. Search engines are effectively a natural extension of the mind, and must therefore be factored into the business models brands use to connect with their customers.

TODAY'S CONSUMERLAND IS AN ECOSYSTEM

The final distinguishing characteristic of the new ConsumerLand is that, despite growing diversity and fragmentation of populations, it is nevertheless a highly connected data ecosystem. (What is DNA, after all?) Everything touches and is connected. Leisure and work, home and mobility, time and place of consumption all morph together into a blurred hodge-podge of life, as consumers flow seamlessly between multiple contact points. Consumers do business at home, take their home life to their business, and act like kids and adults at the same time, while multitasking hundreds of different things each day.

In this ecosystem, people don't define themselves according to strict economic barriers or tidy demographics. They have the freedom to travel the landscape and camp out wherever they want. Earlier in the book, we raised this same point in the context of consumers being like investors, no longer tied to thinking of themselves as part of a single socioeconomic group, feeling instead that they can be stakeholders in any way they please. In the same way, consumers today see themselves as living a lifestyle and seeking products that fit their view of the world. You have to recognize the interconnections among diverse consumers, within a single defined lifestyle.

The secret to communicating with lifestyle consumers is to build multiple pathways to reach them across the wide spectrum of their activities. You need to create hundreds of touch points, not just one or two. The words *holographic* and *holistic* are key here. You seek to build holistic strategies that approach consumers holographically from every angle. And then keep refreshing them. In practical terms, it means you need to learn to deal with all those bloggers, epinion makers, YouTubers, social networks, search engines, buzz WOMers, viral e-mailers, spammers, mobile companies, and content producers all at the same time.

Like all ecosystems, ConsumerLand is complex. We're sure a lot of fundamentals about how to best manage it for optimum health are still misunderstood. What's clear, however, is that too many brands are not engaging with consumers as ecosystem inhabitants. They are still stuck in believing that consumers are just, well, consumers.

LESSONS LEARNED

Once upon a time, business models lasted a lifetime. Blue chip companies built shareholder value for generations of investors from models that remained essentially unchanged. Competition was restrained. Choice was limited. Large manufacturers controlled retail channels. Physical assets provided scale and insulation. Audiences tuned in religiously to the six o'clock news. It was a Newtonian world that ran like clockwork, and from the 1950s through the early 1990s, the market leader could sell its product by simply telling people that it was the solution to their nervous headache using 10,000 GRPs a year.

In that mechanical branding universe, consistency was celebrated because familiarity was important to consumers. Firms defined excellence through endurance. Best practices celebrated what worked yesterday and brand managers were more like maintenance engineers. During this time, doing things differently was not a friend to business, or desired in a brand.

Now what's happening in ConsumerLand challenges almost all our accumulated learning about business, marketing, and brands. What percentage of marketing dollars should be allocated to digital and online activities? What should those activities look like? How much should our brand marketing emphasize search, awareness building, eCRM—electronic customer relationship marketing—social networking, mobile, gaming, or interactive television? How do we measure the effectiveness of various media elements? Can one measure be applied universally or do we need different criteria and benchmarks based on objectives, efficiency, and engagement scores?

Ultimately, the opportunities are endless and the challenges may feel daunting. Worse, everything is constantly changing. Rishad Tobaccowala, CEO of media consultancy Denuo, says, "Three years ago, if you were planning things, you would not have thought about iTunes, YouTube, MySpace, Google. . . . Now you've got a new world, and this whole idea of planning is becoming very, very difficult. In fact, what we basically say is we now have classical structures in a jazz age."

We are all grappling with a world where the rules have changed—the rules about when, where, and how people consume content and advertising messages, and how they discover, engage with, and either endorse or reject brands (and then amplify that decision to their peers). It's changing the business models for companies, the skill sets needed for marketers, the roles for creating and distributing content for media companies, and the rules for how agencies think about creativity for brands.

The problem is, many marketers are applying much of the same old thinking to today's new challenges. *They try to adapt their formulas to the increasingly fractal landscape, rather than rethink them altogether.* As a result, consumers sail further away, while we continue to see brand measures decay and crack. ConsumerLand is taking a harsh and critical look at your business and your brands, creating new principles to abide by:

- We don't control our brands anymore; we simply guide them through the marketplace of consumers. This is especially true of Millennials, who have never known a world where they didn't control the experience.
- We no longer have a linear communication path to consumers. They have unprecedented ability to route around marketers to hear whatever they want, whenever they want, if at all. You can't just go to them. You must attract them.
- Consumers are no longer passive recipients waiting for marketing monologues. Brands must seek out ways to engage. Marketers, long accustomed to being tellers, must also become listeners.

- Some consumers will produce content for brands, regardless of whether we want them to or not. Many want to participate in the creative process. Edit them, tag them—but attempt to exclude them at your peril.
- People trust other people more than they trust brands. They will read blogs, watch videos, search consumer reviews and rating sites, and report on anything they find that is not up to their standards of honesty, fairness, and truth.
- ConsumerLand is a world of personalization. Consumers want to customize products to enhance their own personal brand. Experiences are what matter.
- Consumers want excitement and dynamism out of their brands. They will actively drive WOM, if the content is creative, novel, unique, and makes them look good.
- As consumers interact online, they take on community identities, which lead to more global brand strategies. Ever-larger communities will develop along languages and lifestyles, rather than economic, political, or market boundaries.
- Consumers want information and discovery, and we must allow them to search inside the deepest realms of our brands. Nothing can be hidden from consumers, and there's no use trying to hide anything.
- Consumers live in a vast unified ecosystem that blurs time, space, class, background, and all the usual theories of market segmentation. They live in a fast-paced world with ubiquitous connections. To succeed we need to be there when they are, with relevant content that they might want or need.

No specific formula will guide your operations in ConsumerLand; marketers must instead experiment with various approaches. *Marketing communications need to be marketing conversations.* The good news is that the same technology and social behaviors consumers are using to reverse the tables on brands—all those tools— are available to marketers as well. They can engage consumers in dialogue and recapture their attention with even a small piece of great content. If someone takes the time to respond, or pass that content along, or mash it up, that's to your advantage. After all, participation leads to longer engagement times and begins to suggest someone cares enough to do so in the first place. Perhaps you're more like a brand therapist. You need to get the patient to drop those defenses and simply begin to open up.

The final piece of advice is that you can't participate in this new ConsumerLand unless you honestly feel it. There's a universe of difference between rationally knowing about this landscape and personally experiencing how these innovations make consumers feel and behave. They cannot be understood from a purely intellectual perspective. They need to be felt emotionally and kinesthetically, by living in the same world as your consumer. Do you have a page on Facebook? Have you played virtual basketball with a kid in Finland? What about ordering from Pizza Hut while in character playing EverQuest II? You don't need a ticket to get into ConsumerLand, but you'll never experience the rush unless you ride the rides.

PART TWO

APPLICATION

What does the brand bubble teach us? How can brands bring consumer perceptions back into line with Wall Street's valuations? What actions can enterprises and their brands take to treat consumers as investors, focus on creativity, and meet the expectations and behaviors of customers inhabiting this new ConsumerLand?

The answers to these questions are clear: Many of the old concepts of brand management no longer apply; brands must be managed according to new rules. Brands must become engines of continuous differentiation, fueled by energy and propelled forward by constant creativity and evolution. At the same time, companies must transform themselves around the concept of the brand as an organizing principle. Everyone must become a brand manager. Accountability for the brand must reside in every department. This requires brand leadership in the C-suite, new skills for CMOs and marketing managers, greater openness with consumers, and dismantling old silos of territory and responsibility that inhibit collaboration. The entire company must transform itself into a marketing-driven firm, rather than a firm with a marketing department.

Remember that the brand bubble is built on market expectations. Creating continuous consumer value is inextricably linked with sound brand valuations and future financial performance. For brands to keep pace with consumers, we can no longer accept a static view of their existence. A brand is a constantly evolving idea in the mind of the consumer. We have to work harder, smarter, and faster than ever before. We can't settle for soft brand essences or narrow expressions of brand meaning. Brand strategies have to do more than evoke what a brand stands for. They must provide direction for where a brand has to go.

Yet too much time is spent on thinking about what a brand is, rather than what it can be. We think of a brand as something that can be evaluated and directed as though it were an inert object. We liken brands to trust marks and badges of reassurance. We build brand architectures, pyramids, boxes, and funnels. Thinking like this invariably implies an element of stasis and permanence, which is incompatible with ConsumerLand.

Today, sustaining a meaningful point of difference is more elusive than ever before. The pace of change is accelerating exponentially. Consumers quickly discard derivative brands. After all, it wasn't that long ago that Prodigy and CompuServe were battling for Internet domination; Kodak, Oldsmobile, and MCI were blue chips, Puma, Adidas, and Cadillac were nostalgic. It seems only yesterday that China didn't shop at Wal-Mart and America didn't know of Lenovo. That Cingular was more prominent than AT&T. And that GM was bigger than Toyota.

Our research suggests that only a small number of truly irresistible brands are in existence. They command positions of leadership by constantly reinventing the world as they see it, thrilling their customers and creating future value. As for the rest, their booming brand values are portending a large-scale brand bust.

This is a time of reckoning for business. Collectively, brands make up a massive sector of the global economy. Business has an obligation to shareholders to rebuild brand value by recasting their brands for the new marketplace. For many, there's no time to lose before their bubble bursts.

A Framework to Energize the Brand and the Organization

In Part Two, we walk you through a comprehensive five-stage framework to build an irresistible brand by infusing it with energy and instilling a new vision in your brand management. We show how to identify the energy in your brand, distill it into three fundamental consumer-facing touch-points and ignite creativity throughout your organization. We explain step by step practical ways to become a brand-led, consumer-driven organization that adopts the brand into its being.

As you implement the five stages, the needs of the brand should move to the center of the organization. Brand imperatives become business imperatives. A rigorous focus on creating an irresistible, high-energy brand can transform your entire organization, letting the brand act as a catalyst for collaboration, innovation, and accountability. By looking at the business through the lens of the brand, your management can articulate a stronger creative vision for the company, and people throughout the organization can begin to internalize the company's mission as their own. When this happens, you will create what we call the "Energy-Driven Enterprise." This type of firm sustains its competitive advantage by generating brand, operational, organizational, and cultural energy.

The five stages of our transformation framework were developed from reverse engineering the practices of the highest-energy brands from the nine hundred companies we modeled. We also incorporated learning about consumer behaviors we gleaned from ethnographies conducted in London, Moscow, Mumbai, New York, São Paulo, Shanghai, Singapore, Sydney, Tokyo, and Warsaw. We know that transforming years, if not decades, of traditional brand management does not come easy. By no means is this a formulaic process; what we're describing is a suggestion of steps that will take you toward more brand-centric managerial thinking. For each of the five stages, we address not only the process that must be adopted but also the leading obstacle we have witnessed in companies that undermines the brand-consumer relationship. Many of these challenges will be all too familiar to you as an executive, marketer, or manager, and you may recognize yourself and your enterprise in our analysis of these barriers.

To counter the obstacles, we have developed corollary Laws of Energy. Like gravity, these laws become management tools to control the forces that operate on brands in today's world. The Laws of Energy naturally lead to the corresponding New Rules for Brand Management, which translate each law into practical actions, strategies, and tactics for leaders and managers to induce energy in their brands and transform their brand management to create consumer-centric, energy-driven enterprises.

The illustration on the next page provides a visual overview of the five stages.

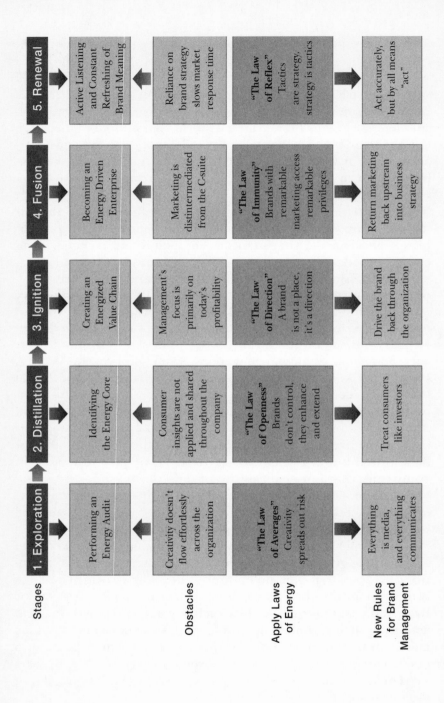

The transformation in brand management called for will take long-term commitment and hard work in your enterprise. But these recommendations have worked in companies to renew their brands and generate positive changes in their organizations, setting them up for a sustainable future. The thinking and behaviors we recommend will move you from simply brand building to powerful brand activation.

Finally, our five-stage brand management plan treats brands as engines of business momentum, because brands are only truly valuable assets when they are leveraged against business challenges—and put to work. Working brands are those with energy. They become so irresistible they change behavior. They move consumers beyond the singular action of buying, into sharing, evangelizing, future contemplation and, of course, buying again and again with a commitment and loyalty that reenergizes the brand, the consumer, and the organization to continuously evolve. In this feedback loop, the company builds momentum in the marketplace and creates brand values worthy of Wall Street analyst expectations.

CHAPTER SIX

STAGE ONE—EXPLORATION
Performing an Energy Audit

The point is not "how creative are you" but "how are you creative."
—SIR KEN ROBINSON, "POWER OF THE IMAGINATION,"
SPEECH AT THE TED CONFERENCE, 2006

The first important thing to know when attempting to instill energy in a brand and alter your brand management is that the process is not random or uncontrollable. Energy can be generated for brands as reliably as it can be generated for homes. Energy can be consciously developed, augmented, channeled, and utilized for your benefit and reward.

Changing your brand management is equally a conscious process, one that can be managed and directed. New skills can be learned. A more inclusive form of brand management can be developed, one that recognizes that everyone in the organization is accountable for the dynamic relationship between the consumer and the brand.

The process starts with an "Energy audit" to assess the level of energy currently present in your brand. Your goal is to capture a baseline measure that identifies the current sources of energy so you can understand your brand's strengths and weaknesses and detect how well your brand management is aligned with the dynamics of the new marketplace. Equally important, the Energy audit allows you to identify potential pathways for building even higher levels of energy. As results come into focus, you'll begin to understand how people respond to your brand's imagery, offerings, creativity, and overall character. These insights will then allow you to inspire ideas that channel energy back into your brand, then across your organization and out into the market.

What's crucially different about an Energy audit, though, is that it is not a simple marketing department exercise to survey what consumers think about the brand. It is an interrogation of the brand experience from every vantage point. The audit reveals the brand's composite perception not only in the marketplace but inside the organization as well. People from all divisions and disciplines must participate because you are setting the stage for creating a more inclusive form of enterprise brand management. Managers across the organization need to get at deep customer insights of who is using their products and why they must uncover the underlying perceptions of their company and brands so that in later stages they have the perspective necessary to connect disparate ideas and offer possible solutions that may otherwise lie hidden inside an operating unit or a function of the business.

As an entry point to an Energy audit with regard to what consumers think of your brand, we invite you to draw upon our proprietary Y&R BAV database, which includes over forty thousand brands. We are opening limited access to readers to see the consumer data Y&R has collected over the years about the energy in their brands—or in any brands, including the leading brands in the world and perhaps even those of competitors.

However, before instructing you how to perform the Energy audit and log in to our BAV, we need to provide some background on how we measure brands so you can understand the scores you will find in our database. Like biology teachers, who need to give students a lesson in cell structure before sending them off to peer into the microscope, we have to give you a brief lesson about the components and subcomponents that make up a brand's equity before letting you run loose in our BAV lab.

THE ANATOMY OF BRAND STRENGTH

If you were to look through a microscope at how brands build equity, the first level of magnification zooms in on the elements of brand growth. As explained in Chapter Two, the BAV measures

FIGURE 6.1. BRAND STRENGTH IS THE FIRST LEVEL OF MEASUREMENT
IN ASSESSING A BRAND'S ENERGY.

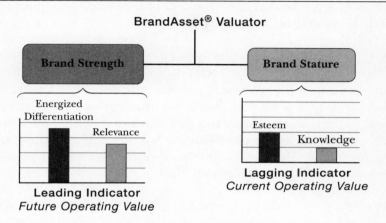

and categorizes consumer attitudes toward brands according to
two constructs—Brand Strength and Brand Stature. These two sets
of measures form the X- and Y-axes of a grid by which we plot a
brand's current status in the market against its potential for future
growth (see Figure 6.1).

- *Brand Stature* forms the X-axis and is built upon two pillars that
  demarcate a brand's current position, *Esteem* and *Knowledge,*
  each of which is measured from consumer attitudes. Esteem
  reflects consumer regard, while Knowledge reflects consumer
  awareness of a brand.
- *Brand Strength* forms the Y-axis and is derived from two additional supporting pillars: *Energized Differentiation* and *Relevance.*
  Energized Differentiation reflects consumer attitudes about
  the brand's unique meaning, with future motion, which
  affect a brand's ability to capture loyalty and margin power.
  Relevance indicates how appropriate consumers perceive the
  brand to be for them, which affects market penetration.

High levels of both Energized Differentiation and Relevance
are required to achieve sustainable growth and broad market penetration. Without Energized Differentiation, even a relevant brand
will stall, lost in the forest of competitors or trapped in the thickets

of consumer disregard. Without Relevance, an energized brand languishes, starving for customers. These two qualities are faster to build than Knowledge or Esteem, but they are also quicker to erode if not constantly nurtured.

THE ANATOMY OF ENERGIZED DIFFERENTIATION

Now let's adjust the microscope to magnify one more level down, probing deeper within the nucleus of Energized Differentiation itself. Here is where the brand attributes that contribute specifically to energy reside. In this view, we now see that Energized Differentiation itself is formed from two dimensions, with each having three elements (Figure 6.2).

- *Energy:* This quality reflects more specifically the consumer's perception of motion and direction in the brand. It sustains

FIGURE 6.2. THE ANATOMY OF ENERGIZED DIFFERENTIATION.

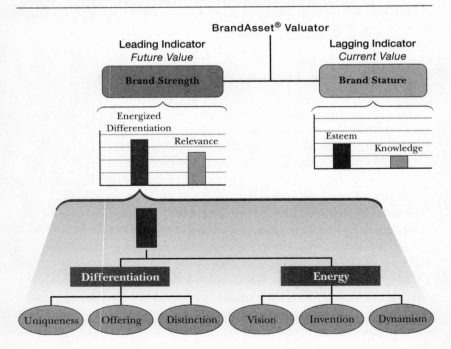

the brand's velocity. Three attribute clusters comprise energy:

- *Vision:* The brand's purpose and aspirations, often originating from the leadership, convictions, and reputation of the company behind the brand.
- *Invention:* The most tangible dimension, demonstrating the brand's perceptions through product or service innovation, design, content, and other tactile brand experiences.
- *Dynamism:* How the brand expresses itself in a dynamic way in the marketplace to create persona, emotion, advocacy, and evangelism through its marketing and other forms of conversations with consumers.

- *Differentiation:* This quality represents the consumer's impressions of the brand's point of difference. It creates the meaning, margin, and competitive advantage in the brand. Differentiation is made up of:

  - *Offering:* The measure of the brand's special characteristics in terms of products, services, and other content that the consumer experiences.
  - *Uniqueness:* The brand's essence, positioning, and brand equity.
  - *Distinction:* The reputation the brand has earned through existing communications and brand image created up to this point.

PEERING INTO THE NUCLEUS OF ENERGY

Increasing the magnification yet again, we finally arrive at the deepest core to pierce the atomic level of energy. Here we explore in detail the three dimensions—*Vision, Invention,* and *Dynamism*—that define an energized brand for consumers. The three elements, a brand's "VID pattern," to use our abbreviation for it, are the actual fuel rods from which brands source their energy and build more of it. Let's zoom in to these energy-building elements to examine each one in detail.

Vision

Brands with Vision espouse a clear direction and point of view on the world. They know what they're on this planet to achieve. Some brands espouse a vision to change the way people think; others seek to shift expectations on the way things are done. They see the world a certain way and encourage consumers to join in. Vision-driven brands see farther; they galvanize and inspire, allowing the brand to travel into new categories and create new meaning. The Vision element of energy reflects breakthrough, category-reframing ideas and higher-order benefits. Vision-driven brands excel in leadership and prescience. They bring more than innovation to consumers: they change behaviors by impacting and improving the way people live their lives.

A parent company's reputation can also play a significant role in driving brand Vision: How does the company act and behave toward its consumers, employees, or the world beyond commerce? Does the company have inspiring leadership that consumers admire? Is the company a great place to work? Does it care about social issues? Is there a unique and powerful culture? Does it operate against a "triple bottom line"? In a transparent society, consumers don't divorce their perceptions of the brand from overarching company values and conduct. They expect visionary brands to stand for higher-order benefits—and that also goes for the company *behind the brand*. For example, Mei-ying, a twenty-two-year-old graduate student we met in Shanghai, told us, "China Mobile is very progressive. Not only are they reaching out to provide coverage in rural areas, they are very active in social issues." That's the type of admiration a visionary brand receives.

Brand Vision in Practice. Here are some brands with notably strong Vision (90th percentile of all brands in our study). They include Amazon, American Express, Apple, BBC, Ben & Jerry's, The Body Shop, Disney, Dove, eBay, easyJet, General Electric, Goldman Sachs, Google, Grameen Bank, Habitat for Humanity, HBO, Hewlett Packard, IBM, Innocent, LeapFrog, Leica, LEGO, Orange, Pixar, Patagonia, Product Red, Rough Guides, Tata Motors, Tesco, Timberland, Wal-Mart, Whole Foods, Wikipedia, Vanguard, and

Zara. The visions they express cut across a spectrum of benefits from making work more enjoyable for their employees to changing the world we live in. Let's look at a few examples of Vision in greater detail:

- One Laptop per Child's stated goal is "to provide children around the world with new opportunities to explore, experiment and express themselves." The company has yet to achieve manufacturing laptops for only $100 each, but it has inspired the competition.
- Visa Green automatically measures and offsets the carbon footprint of consumer purchases through use of its card.
- General Electric, Wal-Mart, and Toyota have led their categories in energy savings, hybrid technology, reduced-emission products, and affordable pharmaceuticals.
- Grameen Bank created "microcredit": small loans without collateral in Bangladesh to help impoverished people. The bank won the Nobel Peace Prize in 2006.
- Southwest Airlines says—and means—"Employees are our first customer." The company sends out birthday cards to each of its thirty-four thousand employees annually.
- IKEA was named one of the world's most ethical companies in 2007 for its employee practices and its promotion of environmental issues and children's welfare.
- Accenture offers paid sabbaticals for its employees to work for nonprofits.
- Cranium has industry-leading recruitment practices that screen and hire future "Craniacs." Cranium has won Game and Toy of the Year awards three straight years.
- American Apparel was named one of the Millennial generation's favorite brands from social networking feedback originating from its staff. Respondents cited they have friends who work there and love their jobs.[1]
- Joost and BitTorrent are revolutionizing the way content is distributed over the net. BitTorrent is now responsible for over one-third of all Internet traffic.
- SUBWAY invented an entirely new category of quick-service restaurant: healthy fast food.

- Fisher-Price promoted children's heath by creating a "smart cycle," marrying active play and learning. The cycle plugs into the TV so kids learn, play, and exercise at the same time.
- Zillow, the online real estate firm, allows buyers and sellers to negotiate directly, bypassing agents and providing access to all home values, not just those for sale.
- Barack Obama was the first truly digital candidate, with easy-to-create personal pages for social networking and fundraising, blogging tools, RSS feeds, and extensions to Facebook, YouTube, MySpace and Flickr.
- Colgate sponsors in-store reading events with its "Reading Is Fundamental" program to promote children's literacy and healthy brushing and washing habits among children.

Invention

Brands with Invention change how people feel and the way they behave. Invention captures the experiential and tangible properties of the brand. The most functional element of energy, Invention is built on the tactile and sensory associations that come from product and service experiences and other physical brand interactions. Invention can be built through innovation, brand iconography, packaging design, applied technology, retail environments, and customer service excellence.

Invention reinforces the brand's presence when there is no other messaging around. Invention energy reinforces product quality and removes dissonance, while stimulating WOM and repurchase considerations. A brand's invention can never remain static. Maintaining consistently high levels of invention require a commitment to continuous innovation, service excellence and new forms of brand experience. A comment from Amandeep, a forty-one-year-old strategist with an Internet portal in Delhi, illustrates the invention energy felt about the new Indian car, the Tata Nano: "This car only costs 100,000 rupees [about 2,000 U.S. dollars], but it's sleek and stylish. This car is changing India." When a brand can change an entire country of more than a billion people, it's clearly commanding invention energy.

Brand Invention in Practice. Brands can demonstrate invention in products, services, and overall brand experiences. The brands that possess demonstrably strong invention include Apple, Bang & Olufsen, BlackBerry, Bose, Callaway, Commerce Bank, Costco, Crocs, Dyson, Febreeze, IKEA, iPhone, JetBlue, Kashi, Land Rover, Lenovo, LG, Method, Microsoft, Netflix, Nordstrom, Pinkberry, Prêt à Manger, SanDisk, SIRIUS, SUBWAY, Shutterfly, Simplehuman, Singapore Airlines, Slingbox, Swiffer, TiVo, Trader Joe's, 3M, UNIQLO, vitaminwater, Vitra, W Hotels, Wii and Zappos.

- Along with WiFi and a bar in the hotel lobby, guests at W Hotels find fashion emergency kits by Diane von Furstenberg and products from Bliss Spa.
- Nintendo's Wii turned gaming into an active social experience with its physical interactive technology that connects millions online.
- Louis Vuitton and Japanese artist Takashi Murakami handbags were sold as part of an installation with Murakami's art exhibition at the Museum of Contemporary Art in Los Angeles.
- Each Four Seasons hotel has a "customer historian" accountable for keeping up a portfolio of every guest's preferences and needs.
- JCDecaux secured the rights to post billboards in Paris by creating a low-cost bicycle rental program. Tens of thousands of Parisians now rent bikes each month.
- Tesco turned its grocery carts into body workout machines with motion-resistant handles.
- Commerce Bank's philosophy is to act more like a retailer, with seven-day service, a penny arcade coin exchange, and dog biscuits in the drive-through.
- MTV.com/overdrive lets the user become program director by controlling content like *Real World,* music videos and artist interviews.
- Nike and iPod teamed up to create NIKEiD, where Nike shoes transfer data to the Nano, including time, distance, and calories burned. It even customizes play lists to a given workout.
- Kidfresh introduced nutritious fast food for kids with playful food presentation and packaging.
- Pinkberry's frozen yogurt groupies have their own corner on Pinkberry's Web site. Their stores are designed to "kindle the senses."

- Neiman Marcus's philosophy is that every one of its stores should feel different. Its new Boston store conjures up the images of a flowing silk dress.
- Simplehuman's products are focused on efficient design to make life easier and simpler, like fingerprint-proof trash cans; its blog gives tips on "efficient living."
- Whole Foods reduced waiting time by creating a single-line system and adding thirty cashiers in its New York supermarkets.
- Webkinz, the plush pet toys, have their own codes that allow kids to adopt and interact with them virtually on their Web site, Webkinz World.

Dynamism

Brands with Dynamism create excitement in the marketplace by how they present themselves to consumers. Dynamism is the most emotional and immediately visible of the three components. The driver of brand imagery and personality, Dynamism reflects the brand's ability to inspire consumer affinity. Traditionally the outcome of a big ad campaign, guerilla marketing event, or highly visible marketplace event, today's Dynamism is increasingly complex and can span a variety of forms of brand engagement—analog or digital, traditional or viral, customized user experience or social media.

Brands with high levels of Dynamism create persona, community, and evangelism among their users. Dynamic brands penetrate popular culture. They give consumers something to talk about, facilitating enthusiastic WOM across consumer social networks and brand ecosystems. Aleksandra, a twenty-eight-year-old retail salesperson from Warsaw, typifies how consumers are inspired by a brand's dynamism: "I saw the Honda Cogs commercial on YouTube or somewhere. It was a really cool clip, so we passed it around." As this statement shows, if a brand stimulates, evokes feelings, and starts conversations among consumers, it has Dynamism.

Brand Dynamism in Practice. This list illustrates the many flavors of brand dynamism: Audi, Axe, American Apparel, Bebo, Best Buy, BitTorrent, BMW, Boost, Burger King, Burton Snowboards, Cobra Beer, Converse, Diesel, Digg, Ducati, ESPN, Facebook, Green & Blacks, Halo 3, Harley-Davidson, H&M, iTunes, Kingfisher, MUJI,

MySpace, Nascar, Nike, Patron, PlayStation, PUMA, Prada, Red Bull, Rock Band, 7 For All Mankind, Shiseido, Stella Artois, Theory, Twitter, Under Armor, Victoria's Secret, Virgin Atlantic, Xbox, and YouTube.

- Each August marks the largest concentration of Harley-Davidson motorcycles in one place on the planet: The annual Harley rally in Sturgis, South Dakota.
- Mozilla Firefox, the open source browser, created a user-generated advertising campaign, using viral clips posted online at Firefox Flicks.
- Twitter has taken SMS to a fluid form of social networking. Millions of kids use this microblogging site to send short text updates to friends across the world.
- An Ecko "Still Free" branded viral for graffiti artists dramatized an artist creating graffiti on Air Force One, amassing more than 130 million views.
- Design Barcode in Tokyo patented its idea to turn ordinary barcodes on products into forms of visual communications.
- Edoc laundry extended alternate reality games through clues woven into its clothing. To play, players had to wear the clothing and could then spot each other wearing the collection and work together to solve the puzzle.
- American Express's "My Life, My Card" Web site hosted a long-form ad from director Wes Anderson, inviting others to create short films and submit them to the site.
- Nike's RunLondon.com created a running community who registered in store or online and then received mobile content, a digital running chip to upload photos, log times, and access to course information to run with forty thousand others.
- Smirnoff Raw Tea concocted a hip hop on Martha's Vineyard to create a hilarious viral music video that more than 2 million people watched on YouTube.
- MINI Cooper drivers were mailed RFID chips with customizable messages that flash up on Mini billboards when they pass by.
- "Black Balloons" viral PSA video was posted on YouTube where it became available 24/7 and integrated into key global warming–related search words.

- Adidas created mobile wrap-enabled outdoor boards, where pedestrians with Bluetooth were offered a mobile mini-movie to download directly to their phone.
- Old Spice Red Zone designed changeable advertising within networked games, included in-game billboards where gamers were allowed to apply graffiti.
- Burger King created customized games for the release of the BK Xbox game series. More than two million copies were sold within four weeks, equal to the top ten best-selling videogames of 2006.
- Diesel promoted its intimates collection through a fake hijacking of its dot-com site featuring live 24/7 streaming video coverage.

THE YIN AND YANG OF ENERGY AND DIFFERENTIATION

Like the tightly integrated duality of yin and yang, energy and differentiation exist inseparably and behave symbiotically. The two forces work together to propel a brand forward. Differentiation grounds the brand, solidifying where it is at this very moment, while energy acts as a catalyst, leading the brand to where it can be tomorrow. Energy accelerates differentiation, while Differentiation gives meaning to energy. Differentiation is more or less static, whereas energy can be reckless and erratic.

When the two work together, the brand achieves both forward progress and strategic accuracy. (See Figure 6.3.)

Brands can find competitive advantage from the energy generated by one of these dimensions—Vision, Invention, or Dynamism—or by all of them combined. For years, Apple has a balanced VID pattern in which its Vision, Invention, and Dynamism all rank equally high. But that hasn't always been the case for everything Apple does, especially the iPod. Apple's culture is legendary for creativity and continuous innovation, as evidenced by such category-redefining products as its computers and even the iPod. This boosted Apple's Invention to the point where, in 2002, the iPod was seen as one of the top 1 percent most inventive brands in BAV. However, according to our research, when it first came out, the iPod was only among the top 30 percent most visionary brands, and the top 20 percent most dynamic brands.

FIGURE 6.3. DIFFERENTIATION AND ENERGY INTERACT TO THRILL CONSUMERS.

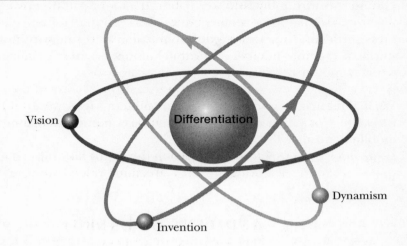

Apple employed tactics that grew and balanced the energy behind the iPod, striving to complement its inventive foundation with a greater sense of Dynamism, further establishing itself as a visionary leader. The results paid off. Today, the iPod sits among the top most energized brands in the U.S. market.

How did Apple accomplish this? One tactic that clearly heightened the iPod's overall VID was when Apple partnered with the band U2, a high-energy brand in its own right. While iPod's energy was built around Innovation, U2's energy was grounded in Dynamism. The two brands worked together in 2004 to launch U2's album, *How to Dismantle an Atomic Bomb.* The first single, "Vertigo," made its way into the market via an Apple commercial for iPod, while Apple designed a limited-edition U2 iPod complete with the band's entire catalog. What's particularly interesting is that, according to our tracking, the two brands literally swapped energy: Over the six-month period of the partnership, U2 increased consumer perceptions of its inventiveness by over 8 percent, while much of U2's Dynamism transferred over to iPod, which saw a 10 percent gain. While maintaining its inventive spirit, iPod is now among the top 4 percent most dynamic brands in America and among the top 2 percent most visionary.

As this story demonstrates, some brands may begin with one strong energy dimension, which then, if managed well, can ignite the others. When they're successfully balanced, they blend into big brand ideas from big-thinking firms.

Nevertheless, in some sectors, we've also seen that a single element is sufficient to power a leading brand in that category. For example, we've noted that each attribute cluster, when strong, can completely power brands in the following categories:

- *Vision:* Financial services, pharmaceuticals, and B2B
- *Invention:* Consumer electronics, personal computing, and mobile handsets
- *Dynamism:* Automotive, alcoholic beverages, and fashion

PERFORMING YOUR ENERGY AUDIT

You're now ready to put away the microscope and move out of the classroom. You've seen how assessing Brand Strength is the key to understanding your brand's sustainable future. To build that strength, a brand must develop Energized Differentiation, through the separate components of Vision, Invention, and Dynamism, each of which can then boost the others, generating even greater energy.

Armed with this background, you can now perform an Energy audit on your own brand. To initiate the audit, we invite you to tap into Y&R's BAV database of more than forty-two thousand brands. Some brands have a long record in our database, having been tracked for more than a dozen years, while others are more recent. For each brand, we have collected and analyzed consumer attitudinal information that allows us to formulate measures of sustainability, including a cumulative "Energy Index," along with separate Vision, Invention, and Dynamism scores.

Your brand's scores provide a top-line perspective of the business issues facing you, and may suggest strategic pathways forward. Your brand's VID pattern especially reveals its strengths and weaknesses, while your competitors' VID patterns can help you identify opportunities to exploit competitive weaknesses. You can also do research to identify unmet consumer needs that might be interpolated from the VID scores of everyone in a category.

These benchmarks can set the stage for you to do your own comparisons between different audiences (for example, your brand loyalists versus users of competing brands). The data also gives you clues about opportunities where you can look for growth and development. And because BAV contrasts all brands against each other, you can go outside your own category to enhance your learning about such areas as customer service, community building, or company cultures. You can also study "stretch" brands you might seek to emulate for insights and opportunities.

How to Access Y&R's BAV

To gain entry into a special section of Y&R's proprietary brand database, go to www.thebrandbubble.com. We'll ask you to provide some basic information in order to get a password but you will not be solicited for any follow-up. (You are welcome to contact us though if you want a personal discussion of your brand.) If your brand is not included in our database, you can still use our data to model your own Energy audit based on related brands in your industry or on leading consumer brands you seek to emulate.

The Energy Index

In the BAV database, the first data point provided for every brand is its Energy Index. This score relates to the brand's overall Brand Strength, derived from the sum of its Energized Differentiation and its Relevance.

Keep in mind that the Energy Index is a snapshot; it reveals only how the brand scored when our BAV took its last measurement, whereas a brand's energy level is constantly shifting. But just as a financial balance sheet is useful to provide evidence of an enterprise's general health, the Energy Index likewise constitutes a powerful measure of a brand's probable energy level and sustainability. The Index is also useful because it yields a comparative value of the brand's stature relative to the thousands of brands the BAV tracks.

Collectively, the energy indexes for all brands in our study result in a relative distribution of scores, using an absolute ranking from 100 down to 0. A higher score indicates greater Brand Strength. We've come to visualize the Energy Index as a thermometer showing how "hot" a brand is, and we've categorized brands into seven levels of heat, from "volcanic" to "inert." Figure 6.4,

FIGURE 6.4. THE ENERGY INDEX.

OVERALL ASSESSMENT: The Energy Index
We've talked about brand value from the perspective of business experts. But what about consumers? The Energy Index is a distribution of Brand Strength (Energized Differentiation and Relevance) from across our brandscape of 2,500 brands we survey in BAV in North America. Since this is derived from stock performance, it gives us a snapshot of greater to lesser potential brand value creation. There are seven levels: (For a specific brand, go to thebrandbubble.com).

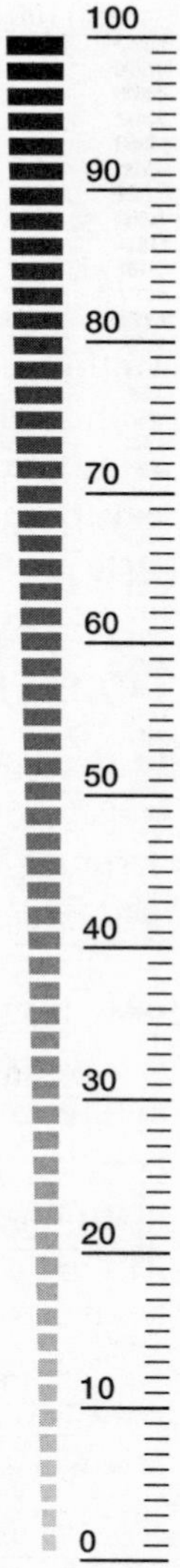

VOLCANIC: Energy Index of 90–100
These are the top 10% of all brands in our study. These supernovas have unleashed luminous Energy on the marketplace. They are weapons of mass devotion. They own the popular consciousness, driving both volume and margin. Of those that have much, will much be demanded: consumers expect brands with this much presence to keep up in spectacular fashion. They must also monitor attitudes of their early adopters carefully. Many could leave the franchise as the mainstream enters. These brands have to prove to their loyalists they still have the heart of an insurgent.

BURNING: Energy Index of 75–89
These brands are sizzling in the marketplace. They've created allure and fandom. Consumers feel their presence in their lives. Now that greatness is thrust upon them, they need to act differently. Brands in this position need to keep converting energy into new forms of surprise and delight. They can't rest now because many brands in this position lose Energy as fast as they gain it.

KINETIC: Energy Index of 60–74
Brands with kinetic Energy are taking notice, and their velocity keeps accelerating. Advocates are forming and chatter is happening. These brands have already come a long way. Perhaps now is the time to think beyond the confines of the market, and the functionality of the product, and consider how to give the brand a wider social relevance.

CHARGED: Energy Index of 45–59
These are brands where Energy is converting from one form to another. Growing sales leads to more marketing. A hot new product inspires a concept store. Often these brands lack a central catalyst for integration. Brands at this stage need more than basic product functionality. They need a champion to infuse emotion and creativity into the brand.

PULSING: Energy Index of 30–44
These brands have latent Energy. They may be doing all the right things in terms of image, saliency and share in tracking, but they still trail the marketplace. They are an upstart challenger brand, or a brand in decline. The firm needs to raise its sights and get its brand to drive the business. It needs to put the brand first.

DORMANT: Energy Index of 15–29
These brands require urgency if they're going to help retain and grow the business. No matter what category, these brands could do with a rethink. Is the existing brand and marketing strategy differentiating enough? Is the brand focused on a sharp target?

INERT: Energy Index of 0–14
These brands are really just a name that people have heard of rather than a brand with real, added value. Now is the time to take a fundamental look at the brand and work out why differentiation levels are so low. Is the firm serious in its efforts to support the brand and bring innovation to consumers? Many are so weak, they are vulnerable to private label, or outright consumer indifference.

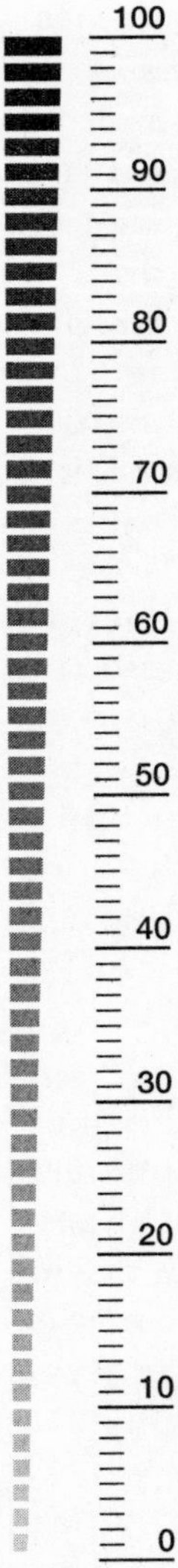

FIGURE 6.4. (*CONTINUED*)

100

VOLCANIC BRAND

Disney, Pixar, Crocs, Google, IKEA, Victoria's Secret, iPod, Harley-Davidson, Swiffer, Nike, eBay, Wikipedia, Starbucks, Target, Dyson, Coca-Cola, Leap Frog, BMW, LEGO, Best Buy, Apple, Sirius Satellite Radio, Toyota, Hewlett-Packard, BlackBerry, Nintendo Wii, Kohler, IBM, Kashi, Microsoft.com, Trader Joe's, ESPN, TiVo, Boeing, Crayola, HBO, General Electric, Dr Pepper, MTV, NASCAR, YouTube, Pepsi, MINI, Amazon.com

90

80

BURNING BRAND

POM, Cadillac, Snickers, Advanced Micro Devices (AMD), Whole Foods, UPS, LG, FedEx, craigslist, V8, Adidas, John Deere, Pepperidge Farm Goldfish, Tazo, Dove (beauty products), Canon, Polo/Ralph Lauren, Xbox 360, Cranium, Sam's Club, Ray-Ban, Linux, DEWALT, Timberland, Nordstrom, MySpace, BitTorrent, Axe, Motorola, Skype, Glacéau Vitaminwater, VISA, PlayStation 3

70

KINETIC BRAND

McDonald's, Mattel, EA Sports, Tumi, Godiva, L.L. Bean, Diet Coke, Starbury (sneakers), Weight Watchers, MasterCard, Madden NFL, Red Bull, Dasani, Facebook, NFL.com, Costco, Ecko Unlimited, Applebee's, ING Direct, Converse, Abercrombie & Fitch, 7 for all Mankind, Curves, Chipotle, Soutwest Airlines, Careerbuilder.com

60

CHARGED BRAND

Nokia, PUMA, Jack Daniel's, Guinness, Firefox, Jamba Juice, Expedia.com, Evian, Method (hand soap), Blockbuster, Staples, Patagonia, Bacardi, Neiman Marcus, Burberry, Foot Locker, Absolut, friendster.com, Weber, Zara, Smirnoff, Marriott, Dunkin' Donuts, Lucent Technologies, Chase, Bulgari, Degree, Comcast, Four Seasons Hotels, Zappos

50

40

PULSING BRAND

Bausch & Lomb, SnackWells, Planters, Kimberly-Clark, Quicken, Aflac, Vespa, Aquafina, Ann Taylor, ChevronTexaco, Equal, 2(x)ist, Tang, Hush Puppies, Parkay, Heineken, Pampers, Fendi, The North Face, Yoplait, Ritz-Carlton, NutraSweet, Perrier, Long John Silver's, Frosted Flakes, Samsonite, Siemens, 7-Eleven, Goldman Sachs, Ericsson

30

DORMANT BRAND

ASICS, Holiday Inn, Huggies, Sweet 'N Low, Kayak.com, Wachovia, Bratz, American Airlines, Papa John's, Fruit of the Loom, AXA, United Airlines, Prilosec, Midas, Ball Park, Oscar Mayer, Michelob, Progressive Insurance, Alcatel, Celebrity Cruises, Hampton Inn, Cap'n Crunch, Gant

20

INERT BRAND

EDS, American Apparel, Esprit, SpaghettiOs, The Athlete's Foot, Commerce Bank, American Tourister, State Farm, Prêt à Manger, Kyocera, AIG, Greyhound, The Hartford, SAP, Foster Farms, Luvs, Motel 6, Haier, Bufferin, One-A-Day, Lipitor, Chef Boyardee, LendingTree, Rolaids, U-Haul, Prell, DRISTAN, Allstate, Taster's Choice, Fab, Prudential, Enterprise Rent-A-Car, Wella, National Car Rental

10

0

which shows how BAV scored a sampling of popular brands as of December 2007, gives you a quick look at the Energy Index.

Interpreting the Energy Index

In general, the Brand Strength score indicates a brand's future potential. Greater overall Brand Strength means greater ability to create future value. More specifically, it's the changes in Energized Differentiation that foretell a brand's true marketplace power. We can see this correlation happening in fast-growing brands like Dr Pepper, Lacoste, Crayola, Method, Heineken Light, and Facebook. Conversely, a drop in Energized Differentiation is a serious warning sign of the eventual loss of overall Brand Strength.

However, note that a single measurement of Brand Strength can be deceiving. A brand may appear momentarily strong to the enterprise, but its specific Energized Differentiation might be stalled or weakening in the consumer's mind. Think of Sun Microsystems, Blockbuster, Sony, and Motorola. This is because differentiation and relevance often take longer to build and are slower to erode, while energy can be volatile. The perception of Energy is the most salient indicator of brand attitude changes, and thus future growth or decline in a brand's differentiation or relevance.

This situation is evident in what appear to be weaker brands where differentiation or relevance trails energy because the brand is new or niche, or its resurgence has not reached the mainstream. Picture Zara, Converse, Prêt à Manger, Samsonite, Gant, or Perrier. In another deceptive reading, energy may appear weak because of limited market penetration and understanding, resulting in low differentiation and relevance—even though the brand is high in energy. Examples are Lenovo, Kayak.com, Commerce Bank, and American Apparel. And Brand Strength can be lowered because pricing or image excludes many customers, thus driving down relevance. Notable examples are Neiman Marcus, Four Seasons, Prada, Fendi, Bally, and e-harmony. For greater accuracy on these brands, study a more specific target audience segment for the brand, rather than just "all adults."

You also need to factor in the *size and category effects* that can impact Brand Strength. Just like the principles of physics, bigger brands (with greater mass) require more energy to move differentiation and relevance, whereas smaller and newer brands with low levels of differentiation and relevance can grow at a faster pace. Citibank, Delta, Burger King, Coca-Cola, and Budweiser need greater energy than Vespa, Ecko, POM, ING, and deli.cio.us.

A brand's category also accounts for differences in the effects of energy. Categories such as computers, gaming, electronics, and automotive are higher-energy to begin with, reflecting greater consumer involvement and interest, compared to low-energy categories such as financial services, quick service restaurants, and household products. In the Energy Index against all brands, category effects often restrain highly energized brands like Aflac, Method, Washington Mutual, Virgin, and Geico. Also, brands in business-to-business, niche industries, or technology often lack familiarity and widespread understanding as well. Think of Siemens, Lucent, Goldman Sachs, Cisco, and Second Life. Yet when we look at their performance within their sectors, these brands' performance is noticeably stronger.

Tracking and Visualizing a Brand's VID Scores

In addition to the overall Energy Index, BAV scores each brand on its three individual components of Vision, Invention, and Dynamism, called its VID profile. It makes it possible to detect whether a brand's three sources of energy are balanced in consumer minds or are based on one dimension being stronger than the other two. It can also reveal a starting point to find competitive leverage. Perhaps your brand has high Vision, while this component is a deficit in your competitors. You might aim to find other sources of energy to harness to drive your vision and thus increase your differentiation over those competitors.

From this audit we can begin to interrogate our product innovation pipeline to determine where to source innovation as well as how to ladder up products to benefits to enhance the brand's equity. As with iPod, brands tend to build one dimension, which then impacts the others. Thus a strong and balanced VID profile is indicative of a highly creative and consistently expressed brand.

THE OBSTACLE TO BEAT BACK

Energy is generated at all points throughout an organization. For energy current to flow across the entire brand experience, each part of the company must not only innovate, it must collaborate. The enterprise must connect consumer insights with new communications, products, services, and other forms of innovation. Ideas must come from anywhere and everywhere. When people come together to think beyond the conventions of their current function, they enhance marketing capabilities of the entire organization. Collectively they can create big-platform brand ideas that reframe consumer expectations and competitors accordingly. As we've learned, limitless forms of engagement have opened up in ConsumerLand. Each of the three drivers of energy—Vision, Invention, and Dynamism—can act as a driver of creativity across their entire brand experience.

Managers often face paralysis. *What actions should I take? Which decisions take priority?* We have observed the barrier to getting big brand ideas off the ground often rests in how firms think about creativity in the first place. Top management may not set a high enough bar at the outset for innovation, customer service, advertising, media and digital, design and retail experience, and so on. Or creativity is applied brilliantly but narrowly. Great one-off ideas happen all the time, but too frequently, they fail to be expressed as a total brand experience. And often what passes for creativity ends up being simply incremental, not exponential.

In many organizations, not enough people contribute to the creative process because most of the workforce lacks access to the creative process, and people can't collaborate with each other. This is precisely the obstacle holding back managers in Stage 1.

Stage 1 Obstacle: Creativity doesn't flow effortlessly across the organization.

Time and again, we've learned that the breakthrough brand ideas that make our top VID list require an organizational philosophy that fosters open-source thinking, as well as champions who can make them happen. Creativity of this sort is still quite rare because structure, P&L statements, reporting lines, and individual key performance indicators hinder big ideas. Top management is too often detached from brand management and fails to stay close to the creative process. The demands of running the daily business can dilute the energy people have available for collaborating. Ideas sit in silos, scattered across the company and difficult for others to access and amplify.

Josep Isern and Caroline Pung are doing some interesting research on what they call "organizational energy" for McKinsey, out of the consultancy's Madrid and London offices, respectively. They wrote, "Just as a car won't move without its engine, so too a combination of energy and ideas is crucial if an organization is to undergo sustained and successful change. Many projects falter because of a dearth of good ideas. Others never make good on their aspirations because the change agents spearheading them, exhausted by the demands piled on top of their day jobs, run out of steam."[2]

We posit that building creativity in an organization is undermined by that fact that *many companies confuse risk avoidance with risk management.* We have examined many instances in which conservative management chases out experimentation as well as collaboration. Few in the organization are willing to take up the mantle of creativity if it is not defined as a managerial imperative. Creativity requires lateral thought and a fair bit of intuition. But many companies aren't built to take creative risks. Managers must meet earnings expectations, and breakthrough ideas are tested against "norms."

But the new reality is that consumers respect brands that are willing to take risks, especially those that push hard on the envelope of creativity. Like investors willing to take on more risk in a bull market because they believe the expected payoff more than compensates them, consumers are willing to accept more uncertainty in a brand in exchange for the greater rewards it might deliver in the future. They're seeking out more innovative and immersive brand experiences. They applaud risk taking because a courageous brand offers more grounding in a groundless world.

THE FIRST LAW OF ENERGY

Getting past risk avoidance is possible if you are willing to believe the statistics. The numbers supporting risk taking are convincing and can help overcome management anxiety if you let them. The statistics are embedded in the first Law of Energy, the Law of Averages: Creativity spreads out risk.

The Laws of Energy

1. The Law of Averages: Creativity spreads out risk.
2. The Law of Openness: Brands don't control, they enhance and extend.
3. The Law of Direction: A brand is not a place, it's a direction.
4. The Law of Immunity: Brands with remarkable marketing access remarkable privileges.
5. The Law of Reflex: Tactics are strategy, strategy is tactics.

When enterprises spread out creativity across their brand, they actually mitigate risk. That's because almost nothing restricts the consumers' definition of creativity. People can sense energy in large, established companies that excel in management and business models, as well as in small, niche companies that stand out for product or service innovation or R&D.

This is precisely the page that business must steal from the playbook of ConsumerLand: The opportunity for creativity today is limitless. No longer constrained by geography, media distribution restrictions, or production resources, creativity can be sourced in any location—and can travel anywhere, to be shared by anyone and imbued with meaning almost instantly. Companies now have a multitude of exciting new ways to have marketplace conversations. Channels for communicating have atomized, while hundreds of millions of consumers access, create, and share content like one global currency.

In a world where consumer creativity has exploded and democratized, the last bastion to fully embrace creativity as a competitive advantage is business itself. Creativity has an economic value that most companies do not understand: a demonstrable multiplier effect on intangible value. Given the dearth of irresistible brands, even the smallest risk taking makes creativity one of the safest investments a business can make to build brand and overall intangible value.

NOT JUST FOR NICHE PLAYERS

A common myth about outside-the-box thinking and creative risk taking is that it is the sole domain of iconoclasts and small, challenger brands. Once a company gains size, complexity, and shareholders, the argument goes, there's more downside. Large companies had better play the game not to lose.

But in our research, we've found statistical evidence demonstrating how creativity correlates with both size of company and amount of energy generated on behalf of the brand. And the surprising news is, when it comes to creativity—big is better.

We first cross-analyzed our BAV data of the leading energized brands with the Forbes Global 2000, a list of the fastest-growing and largest multinational companies in the world. *Forbes* says this list represents "the world's largest companies based on a composite ranking of sales, profits, assets and market value . . . big companies that aren't just ponderous behemoths. . . . These fast-growing, adroit and well-managed companies help set the benchmark for their respective industries."[3] We found that the *Forbes* list of top companies corresponded very closely with our BAV list of brands with substantially higher energy than their categories. The degree of crossover between top *Forbes* companies and Energized Brands (shown in Figures 6.5 and 6.6) is striking.

Then we compared the *Business Week*/Boston Consulting Group's 2007 survey of the world's twenty-five most innovative companies[4] with the leading energized brands in BAV. (See Figure 6.7.)

Look carefully at these two lists: Are these firms small? Are they primarily private companies without shareholders? Are they insurgents operating on the fringe of their categories? No, they're big, layered, complex, and well-respected enterprises that aren't afraid to put some of their (blue) chips on the table to generate energy and growth by embracing creativity in their brands.

These leading companies intuitively understand that *consumers now examine brands from every vantage point* for clues to their velocity

Figure 6.5. Forbes Global 2000: The Fastest-Growing, Largest Multinational Companies.

Company	Sales	Profits	Assets	Market Value	5-Year Average Growth		5-Year Annualized Total Return	Estimated EPS Growth	Debt/ Capital	Country
					Sales	Net Income				
Apple	20,681	2,428	19,461	72,923	30.5%	NM	50.8%	20%	0%	US
Google	10,605	3,077	18,473	137,602	118.1%	158.3%	80.9%	33%	0%	US
Starwood	5,979	1,115	9,280	14,126	6.5%	36.8%	20%	15%	37%	US
Coach	2,402	580	2,001	17,468	30.1%	53.5%	49.9%	20%	0%	US
Whole Foods	5,811	199	2,149	6,716	20.1%	23.2%	17.8%	20%	0%	US
Starbucks	8,209	612	4,528	23,205	24.4%	28.5%	21.8%	22%	0%	US
Harley Davidson	6,186	1,043	5,532	16,962	10.9%	18.7%	6.0%	13%	25%	US
Nike	15,634	1,361	9,822	26,326	10.2%	19.8%	13.5%	14%	5%	US
Hewlett-Packard	94,081	6,518	81,314	106,265	15.0%	25.9%	16.0%	12%	6%	US
Toyota	179,024	11,677	243,598	217,689	10.2%	16.5%	22.1%	n/a	34%	JA
Pepsi Cola	35,137	5,642	29,930	103,425	8.5%	16.5%	6.3%	11%	14%	US
Tesco	69,218	2,754	39,563	67,048	19.3%	17.0%	21.9%	12%	28%	UK
China Mobile	29,792	6,564	51,353	185,314	28.7%	19.0%	28.9%	14%	12%	HK

FIGURE 6.6. *FORBES* GLOBAL 2000 AND THEIR POSITION
ON THE BAV POWERGRID, 2007.

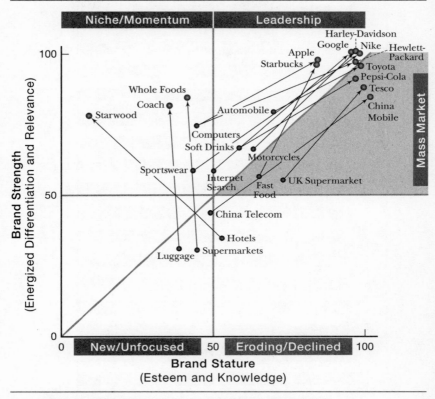

Base: BAV USA 2006, All Adults; BAV UK 2006; BAV PRC 2005.

and future potential. Just as they route around traditional marketing appeals, consumers use a myriad of feelers to sense ideas about
a brand—often from channels that have nothing to do with the
actual advertising the company sponsors. These impressions
form a composite of brand meaning that impacts the brand's overall levels of energy. In our research we found that consumers can
sense the strong presence of energy in new products, PR, CSR,
and other non-advertising-driven initiatives like GE's Ecomagina-
tion, Google's project aimed at digitizing medical records, Dell's
direct-to-consumer business model, Microsoft's Gates Foundation,
Amazon's Kindle, and Toyota's Prius.

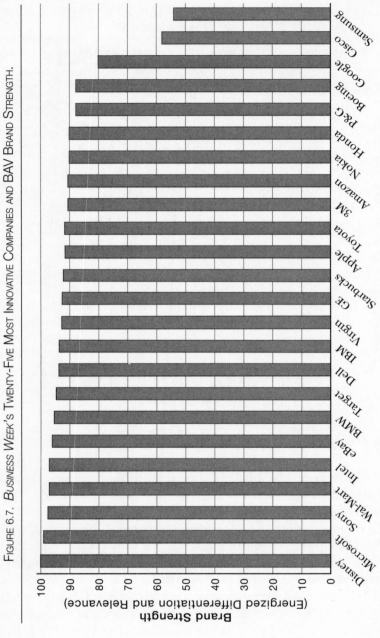

FIGURE 6.7. *Business Week*'s Twenty-Five Most Innovative Companies and BAV Brand Strength.

THE NEW RULE OF BRAND MANAGEMENT

If this stage's Law of Energy is that "Creativity spreads out risk," the corollary take-away is that brands have unrivaled opportunities to stand out, and just about anything can show progress. In ConsumerLand, brand performance is no longer black and white. It is no longer above or below the line. There is no offline versus online. There are no lines anywhere, especially between a brand and the consumer, or a company and its marketplace. This leads us to the Stage I New Rule of Brand Management, which reads:

Stage 1 New Rule of Brand Management: Everything is media and everything communicates.

Companies must embrace the concept that everything is now media and therefore a marketing channel. Today, media isn't just something advertisers pay for. Media is any point where the consumer engages with a brand, or with its company, for that matter. Consumers look everywhere and see everything. The enterprise itself is a series of touch-points, offering endless ways to inspire brand conversations and channel energy back to consumers. These new pathways often detour past traditional marketing practices, but they're still media, and they're perceived by consumers as energy.

Indeed, the very sources of energy in its Vision, Invention, and Dynamism reflect the fact that the entire company itself is effectively a media outlet for the brand. Think back to the VID examples in this chapter: Everything about a company's creativity potentially speaks for its brand:

- A business model is media (JCDecaux)
- Happy employees are media (American Apparel)
- Corporate behavior is media (IKEA)
- Product is media (Louis Vuitton handbags)
- Retail space is media (Pinkberry)
- Clothing is media (edoc laundry)
- Online experience is media (Mattel)
- R&D is media (NIKEiD)
- Architecture is media (Neiman Marcus)
- Distribution is media (Zillow)
- Thought leadership is media (Grameen Bank)

The lessons of energy—Vision, Invention, and Dynamism—also teach us that the consumer now has a holistic and unfiltered view of a brand and its company. To survive, brands must reflect the entire reassurance process that consumers go through before buying anything.

In this everything-is-media world, the burden of creativity no longer rests solely on advertising, because now everything—or even just one thing—communicates to consumers. Swiffer's impressive energy score (98) is due in large part to brilliant product innovation. Glacéau vitaminwater's energy score (82) is driven by product, packaging, and brand identity. We spoke in Singapore with Guangyo, an investment banker who picked up Boeing's energy score (93) on the news of the 787 Dreamliner: "They had been kind of quiet, but this new plane is amazing. I'm going to fly SQ [Singapore Airlines] to Sydney to check it out."

This suggests that the creative canvas inside your company is vast. Ideas can be harnessed from everywhere in the firm—in operations, product development and R&D, business systems and knowledge, customer relationships, investor relations, design, technology, retail experience, and supply chain logistics.

But a company can get misled thinking that brand creativity is simply communications, something to be outsourced to external partners. *Creativity not only spreads risk, it spreads responsibility.* There's far more creative potential in your own people and the contributions they can make to the creative process. Right from the outset, management must set creativity as the new brand mandate. Creativity requires a lot of effort and discipline. You have to will it to happen at the highest levels in the company. You have to create an environment where it can flourish—which means clear-cutting bureaucracies to enable big-brand platform ideas. Your consumers collaborate through wikis and writing online reviews, so why not your employees? Your consumers are creating Super-Bowl-worthy ads, so who's to say your managers don't have a creative eye? Big ideas won't make it through unless you open things up and push your people past their current behaviors. Your creative capital resides in your employees, your partners, and as The LEGO Group learned, your consumers as well.

Energized Brand Case Study for Exploration:
The LEGO Group

BILLUND, DENMARK: Performing an Energy audit to understand your brand's Vision, Invention, and Dynamism is critically important to any enterprise, even when the brand is well established and has a loyal following. The Danish toy company LEGO, a respected household name among parents for almost eighty years, was able to capture new momentum that helped it launch into new areas and skyrocket to enormous new profits once it understood how to evaluate its energy and tap into the perception of inventiveness that consumers long held about the firm's products, despite the huge changes in childhood play brought on by electronic toys.

Today, the LEGO image as the maker of hugely popular interlocking toys hides its humble beginnings. Its founder, Ole Kirk Christiansen, a Danish carpenter, opened his first workshop in 1932, producing wooden toys in the classic European tradition. He delighted children for more than a decade before expanding into plastics, introducing the famous LEGO interlocking blocks in 1949. These improved upon his original wooden design, because instead of loosely stacking one upon another, the plastic blocks could be locked to create sturdy structures and objects that wouldn't fall apart.

(Continued)

Through its decades of history, LEGO has consistently improved upon the original design. From 1962 to 1966, small motors and wheels were introduced to the LEGO world, allowing for mobility. In 1974, LEGO launched tiny figurines that allowed children to make more lifelike toy worlds. With the creation of characters, LEGO expanded to theme-centered products. In subsequent years, LEGO created complete mini-worlds, from medieval castles to film-inspired sets from *Batman, Harry Potter,* and an astonishing array of other popular cultural phenomena.

The strength of the LEGO brand has always been its ability to inspire flights of imagination. The company name itself suggests how Ole thought of his toys: the word *LEGO* comes from the Danish words *leg godt,* "play well." The toys were always created for kids, whose job was to add value to their use through play. "Since the days of the carpenter, each toy—from the simplest to the most elaborate—has left the workshop unfinished. To come to life, each one needs the touch and the imagination of a child."[5] LEGO thus became a helpful tool for child development, as the toys encourage creativity and invention.

The LEGO Group's energy hit the wall, however, in the 1990s, with the dawning of the virtual age. Children everywhere began turning to technology for their entertainment, and LEGO toys were quickly becoming a thing of the past. Trying to keep pace with the changing tastes in children's play, LEGO expanded into new dimensions such as apparel and amusement parks, but they quickly learned that irrelevant diversification is dangerous. Still, these experiments persisted despite lackluster results.

One major barrier to growth for the company became its unbending dislike of selling anything construed as violent. But in the new era of video and computer where most electronic games were built around fighting to the death, LEGO remained steadfastly opposed to the concept of toys simulating harmful actions. Even when it was tapped to create tie-in products for the *Star Wars* films, merely having the word "war" in the title of the products caused conflict within the company. Longtime employees feared selling the merchandise would violate the LEGO Group's core values of peace and goodness. These views made it nearly impossible for LEGO to figure out new ways to reach an audience who spent their time playing Mortal Kombat, the original explicitly graphic violent video game, and its successors.

In time, LEGO began losing traction, desperately clinging to a world that was just as rapidly moving away from the ideals the company held most dear. With an increasing multitude of options for entertainment, the LEGO traditional young male target was not interested in plain creative building. Children no longer came home from school to play imaginatively with toys; they headed straight to their gaming systems or logged on to their computers. LEGO had to take serious action or be vanquished as the old guard and remembered fondly as a relic from the "good old days."

In 1999, LEGO endeavored to adapt by finally creating a toy that appealed to the sensibilities of modern children. In what seems like a direct response to the virtual gaming craze, LEGO launched the Throwbot—a collection of eight characters who came from different planets to battle forces that threatened the safety of their respective worlds. The toy picked up on the themes of many video games of the era—fighting games in which the object was to protect one's realm, with characters that fought each other in incarnations of good and evil. The Throwbot and its successor, the RoboRider—a Transformers-esque series of vehicles sent to save the universe—lured children back to LEGO toys. It helped that some RoboRider packages revealed secret codes that were linked to online games. These toys were affordable and easy to create.

But still, 2001 saw massive financial setbacks—LEGO profits declined by $120 million. Even following the trends was not enough—LEGO needed something more to keep its momentum on the rise. Its fortunes took a turn for the better when its designers began understanding that its customers responded to more intelligent toys. In 2001, it launched BIONICLE®, targeted to five- to twelve-year-old boys. BIONICLE was a line of characters based on Polynesian mythology, using ancient historical storylines so popular in many video and computer games. The company also released multiple direct-to-video films based on the ongoing BIONICLE stories, the company's first foray onto the big screen. There were also books and comic books to further engage children in the story and to create a complete consumer experience.

In this strategy, LEGO took the opposite route from the majority of virtual games. While the gaming companies took their inspiration

(Continued)

from comic books, LEGO created its own product and storyline, and then launched its own comic books. LEGO owned these products from start to finish, and was able to pursue a successful multi-channel entertainment strategy to fulfill consumers' ongoing appetite for more stories.

LEGO's real turnaround came when it partnered with the Massachusetts Institute of Technology to create MINDSTORMS®, a product that allowed users to create and program robots that hooked up to computers. MINDSTORMS was first released in 1998, parallel to the Throwbot and RoboRiders—but this invention truly captured the LEGO emerging technological genius. The product blended motors, touch- and light-sensory mechanics, and computer technology to create a kit essentially made of programmable bricks that could fashion a programmable robot.

Not only was the invention responsive to changing consumer tastes, the product became a prime example of how users can take hold of and modify a product beyond the wildest dreams of its corporate creator. MINDSTORMS not only attracted attention—it also brought on a cult following. Within a very short time, MINDSTORMS acquired a loyal community of enthusiasts, who took it upon themselves to improve upon the toy. Though MINDSTORMS wasn't originally targeted toward older users, it caught the attention of experienced techies, and in 2001, a computer hacker created a program for the robots that proved to be better and more advanced than the original. This was an eye-opening event that caused LEGO to see the strength and wisdom of its passionate users.

The rise of MINDSTORMS caused a sensation in educational communities. In 1999, the FIRST LEGO League kicked off a competition in which entrants used MINDSTORMS kits to build robots to complete certain tasks. Teams of students converged to compete in the contest, with 9,500 participants in total. Each year, the competition sported a different theme, from arctic terrains to ocean odysseys, and in 2006, a mind-blowing 90,000 students took part in the competition. LEGO had created a phenomenon.

LEGO communities had long existed in the shadows, with a few adult hobbyists creating a group called Adult Fans of LEGO (AFOL) who fashioned a Web site to plan events and bring the group together. But MINDSTORMS caused a massive influx of people interested in LEGO products as a hobby. When decided that it was time for a new version of MINDSTORMS, designers realized that no one knew more about the products than their devoted fans, so in September 2004, LEGO chose four active members of the MINDSTORMS world to help test the latest version of the robot kit.

With constant feedback from loyal fans, the product began to morph into something the company never dreamed of. By November 2005 the panel of four became fourteen, and by March 2006, after an application process almost as selective as that of an elite college, LEGO had selected a hundred volunteers who played crucial roles in developing the new MINDSTORMS product, the LEGO Mindstorm NXT, from start to finish. The NXT comprised an "intelligent" computer brick with inputs for sensors and motors, an LCD display, and an easily navigable user interface with root menus. This ultra-sophisticated device was a smash hit for LEGO—in fact, the success of the product resulted in winning the 2006 *Popular Mechanics* "Breakthrough Award" and the International Toy Fair Committee's "Toy Innovation Award."

Although LEGO's passionate users continue to come together of their own accord, LEGO has introduced a number of measures to keep fans involved with the brand and connected to each other. Twice a year, the company opens its doors to a select group of die-hard LEGO lovers for a tour of one of its facilities and introductions to designers, developers, and model makers. LEGO has also created interactive Web sites such as LEGOfactory.com to give enthusiasts a chance to build and share virtual LEGO worlds, which can then be shipped to their homes and created in reality. LEGO.com, the brand's main Internet portal, allows visitors to create a LEGO universe, and offers online games involving LEGO characters. In 2006, the Web site was named one of the top twenty-five "Lifestyle and Children's Web sites" in the United States.

Back in 2004, LEGO tapped Jurgen Vig Knudstorp to help restore its former glory. Vig Knudstorp restructured the company by selling LEGO theme parks and other superfluous brand extensions that were not channeling energy directly back to the brand. Most important, he put an emphasis on consumer

(Continued)

input—consumers now have a voice on which products are launched, and the company takes such opinions seriously. Today, LEGO ranks as the fifth-largest toy manufacturer in the world, with revenues of $1.42 billion in 2007.

By making its brand more elastic, LEGO was able to return to the place it was originally built to live—in the imaginations of today's children. It spread out its risk by innovating across a range of initiatives. And it found ways to use its inner culture as media and open new channels to its brand enthusiasts. LEGO persevered to reinterpret its precious ideals of inspiring creative play to adapt and thrive in a new consumer age.

CHAPTER SEVEN

STAGE TWO—DISTILLATION
Identifying the Energy Core

*We live in a moment of history where change is so
speeded up that we begin to see the present only when
it is already disappearing.*

—R. D. LAING

The Stage 1 Energy audit encouraged you to look inside and out at your brand, gathering data about its overall energy—as an indication of how consumers and everyone within the enterprise perceive the brand's Vision, Invention, and Dynamism. Now it's time to begin looking forward to planning a strategy for energizing your brand, and your company as well.

The audit may have forced some questions: If Energy Index scores are low, what immediate actions can a company take? What does it mean if VID scores are unbalanced, and more important, what should be done about it? Regardless of the state of the brand's health, this stage urges a fundamental change in thinking about the brand inside the enterprise.

Branding endeavors are often done in a vacuum. They're initiated as "marcom" exercises, with little input from others in the organization or oversight from top management. This stage of distillation urges collective brand thinking to begin the process of becoming more consumer-driven and more aligned around the needs of the brand. The core of brand thinking is, *To achieve our*

FIGURE 7.1. THE ENERGY CORE RADIATES IDEAS OUT
TO THE ENTERPRISE.

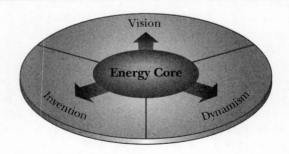

goals, we need to make the brand an organizing principle for the business. This requires finding a central brand thought that everyone can buy into, so they can all work to make it real. We're not referring simply to an advertising idea but to a galvanizing brand idea that creates unity in the organization while bringing the consumer and the brand alive for everyone.

We call this process building an *Energy Core.* The goal is to synthesize a single energy pulse that has the power to infuse and inform every aspect of the enterprise's activities, a Core that can radiate ideas to further enhance the brand's Vision, Invention, and Dynamism. The Energy Core is, in its purest form, the brand's raison d'être. It captures the essential idea behind the brand's existence. It defines the brand's role in the marketplace and within the organization. (See Figure 7.1.)

Often it can be difficult for employees to understand their own impact on the marketplace. How does operating the call center or designing the packaging affect the brand, the consumer, or the share price? The Energy Core is a coalescing expression of the brand's positioning. It helps institutionalize culture and systems around the one powerfully defined idea that underpins the brand. It achieves a common foundation for one operating philosophy and point of reference. A strong, solid Energy Core becomes the central organizing idea that people embrace and mobilize into action.

Speaking of companies he admires, Rob White, CEO of Zeus Jones (a digital strategy company), says,

> It starts on the inside. The corporate culture, working environments, and human resources practices are all based on a clear perspective, set of values, and personality (closely aligned with the founders and CEO in most cases). Then there are the products themselves. Whether retail experience, a piece of software, an electronic device, or a consumable, these types of organizations all share obsessive attention to detail in the way their brands are presented. Design is important at a strategic rather than tactical level. It's as if everyone in the company feels like a brand ambassador. By contrast, companies with weaker brands leave branding practice in the siloed domain of the marketing department. Not only will these brands never reach the same heights, the companies will also suffer from inefficiency since their actions often contradict and at best don't reinforce their communications.

Rob then explains,

> When you ask marketing professionals which brands they admire these days, names like Apple, Starbucks, and Google are often the first mentioned. What's interesting about these companies is that their brands are more an embodiment of their executive leadership than an artifact of their marketing departments. But the consistency and flair with which they present their company to their many publics are remarkable.

This reveals that an Energy Core isn't about advertising—or even marketing. In fact, it's quite the opposite. *An Energy Core is about building a company that acts on what it says.* Which is why a great Core comes from the inside out and needs the imprint of top management. Often the leaders' ambitions, whether expressed as a vision, mission statement, or a form of objective setting, are interpreted as obtuse and difficult to apply by the people in the organization. But placing management's aspirations for the company squarely within the context of the brand creates a message that everyone can relate to and understand. The brand imperative becomes the business imperative. Objectives such as driving profitable growth, enhancing productivity, or improving market share become clearer when expressed in brand language that's consumer-focused.

The Energy Core must be simple yet inspirational. Given the speed and complexity of change, it acts as the brand's "true north," the reference for every turn and change of strategy and tactics in the future. It is the lens through which every aspect of the customer experience, including products, services, and communications, is defined. A strong core allows a brand to segment on attitudes and values, reorganizing its products and services around customer insights and deeper emotional needs. In this manner a brand can unite different target demographics and user behaviors as well as different lines of business. It also reflects a shared sense of meaning that binds together management and employees, business units and their larger obligations, the company with its supply chain partners, customers and shareholders. A powerful Core aligns the organization and allows it to more aggressively shape its future. It brings together the disparate mind-sets and silos around key performance metrics and common goals. It makes the brand fully operational across all business, marketing, and communication channels. In this manner, the brand can travel up through management hierarchy and across lines of business, ensuring greater brand consistency and the selling of potentially bigger, more robust brand platform ideas.

A great Energy Core puts the consumer at the heart of the organization. The organization can begin identifying itself and its markets according to the needs it addresses rather than simply the products it makes or how and where it makes them. By defining customer needs around how the brand exists and operates in people's lives, rather than in terms of the existing products, the Core liberates the organization from the potential of obsolescence. Managers are free to continually reinvent the brand and product offerings as consumer needs and technology change.

And because today's consumer assesses a brand for its future potential, the Core underscores permanence. It helps filter ideas and maintain clarity of the brand positioning as it experiments, innovates, and evolves. It allows the business to provide what today's consumers seek: perpetual brand reinvention.

Right on Target

The retailer Target offers a useful model for how a once-ordinary company found and exploited a powerful Energy Core of innovations and quality in new merchandise at amazing prices. Think back on the Target of the 1990s and contrast that image with what we see today. Target has transformed from a mass merchandiser to a forward-thinking retail brand, part of sparking a colossal cultural trend: *masstige*—that is, mass prestige.

In our analysis, Target built up its Vision into a strong inner expression of the brand that everyone in the firm understands. Its commitment to upward mobility and style also plays out in its extensive philanthropic work on behalf of its customer base. The retailer led all corporations on a cash-giving basis in 2005, especially in donations to schools. From its Energy Core, Target also built out its reputation for Invention, creating exclusive product partnerships with noted designers such as Isaac Mizrahi, Philippe Starck, and Michael Graves, who produced moderately priced clothing lines, housewares, and everyday necessities infused with a bit of chic. Target also garnered distinction among seniors with its convenient Clear Rx, a reengineered prescription bottle that is color coded, turned upside down and flattened to make the label more easily visible. The product was named one of *Time* magazine's most amazing inventions of 2005. And finally, Target's Energy Core inspired a stirring new Dynamism that appears in its highly stylized advertising and especially in its back-to-school promotions with Facebook, where Target allowed college students to design their ideal dorm rooms with Target products.

Target gathered its energy around its Core to create impressive results in a relatively short time. (Figure 7.2 shows the significant increases and rebalancing of its VID profile against its category.)

Between 1999 and 2007, BAV found that Target increased its Vision by 210 percent, its Invention by 166 percent and its Dynamism by 170 percent. People everywhere began pronouncing the store name as if it were French, calling it "Targé" to reflect a sophisticated, fashionable, yet practical brand experience. Target's upward trajectory in brand growth and brand value between 1993 and 2007 is demonstrated in Figure 7.3.

FIGURE 7.2. A MASSIVE SURGE IN VISION DROVE TARGET'S INCREASE IN ENERGY.

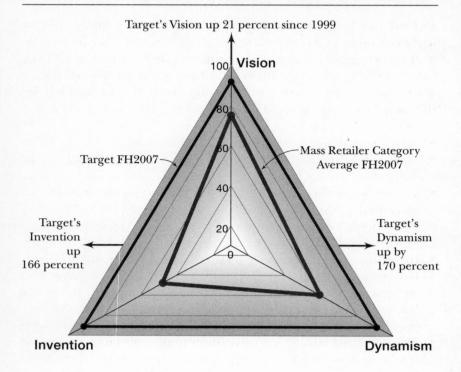

Target's Vision up 21 percent since 1999

Target FH2007

Mass Retailer Category
Average FH2007

Target's
Invention
up
166 percent

Target's
Dynamism
up by
170 percent

FIGURE 7.3. TARGET'S BRAND GROWTH OVER TIME.

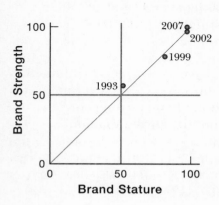

Target's energy and brand performance
- Energy— +44 percent
- Preference— +69 percent
- Innovativeness— +36 percent
- Trendiness— +32 percent
- Stylishness— +22 percent
- Value compared to
  competition— +20 percent

Target's revenue rose from $11.7 billion
to $63.7 billion from 1993–2006

Target's stock price rose from $16 to
$62 over same time period

A FIRST PASS AT YOUR ENERGY CORE

Defining an Energy Core is an iterative process, a matter of trial and error. The task must be consumer-driven and enterprise-wide, and the result must articulate management's aspirations. The Core can arise from the internal culture, proprietary innovation, communications, or many other places. Here are a few examples of Energy Cores fueling successful brands:

- Advertising as mission: "Just Do It"—Nike
- A proprietor's vision: "Be the third place" to spend time—Starbucks
- Technology-led innovation promise: "Organize the world's information and make it universally accessible"—Google
- From the DNA of the product: "The Ultimate Driving Machine"—BMW
- Inverting a category belief: "Household cleaning should be like personal skin care"—Method
- An image of the future: "Imagine a world in which every single human being can freely share in the sum of all knowledge"—Wikipedia
- Espousing social values: "Environmentally conscious makers of quality outdoor clothing"—Patagonia
- Remaking a category for consumers: "Be a challenger brand"—Virgin
- Creating a sustainable corporate social business model: "All you have to do is upgrade your choice"—Product Red
- Brand aspiration that binds a community: "Freedom"—Harley-Davidson

An Energy Core might evolve from an existing brand position or the company's mission or vision statement. Or it might be a completely new thought. If you don't have a strong core already, look over your Brand Strength and VID attributes in our BAV for clues. Is there a single energized attribute for which your brand is already recognized among consumers? If so, you might fashion a first draft Energy Core loosely around this to see if its essence can be extrapolated into the two weaker VID dimensions.

For example, OLPC has an Energy Core built on a Vision of "providing children access to inexpensive laptop computers," even though its actual product reality hasn't reached that Vision; 3M wraps its core around its Invention; while Apple's marketing Dynamism ("Think Different") served as an internal and external mission that preceded actual innovations like iPod, iTunes, and iPhone.

Some brands discover their Energy Core in the sweet spot between a marketplace insight and their brand's inner truth. Unilever's Axe deodorant research uncovered that, in the dating world, young males discussed the perils of other guys who interfere, or in their words, "kill their game." Axe was positioned on the insight: "If you keep your cool, you get the girl." The creative articulation became "Game Killers," how to navigate those potential enemies that inhibit effective dating. Gamekillers.com led to a viral interactive, animated short, as well as to a *Game Killer* reality show launched on MTV, which became the fourth-most-watched program on cable in early 2007. Axe is now the number one deodorant among young males.

The Energy Core can be based on the brand's desire to buck a trend, break a convention, or create a rupture in the usual marketplace. Occasionally, a brand manages to break out from its category by changing the rules of the game. Trader Joe's started out as a chain of convenience stores, then recognized a need to differentiate. Noting a growing appetite for international cuisine, the store stocked its shelves with hard-to-find gourmet items sourced from around the world. It established direct relationships with smaller vendors and obtained unique products, which it could then private label. By avoiding national brands and skipping the middleman, TJ's let consumers enjoy high-quality, gourmet foods without breaking the bank. Miranda, a twenty-seven-year-old New York schoolteacher, says, "I love the home-made signs around the store. They give TJ's the feel of a local food co-op and remind me I'm saving money."

TJ's Energy Core translates to strong ethics in the way it deals with suppliers (not stocking genetically modified foods or charging its suppliers a stocking fee), how it values its employees (paying employees above-union wages, funding a company retirement plan, and frowning upon special treatment for executives), and the way it treats its customers (adapting its stores to local markets and striving to impart transparent, helpful in-store experiences). Even as it taps into new consumer trends such as organic and locally grown foods, TJ's does it in a way designed to maintain accessibility and support its principles, always seeking to keep prices relatively low and avoiding suppliers whose organic standards are not as stringent as they should be. Sales in 2006 were an estimated $5 billion, up from $2.6 billion in 2005, with triple the sales per square foot of the average supermarket.

The impetus for an Energy Core can come from a cultural insight into a new collective consciousness in society. Orange Telecom, Whole Foods, and SUBWAY also rode powerful seismic shifts in society to create momentum for their brands, by building around social optimism and community, quality organic foods, and readily available, healthy fast food. Finally, an Energy Core can reconnect a company with its values, as Howard Shultz is doing in returning Starbucks to its "coffeehouse roots," attacking the problem that its coffee experience is becoming commoditized.

USING THE ENERGY CORE TO SYMBOLIZE A PURPOSE-DRIVEN BUSINESS

Looking at high-energy brands, it is striking how many have defined themselves more by their point of view and values than by any specific product benefit. At their best, these brands have a truly individual voice and a sense of real individual choice having been made. Above all, they reflect two beliefs: First, basic needs are being met, so there is a need to reach beyond them. Second, that it is increasingly difficult to maintain a competitive edge solely by focusing on a national product advantage.

Many iconic brands originated with a values-driven purpose. In the case of Lever Brothers, the factory at Port Sunlight was part of a large community with child care, carefully thought-out housing, and benefits that those employed by a multinational today could only marvel at. The makers of Sunlight (and in a later iteration, Persil), firmly believed that they were engaged on a moral mission: cleanliness is next to godliness. When Unilever expanded the footprint of its washing powder in India by working with local government to bring water to new rural areas, it gave the brand a power among Indian consumers. The company's purpose enabled a better life for people.

Unilever began with a deeply held point of view. Its founders had conviction and strong and singular cultural beliefs underpinning their brand. This insight led us to examine how consumers identify with brands that hold powerful values-driven core beliefs. The idea behind the study emerged from an excerpt we found in Whole Foods CEO John Mackey's blog (www.wholefoodsmarket.com/blogs/jm). In one thesis, John discussed the importance of organizing a business around a core idea that serves a higher master than shareholder value. He wrote:

> Whole Foods has another purpose besides maximizing profits. . . . I believe that most of the greatest companies in the world also have great purposes which were discovered and/or created by their original founders and which still remain at the core of their business models. Having a deeper, more transcendent purpose is highly energizing for all of the various interdependent stakeholders, including the customers, employees, investors, suppliers and the larger communities in which the business participates. . . . While these deeper, more transcendent purposes have unique expressions at each business they also can be grouped into certain well known and timeless categories:
>
> - *The Good: a Core centered around "service to others," e.g. Southwest Airlines, JetBlue, Wegmans, Commerce Bank, Nordstrom, REI and the Container Store*
> - *The True: a Core about "the excitement of discovery and the pursuit of truth," i.e. discover what no one has ever discovered before, e.g. Genentech, Amgen, Medtronic*
> - *The Beautiful: a Core focused on "excellence and the quest for perfection," e.g. Apple, Berkshire Hathaway and Four Seasons Hotels*
> - *The Heroic: a Core seeking "to change the world," e.g. the Ford Company when Henry Ford first created it, Grameen Bank in Bangladesh*

We tested John's framework to correlate it with the presence of energy. We created a factor analysis of the top 10 percent most energized brands, totaling approximately three hundred brands. The factor analysis reduced the forty-eight independent imagery variables to a smaller number of factors, effectively discriminating

FIGURE 7.4. BAV FACTOR ANALYSIS OF JOHN MACKEY
PURPOSE BRANDS FRAMEWORK.

Good → Cares about Customers, Community Minded, Down to Earth, Eco-Friendly Friendly, Helpful, Kind, Original, Reliable, Social, Socially Responsible, Straightforward, Trustworthy

True → Authentic, Best Brand, High Performance, Innovative, Up to Date, Worth More

Beautiful → Distinctive, Glamorous, High Quality, Prestigious, Sensuous, Stylish, Unique, Upper Class

Heroic → Daring, Dynamic, Independent, Intelligent, Leader, Progress, Visionary

the four ways brands build Brand Strength. By identifying the imagery variables that load into each of the four factors, we could better understand the nuances of the factors, and moreover, ascribe factor values to any brand in our database. (For example, Whole Foods scores 12.4 points on "Good," 9.1 on "True," 8.1 on "Beautiful," and 7.8 on "Heroic.")[1]

Figure 7.4 shows the types of factors we ascribed to each category. This allowed us to quantitatively evaluate consumer perceptions of brands using John's construct.

As portrayed in Figure 7.5, we plotted select brands that John cited and additional brands that met his classification in order to visualize the interrelationships between energy in brands and the timeless factors. In large part, consumer perceptions mirrored John's observations: Southwest Airlines, JetBlue, and Commerce Bank are certainly "Good," and Four Seasons is perceived to be "Beautiful." A few of our findings differ, but this may be the result of the category-agnostic approach that consumers take when evaluating brands. For example, Nordstrom, when viewed as part of the entire brandscape rather than just department stores, may actually be more "Beautiful" than "Good."

This study demonstrates that consumers unconsciously borrow social structures to organize brands into archetypes

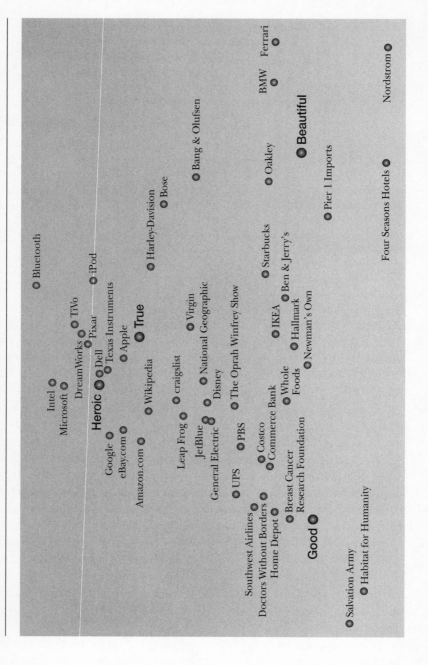

FIGURE 7.5. THE TOP 10 PERCENT MOST ENERGIZED BRANDS CLUSTER AROUND TIMELESS IN SOCIETAL ARCHETYPES.

based on human qualities they find appealing or desirable. Brand personality is therefore far more complex than tonality. A highly energized brand has a deep narrative meaning. Like a highly principled person, a brand with a vibrant Energy Core withstands competitors, product cycles, and inevitable consumer change.

Journey to the Center of the Brand

A brand's search for its Energy Core is a challenging task that cries out for unfettered collaboration. With the VID pattern in hand, you can interrogate your consumers and your organization. Extended reflection and questioning will help you deepen your assessment of your brand and company. Evaluate potential themes for an Energy Core from every point of view, including top management, employees, supply chain partners, shareholders, consumers, external influencers, and value chain partners. Assess how everyone views and interacts with the brand, what they perceive as special. Look at the brand through the lens of each function. Is there a core embedded in a distinct operational advantage? (Zara's fast-fashion.) Is the product a catalyst to company's values? (Innocent's "do some good.") Your customers may do as much to express who you are as anything you can say. (MINI's motoring clubs.)

As you work to distill a strong, unified Energy Core, you'll need constant feedback and refinement, which you can obtain by inviting a consumer panel into the process. "Brand fans"—as the case history of LEGO shows—are a highly useful means to gain insight and inspiration. Through an iterative process, you can expose them to new ideas as you get closer to the center of the brand.

Testing Your Core for Potency

An Energy Core must be vibrant enough to inspire the wide range of people and ideas within most enterprises. Once you have developed a draft of your Core, you can use the following checklist to test its suitability to detect if it can lead to both strategy *and* tactics.

Energy Core Test

Here's a short test to check out if the Core can drive ideas and tactics related to furthering your brand's VID or its corporate ethos among consumers.
Can the Energy Core . . .

❏ Change the way business is being done currently?
❏ Transform the corporate culture?
❏ Inspire partners throughout the value chain?
❏ Shape and drive the customer experience?
❏ Create advocacy and community?
❏ Encourage consumer participation?
❏ Expand the business model or distribution channel?
❏ Integrate the brand into popular culture?
❏ Guide product innovation and R&D?
❏ Inform the retail experience and service offering?
❏ Influence the "Influential"? (Shareholders, analysts, and so on.)
❏ Reach an attitudinal mind-set that transcends demographics?
❏ Be made personal to individual customer selling propositions?
❏ Inform strategic alliances and partnerships?
❏ Translate into promotions, events, and loyalty programs?

Since the Core has to be a company-adopted brand positioning, the best test is simply asking, "Can we execute tactics against this?" The Core is robust if the entire company can get behind it and come up with sources of energy in the form of ideas that keep the brand continually refreshed.

As you move through the process, your team must continually refine the Energy Core to infuse it with the most meaning. Keep stretching it to be certain that your Energy Core is as robust as it can be. The more the Core can force connections among ideas and stimulate tactics, the more energy it will generate in the marketplace.

THE OBSTACLE TO BEAT BACK

An Energy Core is first and foremost a contract between the brand and the consumer. Peter Drucker said, "The purpose of business is to create and keep a customer." But often firms focus the majority of their time and effort on their shareholders. We allow investors to see the furthest horizons of our corporate visions, business models, and innovation, while we fail to show that same side of our brand to consumers. To one group we promise returns tomorrow; to the other group we seek to sell stuff today. Other than Macworld, can you name a "customer as investor" conference?

A narrow, short-term perspective can lead to a common obstacle that negates the hard work needed to fashion an inspiring Energy Core behind the brand:

Stage 2 Obstacle: Consumer insights are not applied and shared throughout the company.

Shareholders permeate the thinking of most companies, but what's the group that generates the shareholder value in the first place? It's consumers! The ability of an Energy Core to stick is clearly predicated on the enterprise becoming more consumer-centric and opening its structure to consumers as well. How good is your company at getting close to your customer, *really close?* Do you study their behavior? Do you bring consumers into your process? And do you go at consumer learning with an eye for the entire brand experience? Are you including product development, retail, sales, and other partners into your discovery process?

From our perspective, the common failure to articulate and apply insights is related to the widespread tendency to forget that *the consumer owns the brand.* We can't ignore consumers' real needs and wants. We can't hear only what we want to hear. We need to embrace the shifts in consumer opinion, rather than develop whatever suits us best. If we fail to enter into honest dialogue with our customers, we will be slow to react and, worse, unable to anticipate their future needs.

THE SECOND LAW OF ENERGY

To surmount the usual corporate shareholder-centric view of the world, to resolve the conflict of agendas within the enterprise, and to ensure that everyone is focused on creating a strong, energized brand, companies should adhere to the Second Law of Energy, the Law of Openness: Brands don't control, they enhance and extend.

The Laws of Energy

1. The Law of Averages: Creativity spreads out risk.
2. **The Law of Openness: Brands don't control, they enhance and extend.**
3. The Law of Direction: A brand is not a place, it's a direction.
4. The Law of Immunity: Brands with remarkable marketing access remarkable privileges.
5. The Law of Reflex: Tactics are strategy, strategy is tactics.

We can no longer doubt that we can control our brands no better than we can control our stock prices. Marketers can no longer rely on the "interruption" business model. They must pursue the consumer's agenda rather than their own, by marketing brands *with* consumers rather than to them. When a company shares its brand, the consumer actually starts to come inside the organization. Through co-creation, real insights can be garnered and swift adjustments can be made.

The Law of Openness redirects the enterprise toward behaviors that support energized brands. As soon as the organization abandons attempts to control the brand, it begins to give itself over to consumer input and co-creation. A.G. Lafley, CEO of Procter & Gamble, owner of some of the bluest blue chip brands in the world, clearly expressed this when he said, "Consumers are beginning in a very real sense to own brands and participate in their creation. We need to learn to let go."[2]

Today, co-creation is accomplished through many types of brand conversations. And brands should not let consumers talk back just to them; ideally, they should facilitate consumers' talking with each other. For brands to stimulate such conversations, they must be experiential and experimental. The former provides consumers with experiences to share, while the latter jump-starts conversations by bringing in elements of surprise and shock that make consumers eager to share the brand and its content with others.

Co-creation and conversation are now paramount for brand success, because getting into the consumer vernacular requires appealing to the language of the people. Being talked about is absolutely critical for a brand because, in ConsumerLand, people trust other people more than they trust the brands.

One of the tactics brands increasingly employ to demonstrate their willingness to give up control is inviting consumers to personalize and customize their experiences. Think back to ConsumerLand, where brands give away portable content or widgets that consumers can drag to their own Web pages or mash up into their own YouTube videos, or take over their home page on MySpace.

One great example of co-creation comes from Mattel, which built a special secure Web site for its young Barbie fans, six to eleven years old. Mattel's research showed that 50 percent of these girls were spending large amounts of time online. The site, BarbieGirls.com, became the first global online community designed exclusively for girls, where they could choose from countless features and accessories to customize their own virtual Barbie character, design their own "room," shop at the mall, play games, hang out, and chat safely with other girls. The online community had 200,000 registered users in the first week, a million within six weeks, and six million within a hundred days.

Some brands boldly entice consumers to enter into dialogue. Converse, for example, put out a call to its audience to create a "political, positive, original, and inspiring" twenty-four-second video to "celebrate the spirit of Converse and the Chuck Taylor All Star shoe." Consumers were given total creative license to film what they wanted; the movies did not have to feature Converse products, but only be inspired by Converse. The company marketed the initiative through street art and graffiti-style posters in cities—reinforcing and preserving the authenticity, history, and street credentials of the brand. The program, along with alliances with designers like John Varvatos, helped Converse resurrect itself after a near collapse in late 1990s.

Pontiac, too, opted for a direct approach to inviting conversation. First, it built its own social networking site, Pontiac Underground, a forum aimed at Pontiac junkies who can post their pictures and videos and discuss anything related to their cars. The site uses Yahoo's social media tool as the foundation and has the slogan "Where passion for Pontiac is driven by you." Tapping into MySpace, it next invited MySpacers to make money from Pontiac by promoting their products to friends. Promotees are sent a free "Friends with benefits" credit card that allows them to receive payments up to $1,000 from Pontiac whenever a "friend" buys one of the cars. Named "Friendonomics," the program added a big incentive to the concept of tapping into social networking. Finally, Pontiac has staked out a presence in the colossal alternative reality world of Second Life, opening "Motorati Island." To draw players to the virtual island, Pontiac offered the prospect of free virtual land for car enthusiasts.

Yet another example of a music artist asserting an experiential and experimental nature was Duncan Sheik's album *White Limousine*. Rather than releasing a standard plain vanilla CD, the album came out in a two-disc set, with Disc 1 titled "Mine" and Disc 2 "Yours." The former was Sheik's new CD, while the latter included software allowing listeners to remix tracks any way they liked. This cool idea effectively erased the distance between the artist and his listeners by inviting them into his artistic development process.

Whatever form they take, co-creation and involvement must be part and parcel of every energized brand's relationship with its audience. This is new territory for most brands, and giving over control is never easy. But if you reflect on it, there is truly no greater expression of affection and loyalty than when your customers care enough to want to help create or advocate on behalf of your brand. We've cited an aphorism that bears repeating now: *Personalization gains greater engagement and acceptance for your message.* After all, if someone takes the time to create a personal radio station, viewing experience, or mashup—what better compliment can a brand ask for?

CONTROL FREAKS LOSE ENERGY

While a few brands are starting to get it right, most still don't trust the idea of losing control by welcoming customer input with open arms. Here are three recent failures from some major companies that should have known better, but instead lost tremendous opportunities to exploit their brand's energy among eager consumers:

• *Mentos and Diet Coke:* A remarkable video showed that dropping a Mentos candy into a Diet Coke bottle results in an explosively fun twenty-foot geyser. Almost immediately, people began posting videos of their own experiments. Mentos responded with a Web site encouraging the craze. But Coca-Cola issued a statement saying, "We would hope people want to drink [Diet Coke] more than try experiments with it. . . . The craziness with Mentos doesn't fit with the brand personality." Beset by ridicule, Coke soon changed its tune, launching its own pro-geyser Web site, but by then, the fizz was flat. One blogger on The Viral Garden titled his posting, "Coke boldly goes where every other clueless control-hungry company has gone before."

• *Polaroid:* Upon hearing the Outkast lyrics "shake it like a Polaroid picture" from the group's chart-busting song "Hey Ya!" Polaroid quickly issued a finger-wagging response cautioning people that taking the song literally (shaking the film) does not help its development and could ruin pictures. The silliness of Polaroid's statement was mocked in hundreds of magazine articles, newspapers, and blogs. Aside from the negative press, Polaroid completely wasted a golden opportunity. Influx Insights marveled at Polaroid's ability to just "sit back and let the phenomenon blow by, as the brand's dying breath mutters, 'Don't shake the pictures.'"

• *Cristal:* The *Economist* asked Frédéric Rouzaud, managing director of Louis Roederer Champagne, whether the hip-hop world's love of its flagship, Cristal, "could hurt the brand." "What can we do?" Rouzaud responded. "We can't forbid people from buying it. I'm sure Dom Pérignon or Krug would be delighted to have their business." Hip-hop artists like Sean "Puffy" Combs, Lauren Hill, Snoop Dog, and Jay-Z had written Cristal into a slew of hit songs, including free product placement in videos. Hip-hop helped make Cristal the eighth-most-mentioned brand on the Billboard charts in 2005. But when Rouzaud called the rappers' attention "unwelcome," the hip-hop community boycotted the brand.

The New Rule of Brand Management

For companies to adhere to the Law of Openness, they must realize their brands are public servants as much as agents of commerce. Rather than working to force consumers to keep the brand top of mind, they must instead work to keep consumers on top of their minds. This thinking is embodied in the Second New Rule of Brand Management, which reads as follows:

Stage 2 New Rule of Brand Management: Treat customers like investors.

Today, brands must think of themselves as being in the business of attracting consumers in the same way their enterprises attract investors. As noted earlier in the book, consumers today make decisions using the same rational behavior as investors. The qualities they seek in a brand are increasingly similar to what investors look for in a company. They have become shareholders with equal clout and influence. They are savvy and inquisitive, actively assessing a brand's current and future returns. They look for momentum and tomorrow's expectations. Those who don't find what they want will readily abandon the brand, just like investors divesting from a poorly performing stock.

By showing your organization how consumers think like investors, you can get managers to look at brand management through a familiar lens—creating shareholder value. Since basic principles of investor management now apply to brand management, customer relations have become remarkably similar to investor relations. That makes it possible to unify various ideologies about how brands and companies should be managed. Once others in the company understand the "two investors" idea, you can begin alleviating the usual spate of concerns that form barriers to building a total consumer-facing organization.

One of the world's most admired brands has put the consumer squarely in its boardroom. And its leaders go from industry to industry remaking lethargic categories in the image of the consumer. This is the story of the true consumer champion, Virgin Atlantic.

Energized Brand Case Study for Distillation:
Virgin Atlantic—Brilliant Basics, Magic Touches

LONDON, ENGLAND: A brilliant Energy Core is a beacon to guide your brand's evolution while instilling an inclusive sense of understanding and application across the enterprise. This is perhaps best explained through the cheeky, iconic British airline—and ultimate challenger brand—Virgin Atlantic.

The entire family of Virgin brands is known for relentless determination to redefine the categories where they compete, while challenging consumer expectations in an entertaining, engaging, and often humorous way. Its businesses, target audiences, and communications are quite diverse, but what binds them together is distinctly Virgin: Virgin enters every new business with the same mission:

- Identify markets where consumers are getting a bad deal.
- Provide an alternative, tangible Virgin solution.
- Inspire consumers by having the conviction to fight in their corner.

Virgin Atlantic is at the heart of this belief and the driving force behind this perception. In some respects it is the archetypal Virgin brand, embodying all that the other members of the family have to live up to.

At a time when airlines had ceased to be distinguishable brands—when most airline business models were focused on subtraction, Virgin believed that passion and evangelism had to be earned through *innovation.* This word gives the airline industry hives. And in 1984, the fledging airline took flight—literally—with one of its founding principles being founded on one mind-bogglingly simple but utterly genius maxim: "Brilliant Basics, Magic Touches."

Virgin Atlantic's Energy Core was predicated on re-injecting a sense of adventure and excitement into air travel and recapturing the imagination of the flying public. Most airlines seemed to care very little if every customer was engaged with the "brand." Their most lucrative passengers were in the front of the plane, and the masses were stuffed in the back and offered consistently sub-par service. International long-haul travelers of all kinds, whom Virgin was courting, had increasingly less preference or expectations

(Continued)

of service, comfort, or any expectation for an experience. Today, air travel is taken as standard, and not viewed as something miraculous or even something particularly special.

This is where "Brilliant Basics, Magic Touches," becomes the rallying cry for the company's contract with the consumer. Virgin Atlantic's Upper Class is the perfect demonstration of this principle: Door-to-door limo service, drive-thru check-in, onboard massages and manicures, a sleek bar lined with leather stools . . . a revolutionary flying experience unlike any other in the sky. Upper Class was introduced as a fantasy world of Magic Touches where the entire experience was mapped out for the consumer, starting on the ground. Research shows that passengers arrive sometimes as much as three hours early, just to hang out in Virgin's swanky "clubhouses." At Heathrow in London, for example, Virgin's lounge offers haircuts in a Bumble & Bumble salon, spa treatments from Cowshed, a serene rooftop garden, a business center with Wi-Fi access, a library, gourmet cuisine served from breakfast through dinner, a quick-stop deli to satisfy the munchies, and a dedicated mixologist at its sleek cocktail bar. These were Magic Touches taken to the highest level of sophisticated luxury; this was what made a brand a consumer-champion, an iconoclast—giving consumers not only what they expected, but also astonishing them with the things they never imagined.

Brilliant basics, magic touches brought to life

Add to this smart, unexpected communications that reinforced the basics with simple, visual messages. With bananas and Cuban cigars made to look like airplanes and sassy, saucy punch lines like "BA don't give a shiatsu," referring to the massages available onboard in the Upper Class cabin and in the clubhouses on the ground, Virgin Atlantic made flying look . . . entertaining. At the same time, Virgin never passes on an opportunity to, as the British would say, "take the piss out of" Britain's giant flag-carrier, British Airways. When BA had trouble erecting its Millennium Wheel, Virgin pounced on its massive rival by flying a blimp over the grounded wheel, crying the message. "BA can't get it up."

The result, a brilliant brand experience that is quintessentially "Virgin"

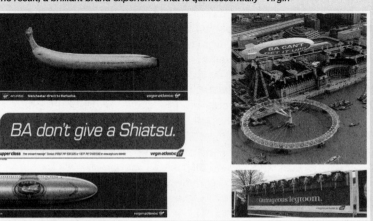

Virgin's irreverence gained immeasurable appeal because it had incredible attention to detail. To Virgin, flying was no longer about being stuffed into a seat for an eight-hour haul across the ocean. It was an experience, something to be enjoyed, savored, like a mini-vacation. Virgin brought cheek, sass, and a killer sense of humor to its consumers through every aspect of the brand experience—from the flight attendants to the crew members to every piece of communications within the consumers' line of sight. Everything related to Virgin communicated style, naughty impertinence, and a sense of undeniable hip. This flair extended to the trademark shade of instantly recognizable and iconic Virgin-red, which permeates all communications, crewmember uniforms, and even the aircraft itself. Red is a color of energy, motion, constant

(Continued)

restlessness and change—a bold color that perfectly captures the unbridled momentum of the Virgin brand.

Challenger brands take their category's standard protocol and turn it in its head. They spot a consistent weakness in a brand experience and annihilate it, giving the consumers something they never before dared to dream about. Virgin has succeeded in doing this across multiple categories. Beginning with Virgin Megastores and Virgin Atlantic Airlines, Richard Branson has taken his vision of fun, spontaneous, and always-evolving style from the skies to communication to trains to music, and soon into space. Virgin reenergizes the consumer-brand relationship, making it something exciting, something palpable, which very few established brands have the ability to do. But Virgin has managed to persevere, changing with the times, keeping up with and moving ahead of category trends—in many cases, starting the trends. For example, Virgin boasts the longest flatbed in the sky, as well as (in its Upper Class section) the only double bed for couples. A flight attendant is always on hand to help turn down the bed (which flattens at the press of a button) and settle the incredibly soft, thick duvet to a passenger's comfort.

Unlike many airlines, which offer First Class, Business Class, and Economy, Virgin has an entirely different spin on the level between Economy and Upper Class—the latter described as "First Class at Business Class prices." Virgin found a way to make even Economy, which so often seems ordinary, cramped, and more a hassle than an adventure, not only tolerable but even desirable. Though the Premium Economy passengers might not receive the same incredible perks as Upper Class, they are offered privileges such as dedicated check-in, priority baggage claim, a selection of preflight drinks, and after-dinner liqueurs—Magic Touches that make the flying experience just a little bit sweeter.

Global BAV data reveals that flag carriers—a nation's official airline—have the highest energy in that country's airline category. For example, Lufthansa and Alitalia soar above the rest of the category in Germany and Italy. But the highest-energy airline in the United Kingdom is not British Airways but Virgin Atlantic. In fact, in 2005, British Airways outspent Virgin at an 8:1 ratio in media and communications, but Virgin still leads the way in consideration and brand popularity. One could arguably say it has become a sort of icon of British pride—just as the world associates Britain

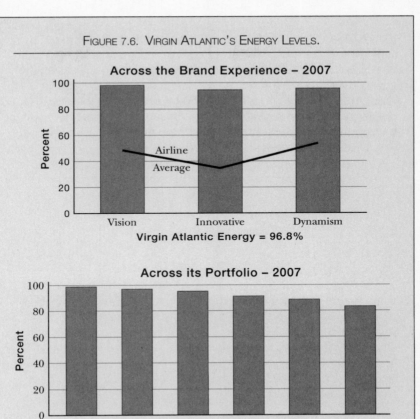

FIGURE 7.6. VIRGIN ATLANTIC'S ENERGY LEVELS.

with Aston Martin, James Bond, and the Royal Family, Virgin has taken its place proudly among the world's best-known popular culture British icons. Figure 7.6 tracks Virgin's energy in terms of its VID profile and its varied portfolio.

Because of this determined push through categories, Branson himself has become the highest-energy "brand" in the United Kingdom. His strategy of rescuing the consumer from mundane and poor-value service and products has made every single brand in the Virgin portfolio immensely strong. Ranking only slightly below Branson in brand energy are Virgin Atlantic, Virgin

(Continued)

Mobile, and Virgin Trains—in all cases, Virgin has perpetuated its signature brand psychology of performing the cost-of-entry basics to the business phenomenally well and then surpassing the consumer's expectations in mind-blowing, creative, and—what's most important—playful and surprising ways. Brilliant basics, magic touches: the keys to sweeping miserable, neglected consumers off their feet and making them fall in love with what should be, what used to be, mundane.

CHAPTER EIGHT

STAGE THREE—IGNITION
Creating an Energized Value Chain

*Somebody has to do something, and it's just
incredibly pathetic that it has to be us.*
                                        —JERRY GARCIA

The distillation phase identified the most discriminating and creative forms of energy for your brand, and helped your company coalesce an Energy Core. In this stage, *ignition,* we launch the implementation stage where you harness that energy for practical use. In ignition, the enterprise takes the fuel from its Energy Core and uses it to drive the brand forward, continuously activating and renewing the sources of Vision, Invention, and Dynamism. This then transfers energy out to consumers and back through the organization.

In chemistry, ignition occurs when the heat produced by a reaction becomes sufficient to sustain it. Similarly, in business, ignition occurs when the excitement produced by the Energy Core becomes sufficient to sustain creativity, customer attraction, and business growth.

The question is, where does that spark come from? It can only come from connecting management with employees, employees with each other, and the company with the outside world. The organization's goals for the brand must become real for everyone. All participants must understand how their own actions boost the energy levels in the brand and fuel the Core.

Companies that operate in multiple channels, in particular, face numerous hurdles in their efforts to build a strong brand. Incompatible inventory management systems, disjointed incentive practices, and different cost and margin structures all dilute the company's efforts to present a clear and unified brand to customers. Brands that overcome these hurdles often find themselves in a powerful competitive position.

Some of the best companies take a command-and-control approach to the brand. They often have a benevolent dictator who takes brand management into the boardroom and forces integration among departments around the brand. But the spark of ignition needn't be restricted to the Shultz, Branson, Dyson, and Jobs dynasties. With commitment to its brands, any C-suite can assume a proprietor mentality and preside over a brand- and consumer-driven culture.

Rob White also told us, "CEOs should care about the signals they send through all the various ways they touch people, inside and outside the company. Not just with words and pictures, but with their actions. Take inventory of these signals. See where they are strong and mutually reinforcing. See where they clash and contradict. The most common transgressions are when the company's actions don't match its words."

How does this C-suite effort begin? One consideration is to create a very closely held team that controls and manages the ignition process. Its members should represent stakeholders from each business unit or division as well as key external partners in the supply chain. The key is to find people who can make implementation happen in the organization, offering a model of egoless teamwork and credibility across the company. Grant them access to encourage collaboration and shape innovation. Link them with vital resources and enable them to synthesize new connections between consumer insights, disparate ideas, and hidden innovation. Hold them accountable for inspiring and connecting actions that elevate levels of energy in the organization and in the brand.

This is not a new cost center. The talented team brings each of the operating units together to build business excitement and implementation around the needs of the brand. In ignition, brand building is not a separate exercise from marketing. The brand is instead incorporated in marketing actions across the company.

To protect them from getting tangled in the thickets of reporting lines and P&L's, they must take direction from the C-suite. They must begin proselytizing the brand into the culture. To build the brand to meet business goals and stimulate growth requires a highly integrated brand platform idea that aligns each business unit to express the Energy Core by systematically identifying how each can best internalize and apply it to their function. For example, if you're working in human resources at GE, how does "Bringing Imagination to Life" impact your job? For everyone in the enterprise, the transformation team examines the question, What Vision, Invention, and Dynamism can I contribute to the brand, or connect to another idea in the company? The team organizes and curates, as each division is constantly supplying new potential sources of Energy in the form of ideas and connections.

When ideas begin flying all over the place and when everyone begins to be accountable for generating energy in the brand-consumer relationship, the firm will begin to own an *Energized Value Chain* like the one depicted in Figure 8.1. This chain relies on everyone contributing ideas and sharing insights across the organization. Through these actions, the brand's Energy Core begins to reach vertically down through the organization to create consistent brand experiences for consumers, and horizontally across divisions to instill brand advocates among each respective stakeholder.

Building an Energized Value Chain is not corporate restructuring. It is more like reawakening and repositioning the current organizational and operational practices to think uniquely from the perspective of the brand. As Figure 8.1 suggests, the model resembles a rechargeable battery, as each part of the organization becomes responsible for replenishing new forms of energy to keep the brand vital and moving in the eyes of the consumer. Every function within the business must contribute juice to the recharge in some form. Any inconsistencies in leadership and direction will compromise the experience and drain energy in the brand and the value chain partners.

When the enterprise gathers around its Energy Core, it creates the environment necessary for big ideas. An Energized Value

FIGURE 8.1. CREATING AN ENERGIZED VALUE CHAIN VERTICALLY
AND HORIZONTALLY THROUGH THE ENTERPRISE.

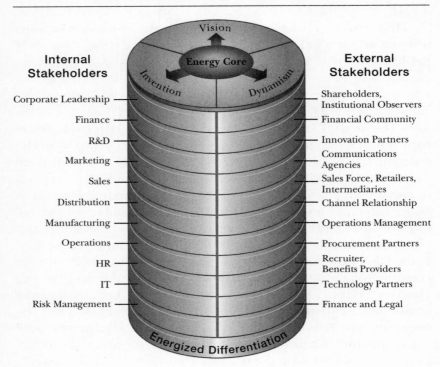

Chain creates cultural loyalty, as all elements of the enterprise combine to elevate the brand above its peers. This loyalty is actually the most salient characteristic of high-energy brands—the ones that end up redefining their categories and completely transforming their customers' expectations.

IGNITION IN PRACTICE

Triggering ignition requires the transformation team to examine the entire array of business activities, seeking out new energy from all areas in the organization. Through the ignition process, they must systematically interrogate how each functional area might impact the Energy Core to inspire new forms of Vision, Invention, or Dynamism. They ask and get answers indicating how each function will institutionalize and implement energy in support of the brand.

Here are a few brief examples to illustrate how different functions or initiatives have contributed to igniting energy for their brand:

ENERGIZED CORPORATE LEADERSHIP

After Hurricane Katrina, Wal-Mart's CEO Lee Scott asked his company how it could reduce the cost of living for its customers. The resulting innovation inspired by his leadership: low-energy compact fluorescent light bulbs (CFLs). The spiral bulbs were proven to generate great energy savings because they lasted as much as twelve thousand hours versus one thousand hours for the average incandescent bulb. But the price hurdle was too high for its customers, so Wal-Mart leveraged its vast negotiating power to persuade GE to lower its price by 21 percent, reducing CFLs' cost to about ten times the price of a regular light bulb, according to *Fast Company*.[1] Manufacturing economies of scale helped lower prices further as CFL demand was generated through Wal-Mart's advertising and publicity from Oprah Winfrey. Wal-Mart's stated goal was to sell 100 million CFLs in 2007, earning it praise as an environmental and consumer advocate.

ENERGIZED FINANCE

Starting with its name and its heritage as the Sex Pistols' record label, Virgin had always been in the business of taking risks. Then it went public, which turned out to be unproductive for a risk-hungry company that needed to fund growth (and avoid complacency), given Wall Street's short-term attitudes and focus on quarterly returns. Virgin founder Richard Branson wanted to expand the brand into increasingly diverse businesses, so he took the business private again, reinventing its capital structure, and in so doing reinforcing its sense of a company that couldn't sit still waiting for conservative fund managers to catch up.

ENERGIZED R&D

Procter & Gamble started to rethink the entire household-cleaning category and eventually the "not invented here" mentality of new innovation. Even though the bulk of its business and the bulk of the market was in liquid cleaning products, the company knew from research that consumers were dissatisfied with these products' messiness and inconvenience. Through a new "connect and develop" model, its developers brought in collaborative technology and design partners to foster lateral ideas. When they found a technology from Japan that used electrostatic energy to collect dirt and dust, they reinvented the category with a brand called Swiffer. It generated the strongest test market results in P&G's history of marketing cleaning products. Customers do most of the marketing—through fan Web sites, blogs, and WOM. P&G now has a burgeoning reputation as a "doors open" creativity company. Outside partners now account for over a third of all of P&G's innovation.

ENERGIZED BUSINESS MODEL

Geico, the iconoclast direct marketer of automotive insurance, had a simple and yet profound idea: eliminate the middleman to give customers a better deal. Then to counter low consumer interest in the category (which resulted in a lot of car insurance business going to the default brands), Geico stimulated engagement with a free online auto quote questionnaire and what it called the "fifteen minute challenge." Using a new insurance business model as its Energy Core, Geico layered its messaging to keep the brand fresh and topical: going from geckos to celebrities to cavemen (and a TV show on ABC). Landor brand consultancy named Geico one of the "Breakaway Brands" of 2007.

ENERGIZED SALES

Apple, with only its tiny share of the computer category, struggled for years to get traction with major IT retailers and resellers. The problem looked particularly acute when the company planned its expansion into consumer electronics with the iPod. Extending vertically by creating branded retail environments had proved a failure for Gateway. But Apple's drive to be a lifestyle, not just a technology brand, created the idea for highly interactive brand showcases. These showcases took the exciting environment found previously only at Macworld and integrated it with selling product. Apple went directly to consumers via its bright, futuristic concept stores, which are equal parts retail environment, educational forum, and brand experience. And by stimulating high levels of store traffic, Apple was able to prove the stores' value as a research destination for consumers who end up buying at Apple's other consumer electronics retail partners.

ENERGIZED MANUFACTURING

General Electric knew that people depended for their life on its jet engines, so it embraced a commitment that failure could be avoided with development of a more rigorous manufacturing process. In response, it adopted and refined a new management approach called Six Sigma, designed to minimize error. Six Sigma contributed greatly to the aura that surrounded GE during the Welch era, and many other companies adopted its practices across the world.

ENERGIZED OPERATIONS

To implement Unilever's "consumer nation," a Booz & Company analysis recommended that the company task all employees (from the finance director to the supply chain assistant) with "experiencing what the consumer experiences." As a result, all employees try new organic deodorants, read teen magazines, and blog with consumers. Their vox pops are tracked and monitored, and learning is shared across the organization. These efforts foster a culture of continuous learning, plus they are fun and add to the work environment. "The company has instilled a consistent, shared understanding of their consumer across the business," according to Kevin George at Unilever.[2]

ENERGIZED DISTRIBUTION

Zara pioneered "Fast Fashion," a method to compress trend-spotting, design, manufacturing, and distribution into a thirty-day cycle. Zara manages 300,000 new SKUs annually and creates 11,000 new items every season. Roving "style detectives" scour the world for the latest fashion trends, then brief designers who interpret and deliver new designs to factories across Europe and Asia. From two main hubs, new merchandise is delivered to two thousand stores worldwide twice a week. Zara allocates small batch allotments per store, limiting deliveries to create a scarcity effect. This has caused behavior change: customers visit stores more often, and they tend to buy new merchandise when it arrives rather than waiting for markdowns—which are no longer a near certainty. To keep its product as fresh as possible, only 40 percent of its goods are produced before the start of the season. Zara books time at its production facilities without even knowing what it will make. Individual store managers direct designers on how to augment merchandise based on local trends, customer feedback, and selling patterns. With a record of same-store sales growth of roughly 9 percent annually since 2000, Zara is now the third-largest clothing retailer in the world.

ENERGIZED IT AND CRM

Harrah's Entertainment started out running the same race as its competitors, but visionary IT and a continuous customer tracking system put the company in the big money. By tracking customers by name, age, preferred gaming method, spending, income, frequency of visits, and other factors—its meticulous databases gave Harrah's a significant edge in customized service. It launched "Total Rewards," a preferred-visitor card program, divided into Gold, Platinum, and Diamond tiers, providing customers with shorter lines and more individualized offerings. Harrah's puts every discovery about a customer into the database, from which slot machine a visitor prefers and which casino location is most frequented to how the customer responds to a telemarketer's offer of free rooms or dinners. Because Harrah's collects its information about customers for years, it can base marketing strategy on longer-term predictions about how much customers will spend at Harrah's over an extended period of time. This data is then used to develop marketing programs targeted at certain types of users, from casual weekend and evening gamblers to those who stay at the hotels and gamble for longer periods. The close partnership between IT systems and CRM has made Harrah's one of the most successful gaming institutions in the nation, going from $4 billion in revenue in 2002 to more than double—$9.6 billion—in 2006.

ENERGIZED HR

From its start, Google has had a clear idea of the kind of people it needs to fulfill its broader corporate mission. It looks for people who approach problem solving in unconventional and unexpected ways, as well as having a detailed grasp of technology. To satisfy its hunger for the right people, the company created a new approach to recruiting, including puzzles that people had to solve simply to get an application form. By making the process public, Google created WOM that added to the company's image as a trend-setting company and a cool place to work.

THE OBSTACLE TO BEAT BACK

Only continuous business innovation will create sustainable competitive advantage. But when management is focused primarily on short-term performance, an Energized Value Chain is never optimized. The distractions that cause managers to fail to take a long-term view form the third obstacle to true brand-centered enterprise integration, which we synthesize as follows:

Stage 3 Obstacle: Management's focus is primarily on today's profitability.

Despite long-range business plans and innovation strategies, firms tend to manage brands in the here and now. The erosion in aggregate brand health is in part the by-product of a world where, all too often, short beats long. Given the pressure to drive quarterly earnings and the relative absence of forward-looking brand metrics, marketing's perceived worth inevitably ends up being judged largely on current sales. This turns marketing into a leaf blower—primarily pushing out current inventory to maximize current quarterly earnings for shareholders.

WHEN SELLING MORE IS EARNING LESS

Brands are the last levee holding back commoditization, but brand managers are often deluged with a very demanding here and now. Don't get us wrong—we love robust quarterly earnings as much as anyone. But brand building takes serious collateral damage when only the short term is emphasized. This view detracts from the real purpose of marketing. In effect, marketing is put in charge of a brand with a business objective that is essentially anti-brand. Marketing must maximize consumer value, not just sales. Too often, though, CMOs are being drawn away from the future and into the present. The steady ongoing process of branding is fast becoming a discretionary expense that can be dialed up or down through ninety-day strategic planning cycles. *Today, most of marketing is no longer marketing; most of marketing is just selling.*

Part of the challenge can be traced to a lack of marketing accountability. While real-time data offers marketers lots of tools and gadgets, little hard evidence reveals marketing's contribution to the objectives of business strategy. How do marketing activities correlate with top-line growth? "Hard numbers drive out soft, leading managers to manage brands by the data they have, not the data they need," Leonard Lodish and Carl Mela point out in their *Harvard Business Review* paper, "If Brands Are Built Over Years, Why Are They Managed Over Quarters?"[3] This is, in part, because promotions and events that drive sales can also be considered as brand building. These tend to supplant long-term brand building, which is more soft and squishy.

Focusing only on near-term brand managing turns the eye away from the world constructed by today's consumers, where brands play a key role in the emotional landscape. We can discern this shift in the distinct turn over the past few decades toward emphasizing tactical price promotions over strategic brand building. Between 1978 and 2001, trade promotion spending—or discounts—increased from 33 percent to more than 60 percent of marketing budgets, while spending for advertising was down from 40 percent of marketing budgets to 24 percent.

But with an increased reliance on price promotions to move product and bolster near-term earnings, consumers will begin to abandon brands and commoditize the categories. Why wouldn't they? If that's all marketers have to say about their brands, why wouldn't consumers follow suit?

Which brings us back to the paradox: We woo investors to see our company's vast horizons, shiniest forecasts, and glossiest annual reports, but we don't often position our brands in that same context. How do you create a sea change if you can't see above the waves?

THE THIRD LAW OF ENERGY

The way to break through a static, short-term cycle of brand management is to embrace the third Law of Energy, the Law of Direction: A brand is not a place, it's a direction.

The Laws of Energy

1. The Law of Averages: Creativity spreads out risk.
2. The Law of Openness: Brands don't control, they enhance and extend.
3. **The Law of Direction: A brand is not a place, it's a direction.**
4. The Law of Immunity: Brands with remarkable marketing access remarkable privileges.
5. The Law of Reflex: Tactics are strategy, strategy is tactics.

ConsumerLand runs on a Darwinian principle. Like animals in the wild, consumers handle a vast, diversified brandscape by staying alert to movement. Consumers now cope with life by making decisions based on pieces of the picture that are changing, rather than by what stays the same. Sameness recedes into the background. With change occurring at such an accelerated rate, and confronted with such an astonishing number of products and choices, consumers worry about falling behind the learning curve, betting on the wrong technology, or investing in a product that rapidly becomes obsolete.

To compete in today's world, brands must be verbs. Rather than being a fixed, stationary promise, the brands consumers notice and attach themselves to are the ones that are heading somewhere. If a brand isn't moving, it's invisible.

Irresistible brands move their culture by leading, changing, adapting, and evolving. We see this in the entertainment world, where the most highly acclaimed artists today take on new and diverse roles. Madonna's enduring fame is due, in part, to her effort and ability to constantly reinvent her brand. Johnny Depp has played diverse roles in *Edward Scissorhands, Pirates of the Caribbean,* and *Sweeny Todd.* Music artists from REM to U2 to Beck have taken new paths as ways to stay surprising. These artists implicitly understand that celebrities who remain overly consistent fall prey to being typecast. Even a brand like Woot (woot.com) has created a huge following on the premise of selling a new item (and only one item) each day, for one day only.

The same is true for consumers, who want, and even respect, brands that "change things up." The Law of Direction dictates that a brand must constantly prompt people to consider and reconsider. Consumers want brand relationships that are as differentiated and evolved as they are so they can navigate through constantly new and unfamiliar territory. They need brands that will help them, not pull them back, even in the most mundane of categories. Wanting innovation from their brands becomes at least a habit, if not a necessity, even if there is no rational need for it.

The Law of Direction means positioning can no longer be static. We can no longer rely on positioning a brand with the hope that it will stay in place. We used to think of positioning as a hole in the ground in which to plant a brand. Water it with repetitive messages and Gross Rating Points until it bears the fruits of brand equity. But the marketplace is in constant motion. Competitors, consumers, and culture are constantly reordering brand meaning.

It's no longer effective to stake a claim to a perpetual territory and defend it through repetition. Instead, *the best way for a brand to own a position is to be constantly dynamic within it.* The only positioning that works is to continuously redefine and refresh what the brand means to consumers. This also helps the brand respond to threats better and faster, and recognize when consumers are giving it opportunities to evolve and change. When brands allow themselves to be episodic and surprising, they are more apt to be believed. In the consumer mind, flexibility makes the brands theirs (and not the object of some brand manager's control fantasy). Position a brand and you create users; energize a brand and you create followers.

Today's leading brands often come from companies that are eschewing short-term performance metrics as the only metrics that matter. Many instead are thinking about the long-term direction in their companies and brands. They are reversing the stream of influence and focusing instead on pleasing all stakeholders— customers, employees, and partners in their value chain. Some are dispensing with quarterly earnings forecasts, staking out longer success criteria, and allowing more time for brand initiatives to take hold.

A firm that embraces the Law of Direction knows that "the brand" is the only real business, and without that, it's out of business. Its people see past the immediate challenges to fold long-term brand health into their decision making. They know consumers are a temporary blessing and will only stay with those brands that are moving, engaging, and acting different, continuously.

PUTTING A VALUE ON FUTURE VISION

The value of brands' being direction seeking and forward thinking seemed so critical that we put the concept to a test. We performed an analysis to find out if companies that looked beyond today were perceived to have more energy by consumers. We constructed the premise that "stakeholder-centered" firms—those that set out to optimize value for *all* constituents involved, including investors, customers, employees, and partners with more or less equal regard—have a broader purpose in creating value in their brands and company than what we might call traditional "shareholder-centered" firms.

We borrowed a list of stakeholder-centered firms from David Wolfe, Rajendra Sisodia, and Jagdish Sheth's book *Firms of Endearment: The Pursuit of Purpose and Profit,* which identified thirty such stakeholder companies, including Amazon, Best Buy, Caterpillar,

FIGURE 8.2. MORE ENERGY IN STAKEHOLDER-CENTERED COMPANIES.

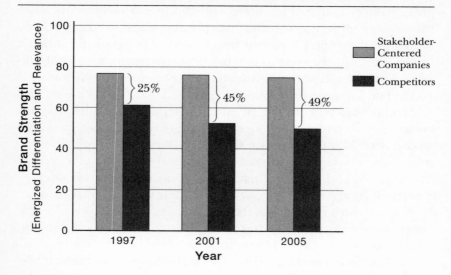

Commerce Bank, Costco, eBay, Google, Harley-Davidson, Honda, JetBlue, Johnson & Johnson, Progressive Insurance, Southwest, Starbucks, Timberland, Toyota, UPS, and Whole Foods. Using their list as an informed starting point, we compared those companies to their non-stakeholder-centered competitors within their respective categories to contrast the levels of Brand Stature (Energized Differentiation and Relevance) among consumers.

Sure enough, stakeholder-centered companies achieved significantly stronger results than their shareholder-centered competitors. Moreover, the results showed their competitors consistently lost energy over the years, while stakeholder-centered firms maintained healthy levels (Figure 8.2).

Stakeholder-centered firms also achieved 115 percent more "emotional consideration" on average than other companies in our study (defined as "is this brand the only one you prefer?"). We also uncovered the point that companies that stake out a longer-term vision and are oriented toward future value actually have greater margin power: Stakeholder-centered companies were worth 51 percent more in pricing power than the norm in the comparison time frame.

This test demonstrates the widening gap forming between stakeholder- and shareholder-centered firms from a consumer view. Stakeholder-centered companies are more energized, indicating a longer-term focus on energy and creating future value in the marketplace. What this means for marketers is that consumers are more attuned than previously thought to a company's motivations. They are acutely aware of the emphasis, or lack thereof, that companies place on them as constituents. Consumers, being investors, want a vision for where the brand is heading. They reward brands from companies that see further.

THE NEW RULE OF BRAND MANAGEMENT

Through a brand, consumers expect future utility on the part of the entire company. Managing the brand and its momentum and direction is now everyone's responsibility. Every link in the value chain needs to be devoted to the brand and consumer to align strategic decisions with product and service innovation, brand management, customer experience, and marketing. To achieve this, the brand and its Energy Core must be used as a basis for guiding the business forward, rather than simply as a brand-building communications function detached from business strategy. The New Rule of Brand Management for this stage is

Stage 3 New Rule of Brand Management: Drive the brand back through the organization.

Instead of simply sending a brand into the marketplace, a company with an Energized Value Chain constantly thinks, plans, and acts from the viewpoint of the brand. This company is able to balance the short with the long and maintain the energy supply necessary to propel the brand forward. Together these moves create a culture that consistently champions creativity and embraces change.

And once in a while, a chain is put to a great test to see if each link can hold in the face of seemingly inevitable collapse. This is when a company is at its best, or at its worst. Xerox was pushed to the brink and an unlikely leader was about to emerge.

Ann Mulchay
CEO and Chairman, Xerox

Energized Brand Case Study for Ignition:
Xerox—The Energy Inside

At the beginning of this chapter, we said that ignition occurs when the heat produced by the Energy Core becomes sufficient to sustain continuous creativity, customer attraction, and business growth. Ignition requires the entire team to come together, remove their own personal agendas, and break down silos and self-interest in favor of the larger brand goals. For most organizations, this challenge is enormous, but it can be done. The story of Xerox's reinvention of itself to become one of the leading brands of the world exemplifies both the effort required and the rewards.

For half a century, Xerox symbolized a golden icon of breakthrough ideas and innovation. As the inventor of the world's first photocopier, launched in 1959, the company had a product that was critical enough in business to become its own verb. By 1975, Xerox possessed an astonishing 70 percent share of the photocopy market. Its monopolistic lead was so far ahead of competitors that the Federal Trade Commission directed it to license its technology to other firms as a way to boost consumer choice.

Over the next two decades, Xerox became locked in fierce competition with its rivals, who challenged the firm for innovation, especially over color copiers. But then in the 1990s, as digital technology came to the forefront, Xerox found its Achilles' heel. For a company rooted in analog programming, making the switch to digital was an especially slow and painful process.

Xerox's board brought in Richard Thoman to do for Xerox what he had helped to accomplish for IBM. But attempts to recreate Xerox as a total document solutions firm and prove to consumers it was not merely a "one-trick pony" did not work as well as the firm had expected. The company's efforts to make the sales and billing divisions more efficient backfired and Xerox lost many key contracts due to relationship disputes and administration problems. Around this same troubled time came SEC investigations into Xerox's accounting practices in its Mexico offices. Competition pounced while Xerox was struggling to get back on its feet. As a result, investors lost confidence in Xerox's ability to recover from the blows. Things looked very bad indeed.

When returning CEO Paul Allaire approached Anne Mulcahy in 2000 and chose her as his successor, the firm was staggering beneath $18 billion in debt and the stock price had taken a nosedive from $65 to $27 in less than a year, only to fall even further—to a scant $6.88—before the year was out. From the very beginning, Anne Mulcahy did not see her task as merely "saving a corporation." It was about saving something precious—something that had changed her life and that of thousands of other families. While Xerox had given them jobs, it had also inspired passion and devotion in them all. It was not the sort of company that people joined just for a few years. Employees worked at Xerox for, on average, fourteen years, and they threw retirement bashes for their departing colleagues. And unlike many other corporations, which had become uncaring in the high-flying nineties, the firm had retained its people-centric culture. Xerox offered not just a job, but meaning—and family, literally. Employees met and married each other. In fact, Anne's own family had taken root at Xerox when she met her husband during her years in sales, and when she was appointed CEO, he had just recently retired after thirty-five years with the firm.

(Continued)

But dark skies put even great families to the test, invoking in employees a natural instinct to flee to safety, especially in a robust economy with plentiful job opportunities. It is during such times that leaders are most desperately needed, and indeed, that great leaders are made. Anne Mulcahy was one of these.

Because of her long experience in sales, she had a natural empathy with people; she could read them easily and see what made them tick. She also knew that Xerox was mired in crises too massive to solve without the stubborn determination of every member of its family. Changing just one thing—sales, operations, or whatever—was not enough. Xerox needed help from every angle; it needed a change from its very roots to its outer limits. As Anne says, "The critical component [of progress] is the alignment of your people around a common set of objectives."[4] For her, the only way to save Xerox was for its people to rally behind it.

In a series of meetings with a hundred senior executives, Mulcahy asked each point-blank if they would agree to stick with company for the long haul. Only three walked away, and those who remained were as passionate as Mulcahy, vowing to work together toward the new goals. Mulcahy's challenge also extended to Xerox partners, including our company, Y&R. We had been Xerox's longtime agency. Along with others who signed on, we were asked to make sacrifices, such as forgoing our fees while working with the team to drive the turnaround effort. Some left, fearing Xerox would never recover. But those who remained began to see more clearly who the Xerox community really was. This group simply loved the company and was not going down without swinging. The hard work began, but energy built among those who stayed to fight another day.

Mulcahy communicated with employees through videos and constant messages, but most often in person. "In a world of voicemail, e-mail, teleconferencing, and Web conferencing, face to face cannot be substituted for."[5] Great leaders let their people know they have support and encouragement, that they are never alone in their fight for the company's survival. Mulcahy made absolutely certain her Xerox family knew that.

In late 2000, when Xerox had close to no cash in its coffers, and the S&P downgraded the firm's debt rating to BBB, Mulcahy's advisers began pushing her to file for Chapter 11 bankruptcy. At the rate Xerox was going, all they had to rely on was a revolving credit line of $7 billion, but with no security or improvement in sight, the fifty-eight banks that held the reins were beginning to get nervous. Ever the warrior, Mulcahy stood her ground against all advice, and refused to give up hope. In her mind, Xerox could never again be Xerox once it was branded as a firm that had had to file for bankruptcy.

While Ignition can perpetuate an already strong brand and make it a mega-icon in the eyes of consumers, it also can harness incredible power to resuscitate and revive a dying brand. But Ignition must begin from within—in the passion of people. Mulcahy's assumption of leadership was a powerful spark that renewed Xerox's Ignition. Already known for innovation, she set in motion a chain of events that led to an explosion of passion and ideas. For Mulcahy, the key to driving employees toward a catalytic change was responsibility. As she said in a 2006 speech at McGraw-Hill, "My instincts told me that complex organizational matrices create complexity and lack of accountability. So we made clear choices, eliminated the matrix organization, and created clear accountability."

Mulcahy bonded especially with Ursula Burns, senior vice president of corporate strategic services, who herself had pledged her loyalty to Xerox at a young age and remained committed to the ailing giant. She and Mulcahy oversaw the difficult task of restructuring internal operations, especially the manufacturing divisions, weeding out the unprofitable ones and either selling them off or closing them altogether.[6] It was a process that took a very gentle human touch. Both Burns and Mulcahy were forced to lay off employees, many longtime friends. But they forged forward with grim determination, relying on the collective energy and the energy of each other to guide and sustain them.

One night, when all still seemed bleak and dreary, Mulcahy received a phone call from Jim Firestone, her chief strategist.[7] He had some encouraging thoughts for her, telling her he believed in her and that "this company will have a great future." Those weren't mere words—everyone at Xerox passionately believed they were true and lived by the hope that one day, Xerox would once again be whole, healthy, and thriving.

Mulcahy involved everyone from senior management to the sales force to customers in the turnaround, moving her energy throughout the company and out into the marketplace. She flew all over the country to reassure clients that despite investor concerns

(Continued)

and negative press, the firm was there for the long haul. Though some customers defected out of fear that Xerox would file for bankruptcy, leaving them high and dry, she received enough loyalty from customers to help Xerox come through the dark tunnel and emerge into the light. As Mulcahy says, "I made it personal. They had my personal commitment that we wouldn't let them down. . . . The great thing is that the customers really wanted the brand to survive and the company to be successful."[8] In the end, when long-standing clients refused to abandon ship, it became clear Xerox's people were doing something right by fighting for survival.

To build more of the heat needed for ignition, Mulcahy also insisted on investing in R&D, even during the bleakest of financial moments for Xerox. If repositioning the brand as a "document solutions" service, rather than a one-trick pony, was to be successful, she knew Xerox would have to prove that it was still an innovation leader, worthy of its storied heritage. As she says, "Even as we dramatically reduced our cost base, we maintained research and development spending. In fact, we didn't take a single dollar out of R&D in our core business—not one . . . our financial advisers thought that slashing R&D was a no-brainer . . . but we knew it would have been a hollow victory if we avoided financial bankruptcy today only to face a technology drought tomorrow."[9]

Mulcahy's leadership began to pay off. In 2007, Xerox's new offering of services brought in $3.4 billion in annuity revenue, up an impressive 8 percent from 2006.[10] According to Mulcahy, "Two-thirds of our revenues are coming from products that were introduced in the past few years." Meanwhile, the Xerox brand has been entirely reinvented, from the inside out, pushed beyond the limits of what anyone in its early years ever imagined Xerox could be. Even the company's logo was modernized, which one article in *Ad Age* referred to as "future-proofing," because "the red X sphere . . . will be important in mobile and Internet applications."[11]

Today, what's key is that Xerox is thinking way ahead into the future, past copiers and document services into new, fresh arenas. The firm has launched over a hundred products in three years, and not a single one is a plain paper copier, proving that Xerox has, in effect, come to understand the Third Law of Energy: "A brand is not a place, it's a direction." As Xerox recovers its past respect and reputation, it is constantly moving, reinventing itself, and surprising consumers with its ability to keep the marketplace on its toes.

CHAPTER NINE

STAGE FOUR—FUSION
Becoming an Energy-Driven Enterprise

*The world is changing very fast. Big will not beat
small anymore. It will be the fast beating the slow.*
—RUPERT MURDOCH

Having established a working Energized Value Chain, management must now focus on formalizing this way of working throughout the organization. Stakeholders need to transfer their energy and passion to their business units and functions. At this stage, management is asking, "How do we know this is working? Are our plans taking hold?" When management's aspirations for the brand and business are becoming part of the culture, that's the start of the final stage of transformation we call *fusion,* a defining characteristic of companies that launch out of their categories and exceed customer expectations.

The added challenge of this stage is that a constant flow of energy and ideas is needed to propel the brand forward. Management must sustain the positive energy that's been building in the organization. As everyone knows, ideas lose energy and people lose energy. A new issue can distract focus and waste the energy in the team. Whatever the factors, the key to making progress stick is when people in the organization begin to own the brand, the business challenges, and the culture as well.

Xerox's fusion began when Anne Mulcahy forced commitments from each manager. Like stripping off varnish to see the wood grain again, forcing these commitments made detractors and fence sitters fall away at various levels and functions, leaving an organization that everyone could see with clarity. Self-interest and ego gave way to believing in each other and tackling the challenges with a common love for the brand and the company they had been such an instrumental part of building.

In fusion, there's a transfer of power. The burden of leadership shifts to the enterprise. The brand and the customer become the window into how people perceive their jobs and their contributions to the overall direction of the company. At this point, people can recognize the Core Values of the company. Xerox returned to its values of innovation, customer-centricity, and family to get back on its feet. Core Values have always guided proprietor-driven cultures like Starbucks, Virgin, Innocent, and many other cherished brands. They attract employees and customers alike because they convey brand integrity. They also suggest that working for the company is worth something much more than a paycheck. People are building something more. Core Values guide the company through change and adversity and act as a reference point for unity. By making the brand part of people's working lives, fusion provides the reason to get up out of bed and come to work.

We've consistently identified stronger levels of energy and overall financial performance when a "brand as culture" mentality is present in the organization. The brand is perceived as something as sacred and valuable as anything the company owns. When the purpose of the company is the happiness and satisfaction of each stakeholder, the firm becomes an Energy-Driven Enterprise—another illustration of the advantage of stakeholder-centered companies.

An Energy-Driven Enterprise reaps many benefits. Aside from garnering customers and fame more readily than its duller fellows, it more competitively attracts and retains talent. In a recent Deloitte & Touche survey of CEOs, one-third said they believe that company vision is the primary reason employees stay with their companies. An Energy-Driven Enterprise can also garner greater investment and source materials at preferential rates. It secures the most desirable strategic alliance partners and encourages consumers to join in, reducing the expense of marketing.

Even as it asks the organization to live the brand and core values, only the C-suite can create the environment for progress to stick. Top executives can shape policy to bring brand and consumer principles into management decision making. They can encourage streamlined approval processes, while allocating reserve budgets for tactics and short-term responses. The C-suite can alter systems and structures that inhibit collaboration, can realign the organization to be idea-led, and can hold divisions accountable for embedding a marketing ethos into their operations by expanding the purview of the CMO or by introducing marketing skill sets in each part of the company.

In most instances, great ideas only emerge and take hold with support from the top. The C-suite must think of itself as a creative director, because a big brand idea can do more for a culture than almost any other type of management activity. Just ask Nike or Apple. Big ideas are simply irresistible. They grab hold of people and make them proud. People then work harder at keeping them alive and making them better. They start to believe. Consumers begin to believe that people at Nike or Apple must be cooler, more creative, and more in love with their work.

Big ideas offer a more immersive consumer experience. Think of newer high-energy brands like American Apparel, Innocent, Method, Simplehuman, Pinkberry, and MUJI. In each case, the brand experience is seamless. This is "brand as theater." Everyone in the organization is consumer facing. Each has a responsibility to create ideas that set the brand alight.

EXAMPLES OF ENERGY-DRIVEN ENTERPRISES

An Energy-Driven Enterprise feeds off human energy—the energy of its people. Ideas come and go, but individuals sustain the activities and beliefs that keep the brand energized. We examined some of the more laudable cultures around today and found many examples of this kind of energy in action:

GOOGLE

Fortune ranked Google no. 1 in its 2007 survey of "100 Best Companies to Work For." Without a doubt, Google's wild success over the past few years is intricately tied to its unique company culture.

The "Googleplex," as its campus is known, recreates the feel of a college campus where the hard-core geek rules. The company keeps its employees keenly focused on its mission by providing them with innumerable perks that help keep them optimally engaged in their work and spending as much time as possible on campus.

Some of the many offerings at Google: free meals at any of the eleven company-sponsored gourmet cafeterias, a gym, a swimming pool, a climbing wall, pool and foosball tables, videogames, roller hockey games, beach volleyball courts, massage chairs, weekly TGIF parties, a hairdressing salon, free doctors onsite, shuttle buses for commuters, and even a laundry! All Google's workspaces are open and shared, to the point that employees are joyously cramped in order to recreate the fun teamwork environment typical of university campuses. This also reinforces the flat organizational hierarchy, which rewards creativity and abilities over experience and position. And, probably most important, Google allows employees to spend up to 20 percent of their time on independent projects—a relevant benefit for the type of innovative, overachieving employee that Google seeks to hire.

In 2006, Google had sales of $10.6 billion versus $16.6 billion, with profits of $4.2 billion. It had 76 percent more Energized Differentiation than the BAV average for brands in 2007.

WHOLE FOODS

Widely known for its energized culture, Whole Foods is no. 5 on *Fortune*'s "Best Companies to Work For" survey. The motto "Whole Foods, Whole People, Whole Planet" characterizes the company as not just a grocery chain but a lifestyle choice. The company has stringent self-imposed quality standards on its products and sells only those that meet them. It does not sell any products containing trans fats or meat from cloned animals, despite FDA approval that the latter is safe to eat. It has banned the sale of live lobsters and foie gras, due to animal cruelty concerns.

Whole Foods pays its employees above-industry-average wages and imposes a salary cap for top executives at nineteen times average full-time pay. CEO John Mackey cut his salary to $1 a year in 2007, donating his stock options to the company's two charitable foundations and setting up a $100,000 a year Team Member emergency fund for employees in need. The company has a policy of donating at least 5 percent of its net profits to charitable organizations and, four times a year, generously offers 5 percent of that day's net sales to local nonprofits.

In 2006, Whole Foods sales from its 187 stores were $5.6 billion, with a same-store sales increase of 8.4 percent. The company had 55 percent more Energized Differentiation than the BAV average for brands in 2007.

NORDSTROM

Nordstrom is no. 24 on the *Fortune* list and is another legendary example of an energized culture, focused on its mission of providing outstanding customer service. Rather than following a strict set of rules, salespeople and managers are given a wide range of responsibilities that allow them to operate the store as though they were the owner of their own shop. At the center of Nordstrom's customer-service orientation is its unconditional money-back guarantee return policy, which leaves the decision on whether an item can be returned up to the salesperson. While this type of policy might invite abuse, Nordstrom's perspective is that it caters to the 98 percent of customers who are honest and who will generate positive word-of-mouth for the company. Nordstrom also frees salespeople to sell merchandise to their customers from any department in the store, emphasizing a total customer-centric shopping experience.

Managers in the company start off as sales associates, which signals to employees that ground-floor experience is valued in the company. Buyers in each region are given the freedom to acquire products that reflect local styles and tastes, and salespeople are encouraged to report customer feedback on merchandise to the buyers. All employees must strive for excellence, tracking sales on a daily basis, and top performers are compensated accordingly. Nordstrom pays its employees' commission plus profit-sharing into a retirement plan, producing the highest levels of employee compensation in the industry.

In 2006, its sales were $8.6 billion, with a same-store sales increase of 7.5 percent from 2005. Nordstrom had 40 percent more Energized Differentiation than the BAV average for brands in 2007.

THE OBSTACLE TO BEAT BACK

We've addressed three obstacles already. We've started connecting creativity across the firm, becoming more consumer-centric, and thinking longer-term about brand building and satisfying consumers as investors. Inherent in these steps is a more inclusive practice of marketing. Now we need to connect marketing more closely with the C-suite.

Top management and marketing have plenty of reasons for not winding up on the same page: Corporate managers may delegate the marketing function. They might see marketing as having soft metrics and therefore diminished strategic value. They might limit marketing's access to the larger organization. They may not embrace the wider skill sets needed of today's marketing function.

Whatever the causes, this disconnect limits the sustainability of the Energy-Driven Enterprise. When marketing is not linked into top management, brand strategies don't align with business strategies. Consumer insights fail to fertilize new forms of innovation. In the end, marketing's lack of support and inability to influence and interact with other parts of the organization results in lost opportunities for growth and eventually, lost market share. This is the Stage 4 obstacle:

Stage 4 Obstacle: Marketing is disintermediated from the C-suite.

Some organizations are R&D-led; others are led by technology or finance; still others by operational excellence. But all must give way to becoming brand-led. "Brand as organizing principle" in the company creates a new imperative for business. The brand is the central focus of all decision making. Consumer insights are a catalyst to internal collaboration and marketplace conversations. The brand and the consumer are at the heart of business strategy.

In too many companies, however, marketing has suffered a long and steady decline in scope and influence, right at the time when it has never been more important. In fact, the Chief Marketing Officer position is steadily under fire. Greg Welch from Spencer Stuart talked with us about his research showing that the average tenure of today's CMO is less than twenty-five months. Greg says, "I can't tell you how many CMOs ring me each month to say, 'Hey, I made it to month twenty-six!'" Even *CMO Magazine* itself went out of business after only nineteen months, not even lasting the average life span of its beleaguered readers.

Although marketing was once a traditional path to the C-suite, today only about 18 percent of Fortune 500 CEOs have a marketing background. Greg said, "I'm worried about the next generation of leaders who are making career choices and seeing the current environment such as it is. They see CMOs expected to perform at superhuman levels. I worry about the talent pool of the future." In reality, the marketing function keeps moving further away from the boardroom, even though it acts as the guardian of one-third of all shareholder value. The brand should be worthy of investment and focus made in similar value-creation engines, such as R&D, innovation, and other intellectual property. Remember Joanna Seddon's research? She pointed out, "If 30 percent of companies' value is generated by brands, that means that 30 percent of companies' resources should go toward managing brands and optimizing their impact on customer behavior."

Resources mean money, people, and capabilities so that marketing can be a way of thinking across the company. You don't need a bigger marketing department; you need a marketing mindset that permeates the entire organization. In the everything-is-media world, everything about the organization is now marketing. As Joel Steckel, professor of marketing at NYU Stern School of Business, has notably said, "Marketing is too important to leave to the marketers."

THE FOURTH LAW OF ENERGY

Remarkable brands often have remarkable marketing. And when brands are remarkable marketers, they do great work, which attracts greater resources both inside and outside the company. Consumers give them permission to be ever more daring, to experiment and explore new frontiers. If something fails, they absolve the brand and forgive the error, appreciating the effort. They even build communities to insulate the brand from competitors and criticism. This thinking is embedded in the Fourth Law of Energy: the Law of Immunity: Brands with remarkable marketing access remarkable privileges.

The Laws of Energy

1. The Law of Averages: Creativity spreads out risk.
2. The Law of Openness: Brands don't control, they enhance and extend.
3. The Law of Direction: A brand is not a place, it's a direction.
4. **The Law of Immunity: Brands with remarkable marketing access remarkable privileges.**
5. The Law of Reflex: Tactics are strategy, strategy is tactics.

As category disruption happens more frequently, brands must increasingly extend their reach, reinvent their business models, and head into new frontiers of growth and profitability. Brands with immersive and highly integrated marketing can command greater levels of support and more leeway to experiment and explore. Consumers, in acting like investors, will champion brands that take calculated risks while penalizing those that play it too safe.

As a result, many brands build themselves up to a broad scale without cost, courtesy of their advocates, social networks, and brand fan clubs. They become reference points in popular culture, earning them the ancillary respect of noncustomer audiences. Supply chain partners give them special treatment. And they're allowed ample latitude to innovate in more forms and to transfer brand meaning into new products and categories. No one ever questioned whether a coffee chain had the credentials to sell books and music. No one admonished iPod for the highest cost per gigabyte in its category. JetBlue's customers, according to BAV, forgave it for its logistical failings by restoring established levels of trust. Google's aura was enough to get it landing rights at a NASA-managed airstrip seven minutes from its offices.

Well-marketed brands are also given the occasional permission to fail. In wanting the brand to bring more benefits in the future, consumers will accept some degree of "brilliant failure" as a necessary by-product of the brand's search for progress.

Remember, Apple had the Newton, the Lisa, and Macintosh TV, but Apple's inventiveness constantly supplies the evolutionary learning for the company's new products, including today's Nano video and iPhone. Apple knows that consumers perceive its products as so attractive that it was able to disrupt the cell phone industry by designing its iPhone to its own specifications, dictating all terms of compliance in exchange for exclusivity from AT&T. Starbucks flopped with Café Starbucks (a full sit-down restaurant), Mazagran (a coffee and soda drink), and *Joe* (a lifestyle magazine), but the company's willingness to experiment with marketing built the foundation for its expansion into premium drinks, as well as into music, movies, and books, all brand meaning transfers that didn't faze consumers one latte. Doubleshot and Frappucinos were successful evolutions of Mazagran, and, with music sales only a year old, Starbucks managed to account for 25 percent of all sales for Ray Charles's Grammy-winning recording *Genius Loves Company*.

Harley perfume and ESPN mobile phones were both product failures that never hurt their brands. American Express Optima set the stage for American Express Blue. All these are essentially great marketers. Despite their flops, they managed to create competitive advantage from the fact that marketing in other firms is about as central to their business strategy today as Pluto is to a contemporary understanding of our solar system.

The New Rule of Brand Management

Rather than being insular, marketing needs to pervade the mindset of the entire enterprise. Our new rule here is as follows:

Stage 4 New Rule of Brand Management: Return marketing back upstream into business strategy.

Why is it that some of the best CMOs are CEOs? People like Jobs, Murdoch, Schultz, Branson, Nordstrom, and Whitman. The approach they take to their brands is evidence for a more broadly defined role for marketing. These leaders coalesce marketing into a generalist capability in the organization, rather than segmenting it into specialties and silos. Greg Welch says, "I hope the CMO function evolves to be more of a general manager job that just happens to look over marketing. This person needs to be spending the most time understanding the call center, embedded in the supply-chain issues, and learning the business units, not scouring over advertising copy."

The lesson to the C-suite is don't outsource marketing. *The brand is your baby.* Marketing is not a department or a cost center; it's a catalyst for creative collaboration. When marketing becomes a common cultural language, it can create highly integrated and immersive brand experiences. Like the brand and consumer, place marketing at the center of the organization. Align the "O"s (CEO, CMO, CFO, CIO). Ensure each division is working with marketing and thinking from a marketing perspective. And hold marketing accountable for addressing business challenges and not just communications challenges.

Marketing must also adopt a wider set of skills to exploit new ways in which consumers now connect with brands. Just as with the blurring of behaviors in ConsumerLand, everyone is in marketing, whether or not it's on their business card. Everyone must think in terms of the consumer and act like a guardian of the brand.

For marketing to have a seat in the boardroom, marketers need to develop greater business acumen. A Spencer Stuart Survey of three hundred senior-level marketing professionals found that among the top skills a CMO should possess is strategic vision; other requirements include an ability to build relationships throughout the organization and a capacity to act as strategic adviser to the CEO, supporting work as a change agent. Coincidentally, these were precisely the same skills respondents thought CMOs were most lacking.[1]

In an increasingly intangible world driven by ideas, business is now in the Age of Marketing. In a world left with few "unfair advantages" of the sort businesses cherish, marketing is still one of the most potent forms of driving intangible value in brands and businesses. And sometimes marketing shows itself in wondrous new ways, as is the case of a brand you've probably never heard of that rules the hearts of one the world's fastest-growing economies.

Energized Brand Case Study for Fusion:
Mumbai Tiffin Box Suppliers—Human Energy

Let's assume you have a well-known brand. You have working capital and maybe even state-of-the art infrastructure. But do you have human energy? Can you truly harness the people power in your organization? The true test of management's leadership is when there's desire inside your organization to take your vision and mission and live it each day. Mumbai Tiffin Box Suppliers exemplifies to the extreme the effort that can be attained and the astonishing results that are achieved when an enterprise fuses energy into every individual.

This remarkable company's business model is quite simple: Deliver home-cooked meals to over 200,000 workers among millions scattered throughout vast city office buildings every workday in Mumbai. Its product has a five-hour shelf life and requires a logistics system of 2.4 million hand movements each day. And yet the company's workforce is nearly 100 percent illiterate, equipped only with pushcarts and bicycles. Other than a train ticket, they employ zero technology. Yet they achieve nearly a 100 percent accuracy rate, making only one mistake in 16 million transactions. The results are so impressive that management and logistics experts have come from every part of the world to study these workers. Business schools have taught their practices. Management strategy expert C.K. Prahalad said of the company, "It's a model of managerial and organizational simplicity."

We spent a week in Delhi with Raghunath Medge, who oversees the Nutan Mumbai Tiffin Box Suppliers Association. He explained that the name for his delivery workers, *Dabbawalla,* means "lunch-pail man," and *Tiffin* is the old-fashioned English word for a light lunch in a box, usually in a cylindrical aluminum container. His assets are his people—and not much more. Says Mr. Medge, "Their computer is their head and their cap is a cover to protect it from the sun and rain."

Home-cooked food has a place of reverence in Indian society. Mumbai Tiffin Box Suppliers fulfills a passionate connection in this food tradition by ensuring Mumbai's workforce receives home-cooked lunches, usually prepared by stay-at-home women relatives. Even in households where both partners work, or where

(Continued)

Tiffin Box

hired help does the cooking, running the kitchen is still the woman's responsibility. Cooking fresh food from scratch each day is a virtue, while bulk cooking and freezing are signs of laziness and self-indulgence. This is the reason why ready-to-eat frozen foods have not yet carved out a respectable market

(Continued)

share in India, and why Kellogg's is still trying to knock over the freshly made *Parantha* or *Idli* that Indian households eat for breakfast.

The craving for home-cooked food (or *ghar ka khaana*) at work in India traces its roots back to the Empire, where many Indian people who worked in British companies disliked the food and wanted their lunches brought to their workplace from home. In addition, a very extensive and prevalent religious notion of purity and pollution exists about food, and it is defined differently among the region's multiple religions. A Hindu will not risk accidental consumption of beef, while a Muslim will not risk pork. A Jain (a sect of Hinduism) won't eat onions and garlic, and strict vegetarians won't eat dinner from a plate that might have served chicken during lunch. Each group has a strong preference for specific tastes. Indian food is time-consuming to cook and needs multiple ingredients, and therefore tastes best when made in small quantities at home. And much of India lacks affordable and hygienic out-of-home dining options.

The company's operation is a marvel.[2] Every workday an army of Dabbawallas pick up more than 200,000 hot lunches from homes and deliver them directly to desks all over Mumbai at 12.30 P.M. when office workers break to eat. Then they collect and return the Tiffins, amounting to 400,000 transactions in all.

Honor and respect of the different traditions around food are taken seriously by each and every Dabbawalla, who takes great pride in delivering the right Tiffin to its respective owner every time. They believe they are *Annadaatas* (providers of food), and this profession has given thousands of impoverished men self-esteem and worth. The Dabbawallas are the personification of the company's values.

Besides pledging his commitment upon joining, each Dabbawalla has to make a small financial investment in the enterprise, which gives him a tangible stake and a sense of ownership. The minimum investment is two bicycles, a wooden crate, at least one white cotton kurta-pyjama (loose shirt and pants), and one trademark Gandhi hat. From his earnings of between Rs 5,000 and Rs 6,000 (around US$140) per month, every Dabbawalla also contributes a few cents back to the association. The amount is used for community programs, loans, and booking marriage halls for their children.

The company's operational logistics perform daily delivery miracles. To compose the pickup teams, the Dabbawallas are divided into groups of fifteen to twenty-five members. Each group is financially independent but coordinates with other groups on deliveries. The process is competitive at the customers' end but united at the delivery end. Their rationale is to push internal competitiveness among the groups, though individual group members do not compete against each other.

Coding System

To overcome illiteracy, an ingenious system of codes was developed to identify the thousands of Tiffins delivered every day. Because a Tiffin can change hands as many as six times in five hours, each is marked for sorting by originating neighborhood as well as final delivery destination, right down to the office and floor.

It's hard to imagine a workforce with greater motivation. Critical to success is the sheer physical energy each member puts into the brand every day, six days a week, traveling an average

(*Continued*)

of twenty-five kilometers per day on public transport and ten kilometers on foot, all involving multiple transfer points using Mumbai's local train network, bicycles, and pushcarts. The entire system depends on teamwork and meticulous timing.

On the pickup leg of the journey, the Tiffins are collected from people's homes between 7:00 and 9:00 A.M., strung on the backs of bicycles, and taken to the nearest local train station. At various intermediary stations, they are hauled onto platforms and sorted further for subsequent distribution. We watched the process at one train station, with four groups of Dabbawallas, each with twenty members, each member serving forty customers. That totaled 3,200 Tiffins collected at this station alone by 9:00 A.M., where they were then sorted according to their destinations by 10:00 A.M., in time for the "Dabbawalla Special" train's arrival. The railways provide sorting areas on the platforms and special compartments on trains traveling south between 10:00 and 11:30 A.M. During the sorting process, each Dabbawalla concentrates on locating those Tiffins under his charge.

Collection

Sorting

Then along Mumbai's several downtown train stations, the last links in the chain, eighty Dabbawallas regroup according to the number of Tiffins to be delivered in each particular area, not according to the groups they belong to. If 150 Tiffins are to be delivered in the Grant Road Station area, four people are assigned to that station because one person can carry no more than

(Continued)

thirty-five or forty Tiffins. The lunches are delivered to the rightful awaiting bellies by 12:30 P.M. without fail. When lunch hour ends, the whole process moves into reverse and the Tiffins are returned to their suburban homes by 6:00 P.M.

As Mr. Medge puts it, "The reason we don't have any errors is because we don't have any technology." Recent BAV data

Delivering to Offices

showed that the Mumbai Tiffin Box Suppliers had a 90 percent energy rating, ranking it among many of the most innovative and dynamic Indian brands such as Titan, Kingfisher, and Tata Motors. Lacking any modern infrastructure or fancy marketing, the Mumbai Tiffin Box Suppliers share Mumbai's unique culture of resilience, hard work, family, and multi-ethnic identity. And this beloved brand mirrors India's "anything is possible" culture, where hope, optimism, and human energy lead to Six Sigma excellence. As Mr. Medge concludes, "People study business books and then practice. We practiced and are now studied in business books. The world's a funny place."

CHAPTER TEN

STAGE FIVE—RENEWAL
Active Listening and Constant Refreshing of Brand Meaning

Consistency is the last refuge of the unimaginative.
—OSCAR WILDE

In business as in nature, those who fail to adapt become extinct—while those who continue to evolve survive. Giraffes grew long necks to reach branches of acacia trees, the only source of vegetation to dot the open landscape of the African savannah. Then the acacias adapted by secreting poison into their leaves and releasing a chemical into the air warning neighboring trees to do likewise. Giraffes adapted again, learning to graze into the wind, thus getting to leaves before they became too sour. Acacias responded by growing nasty spikes, to which, in turn, the giraffe evolved its tongue to reach in between the prickly branches. Both species have adapted over and over, and now both continue to coexist and thrive.

Science commentator James Burke has suggested that adjusting to a rapidly changing environment is highly uncomfortable. In *The Pinball Effect,* he says "The rate of change will be so high that for humans to be qualified in a single discipline—defining what they are and what they do throughout their life—will be as outdated as quill and parchment. Knowledge will be changing too fast for that. We will need to re-skill ourselves constantly every decade just to keep up."

Consumers have, in fact, already taken the first steps, adjusting to this new world of constant surprise and endless motion. From hi-fi to Wi-Fi, break dancing to breaking news banners, the blurring of work and home to the blurring of professional and amateur media, consumers have adapted. Have brands?

Today, brands must be in a state of constant *renewal*. They must subject themselves to never-ending feedback. They must be ready to reshape themselves over and over again, in whatever form that takes. Brands, like business, are in permanent flux. While brands are decaying in ever more compressed cycles of time, energized brands are leading, adapting, surprising, innovating, involving, and responding—behaving differently at different times with different customers, and collaborating, not just persuading. With expanding consumer power and limitless choice, brands cannot possibly stay the same for long. All focus is on what's moving and what comes next.

In today's world, market position has never been more temporary. Success is often a momentary high, followed by a tumbling fall. We must listen carefully to the market and learn from its mistakes in a forward-looking way. We must continuously modify, personalize, share, and improve upon ourselves. Our brands must be an agent of constant surprise.

Part of reinvention requires discarding all the linear and restrictive models of consumer behavior. These might serve brand managers' fantasies of control, but consumers now define brands in their own personal, random, and unexpected ways. That somehow consumers could be corralled into brand choices through a mechanistic A-I-D-A (Awareness, Interest, Desire, Action) model is obsolete. Purchase funnels are really purchase pretzels. Any picture of an orderly, patient, and controllable consumer marketplace is presenting something that just doesn't exist anymore. Let it go.

Striving for steadiness and consistency is futile. Brands need to create their perceptual difference by moving faster and never staying the same. To uncover new insights and connect new technology and innovation with untapped needs, we need relentless curiosity and attention to nuance (and contradiction).

Even when it achieves a success, a brand can't rest on its laurels. As much as we'd like to think otherwise, brand management is a never-ending process. An energized brand is never really finished. It is always a work-in-progress. There is no finish line. Like Mayor

Koch (who famously asked, "How am I doing?"), a brand must be constantly in the market, surveying, learning (and unlearning), assessing, and evolving. This helps keep passion and ideas flowing in the company as well. By establishing a consumer-centric listening post—and by constantly feeding and sharing insights across the organization—management can create renewable energy.

We have no choice but to move to the beat of a capricious marketplace. Only then can we understand the new twist on the French saying, *plus ça change, plus ça change!* The more things change, the more things change. To have consumers fall in love with our brands—and stay in love with our brands—we need to keep things fresh, new, and just a tad off-kilter. This takes listening, anticipating, reacting . . . and sometimes pulling off a surprise. But these qualities are, after all, the foundation of a steamy enduring romance with pizzazz, exactly the kind of relationship we want consumers to have with our brands.

THE OBSTACLE TO BEAT BACK

This brings us to the final and perhaps most challenging obstacle blocking the way for rebuilding brand value. To constantly refresh our brands, we need to maintain a much greater regard for the value of change. The realities of daily business demands and short-term results tend to lull us into a dazed, automaton-like sleepwalk, and we miss the forest through the trees. The obstacle to beat is simply this:

Stage 5 Obstacle: Reliance on brand strategy slows response time.

The fact is, everything is moving faster today, creating unparalleled pressure on brands to be quicker, smarter, leaner, more responsive, and able to innovate more quickly. A critical factor slowing momentum is often the need to protect and vet the sacred strategy. Strategic accuracy often trumps the needs for the brand to respond to meet consumers' changing needs. This inability to change lies at the heart of consumer discontent we found with so many stagnant and predictable brands.

THE FIFTH LAW OF ENERGY

The Fifth Law of Energy points the way to break out of this dilemma—the Law of Reflex: Tactics are strategy, strategy is tactics.

The Laws of Energy

1. The Law of Averages: Creativity spreads out risk.
2. The Law of Openness: Brands don't control, they enhance and extend.
3. The Law of Direction: A brand is not a place, it's a direction.
4. The Law of Immunity: Brands with remarkable marketing access remarkable privileges.
5. **The Law of Reflex: Tactics are strategy, strategy is tactics.**

Conventional wisdom states that strategy is what matters and tactics are just short-term initiatives that don't build brands. Marketers devote an excessive amount of time to thinking about, developing, researching, and selling strategy. Meanwhile, they ignore a real-world truth today: strategy doesn't always come first, nor does it necessarily have to. Approaching a strategy vortex, you can easily get sucked in and lose focus on your customer, or you can strategize too far out into the future, preventing yourself from maximizing opportunities in the here and now.

Strategic development can be a huge time drain. By the time a strategy is developed, pretested, executed, and posttested, the market may have moved elsewhere. While networks debated the viability of television downloading models, 45 million programs were sold on iTunes in 2006. Now, nearly 80 million Americans (43 percent of the online population) watch television shows on the Internet.[1] Veronis Suhler Stevenson estimates that by 2010, spending on downloads for TV programs will total $625 million, up from just $12 million in 2005. When revenue from pay-for-download via cable is added in, the total is put at $938 million for 2010, up from $82 million in 2006.[2]

The Fifth Law of Energy settles the dispute in a King Solomon kind of way between strategy and tactics: neither counts more than the other. In fact, they are really one and the same. A sailboat tacks (that is, changes direction) to maximize the benefit of the wind, but it keeps its destination point fixed. Similarly, a defined brand strategy may be the end point, but it needs tactics to respond to the winds and reach its destination.

Thinking simultaneously about strategy and tactics also provides tangible evidence of progress to people in the organization. It makes change visible and real. It can be especially encouraging when it comes to keeping the organization moving the brand forward with more ideas. Tactics make strategies real.

The ability to think tactically and respond quickly to developing opportunities is also ever more critical to defending a market position. When strategy and tactics are intertwined, a brand can exploit competitive missteps, address crises proactively, and capitalize on ideas that emerge from cultural shifts. Juggling the two at once helps brands learn from experience and respond to the marketplace with less lost time.

JetBlue's infamous February 2007 ice-storm debacle caused operational and logistical failures at its JFK hub, canceling over 1,000 flights, trapping people on planes for up to nine hours, and stranding more than 2,500 passengers across the country. Overnight, the brand went from Harvard Case Study darling to late-night talk show fodder: Conan O'Brien quipped, "JetBlue airlines is experiencing more flight delays and cancellations because of another winter storm. In their defense, JetBlue says we're really more of a May through August airline." Ouch.

Then-CEO David Neeleman drafted a "Customer Bill of Rights," offering cash refunds to travelers who did not reach their gate within allotted times. At its peak in 2003, JetBlue was generating $100 million in profits. But as expansion and fuel costs cut into profitability, it would have been far easier to ride out the storm. JetBlue realized that it had to act differently. By the end of 2007, JetBlue had recovered in BAV. And according to Compete Inc., a consumer intelligence firm, even after the incident, JetBlue enjoyed 43 percent preference among travelers, the highest of any U.S. airline.[3]

Yet now there's the case of the passenger who had to fly cross-country in the bathroom. Think fast again JetBlue!

Jones Soda was born out of an initial small tactical idea. Peter van Stolk, a former Canadian ski instructor who never went to college or studied marketing, founded the company in 1996. He began selling drinks out of ice chests in snowboarding shops and tattoo parlors. A photographer friend, Victor John Penner, suggested that Stolk use his own image as bottle labels. Stolk loved the idea but thought it would be cooler to open the idea to everyone. Rather than one singular identity, Jones Soda now relies on constantly refreshing its image by continually changing the photographs on its labels using images submitted by its customers. The customized labels generated the brand's under-the-radar appeal and set the stage for its unique identity.

Personalization is now the heart of Jones Soda. Customers can submit creatively written fortunes and winners are printed under the bottle cap. Since the birth of the company, 187 million bottles have been sold. Sales moved from $2.4 million in 1997 to $54 million in 2007. The small start-up company has produced 30 percent yearly revenue growth in a flat beverage market, attracted major distribution partners such as Starbucks and Target, and in a major marketing coup in 2007, unseated Coca-Cola for the exclusive nonalcoholic beverage distribution rights at Seattle's Seahawks Qwest stadium.

In contrast to these successes, many companies do not give even the slightest credence to the value of tactics. In 1998, Blockbuster rejected a deal from Warner Brothers to bring DVDs into its business model. It then turned down the opportunity to buy Netflix for $50 million, as an online component was not a part of its brick-and-mortar video rental model. By 2005, Netflix had signed more than 3 million subscribers, while Blockbuster acquired a lesser-known competitor (Movielink) in 2007. In 2006 Blockbuster, the company that had been bought by Redstone in 1994 for $8.4 billion, had a market value of under $700 million. In the first quarter of 2007, Blockbuster announced a loss of $49.2 million compared with $4.7 million a year earlier. By not being consumer-centric and actively evolving its business model to meet the changing market, it had to sit and watch revenue decline as video-on-demand eroded its core business of movie rentals.

The New Rule of Brand Management

Strategy and tactics are more powerful when they lean on each other. Tactics propel strategy forward into action, and action helps a brand be more strategic. Both contribute value, because learning is a by-product of action, not inaction. The new consumer media and digital environment offer brands endless opportunities to be constantly surprising and refreshing. Tactics can keep a brand fresh and prolific, and its creativity becomes more disciplined in the process. When all those wonderfully creative tactical ideas start flying in the same direction, an energized brand becomes energy efficient and begins to gain speed and momentum. Thus, we arrive at the new rule for this stage:

Stage 5 New Rule of Brand Management: Act accurately, but by all means, act.

Taking action any time it's called for is why irresistible brands prove themselves to be endless fonts of creativity and reinvention. An energized brand places itself in a state of constant change–fueled by its ever-renewing Vision, Invention, and Dynamism. While inefficient brands stall and restart, an energy-efficient brand applies continuous force, renewing more energy with each action. With enough action, a brand's energy becomes greater than its mass, and it actually needs less force to keep it going. Less advertising and promotion. It rarely if ever offers a discount. Instead, consumers create the energy around the brand, advocating and propelling it forward.

You may be asking how you can act accurately if you don't know if the action is strategically sound? Science demonstrates that thinking tactically is representative of the most highly intuitive and successful managers. Weston Agor, former management professor at the University of Texas at El Paso and president of El Paso's consulting group ENFP Enterprises, conducted intuition tests on more than ten thousand executives. After his analysis, Agor concluded, "The findings are unequivocal. The higher the level of management, the higher the raw ability to intuit solutions, and the more reliance placed on intuition." Similarly, in a Harvard study, 80 percent of surveyed executives credited their success to intuition.[4]

Other researchers also confirm that experts often rely on their instincts during stressful situations. Gary Klein (chief scientist of Klein Associates, Inc.) and his research team studied men and women working in intensive care units, Black Hawk helicopters, fire stations, multimillion-dollar corporations, and M1 tanks. They found that these expert decision makers, from veteran firefighters to battle-tested software programmers, are unable to explain how they make decisions. As Klein concluded, "Their minds move so rapidly when they make a high-pressure decision, they can't articulate how they did it." But what's clear, according to Klein, is that these individuals react immediately, using instinct as a guide to good decision making—and it works for them. In the same way, experienced marketers should realize they've actually encoded the skills needed for on-the-spot brand management and can trust them.

So when faced with a decision about your brand, consider it your opportunity to act, to be unlike so many brands looking to repeat past glories through an endless recycling of the same tired formula. Today, the biggest asset a brand can possess is its capacity to change. Brands that break free from monotony and lead consumers to hope and dream, to socialize or simply amaze—these brands are proven to derive superior economic performance. They prove to be the best defense against the vicissitudes of time, of which there will always be plenty. Given that we can no longer count on anything to stay the same, a constant devotion to flexibility must dominate our culture.

The spirit of constant renewal typifies Japan's largest and most profitable chain of retail clothing. And now it's a brand making substantial inroads into Europe and America.

Energized Brand Case Study for Renewal:
UNIQLO—Seeing Farther

Today, change can strike at the heart of any brand in the world. The story of Japanese fashion retailer UNIQLO exemplifies how a company prospered from huge social change, yet maintained a state of perpetual metamorphosis in its business model to stay ahead.

Founded in 1984, UNIQLO began as a relatively staid brand in a highly static Japanese fashion world. For much of Japan, fashion has always symbolized expressiveness cloaked in order and uniformity in the culture, even among teens. During most of the postwar twentieth century, the majority of urban Tokyo kids have dressed to show their belonging to one of the cliques. The largest of these is the *Ko-gal* ("young girl"), with roughly 30–40 percent of all high school girls dressing in their school uniforms with a small degree of customization, most typically baggy socks and perhaps dyed hair. The hard core of this group are known as *Yamamba,* girls whose eye makeup gave them a sort of panda-bear look. The Ko-gal were thought to be a bit vacuous, like the "Valley Girl" stereotype. Other groups included the *Goths* (similar to those in the United States), the *Lolitas* (with the Little Bo Peep look), and the *Fruits* (the crazy-looking rainbow of color kids that made Harajuku street fashion famous).

Tokyo Street Fashion

In older circles, Japanese adults too dress in predictable fashion. There was the "OL" look, that is, Office Lady, the female equivalent of the Japanese salaryman. That look was clean and tidy, with skirt and jacket—feminine but not flashy. Those who aspired higher become *Shirokanese,* named after the wealthy Tokyo area of Shirokane. This was an older head-to-toe look of the wealthy businesswoman or housewife, with conspicuous use of expensive French and Italian designer brands.

However, an economic and cultural shift happened in the early 1990s that altered Japan in significant ways. Fathers were laid off. Some families lost their homes. Institutional corruption disrupted the social faith in honor and integrity. Slowly, Tokyo's youth began to realize there was no safety net, no real order, no use for conformity. By the late 1990s, youth culture became withdrawn, more introspective and less concerned with outward appearance. Their statement was an anti-statement.

Throughout these turbulent times in Japan, UNIQLO was going through its own revolution. The company was suffering from being thought of as *dasai*—"uncool." Throughout the hip neighborhoods of Harajuku and Shibuya, teens described the UNIQLO brand this way. UNIQLO entered a deep funk that mirrored the mood of Japanese society. Japan was in the midst of a decade-long recession, with no end in sight.

Being open to change, the company recognized an opportunity to create a new brand identity that reflected the social trend. Concentrating on urban areas, UNIQLO's cheap and cheery clothing set out to outfit the new youth movement. With the launch of a line of brightly colored fleece garments in 1999, its products quickly became the uniform against hype and ego. "Clothing says a lot, but you can say it better," became UNIQLO's mantra: "It's what's inside that matters most." Suddenly the brand was 格好いい —"cool."

UNIQLO became the ultra-hip, ultra-practical, anti-fashion fashion brand. Whereas fashion usually dictates the look, UNIQLO gave people the license to create their own style. The company made the red UNIQLO logo nearly invisible, tucked away inside each garment. One blog posting from a Japanese fashion writer said, "UNIQLO has an attitude: 'I don't need that sort of fashion' is the fashion that UNIQLO offers."

(Continued)

Today, the company is becoming an international clothing empire, with operations extending beyond Japan to South Korea, the United Kingdom, China and the United States. Touting its clothing as affordable quality, simple yet chic, UNIQLO has quickly become a fashion and pop culture phenomenon. It aims to sell fashion at a reasonable price so that people will purchase it steadily as long as a trend lasts.

As a specialty-store retailer of private-label apparel (SPA) company, UNIQLO integrates the value chain from design to production, quality control, distribution, sales, and promotion. It embeds itself deeply in its manufacturing process, down to procurement of raw materials and inventory management. So UNIQLO is able to source the latest materials more quickly and stay in line with the latest fashions, while developing higher profitability and high performance.

Shinichiro Shuda, chief marketing officer of U.S. operations, summed up the company's strategy when he told us, "Our corporate mission is to provide high-quality, classic, yet on-trend casual garments at prices that are way too low for the awesome value it brings. We don't represent a lifestyle, as we're more utilitarian and industrial. Yet we have design studios in Tokyo, New York, Paris, and Milan, and this includes an incredible team of designers. I guess we always strive to create the perfect balance between price, quality, and style. A very hard task, but we like challenges."

One tactic UNIQLO employed was finding ways to be present wherever customers frequent the most. Using diverse store formats and locations, including urban roadside shops, UNIQLO's incongruousness helped generate a large proportion of the company's income in Japan. And to further enhance its business infrastructure, especially for its growing overseas operations, the global design studios collect information on product and market needs and design and commercialize new products by coordinating the international supply chain.

UNIQLO has remained open to continuous evolution. While it achieved substantial growth in the 1990s, by the end of 2003, sales and profits had again plummeted. Saturation of the fast-retailing industry from competition like Zara, Gap, H&M, and others put downward pressure on sales and profitability. The business again needed to embrace Yanai-san's words: "We never hesitate to create something new from scratch by ruining our success stories in the past." Rather than continue down the same path, it took aggressive steps to reinvent its business model once more.

The company developed a three-pronged approach to promoting growth. The first was to review personnel, evaluation, and compensation systems. It modified employees' approach to working within the company, while converting its business format to a structure focused on expansion to drive better results. By August 2004, it made a second turnaround, increasing sales and income through its "scrap and build" strategy, aimed at extending its store network.[5]

The company now focuses on international growth and use of its large-format stores as a driver to accelerate new store openings worldwide, including its first flagship store in Soho. UNIQLO USA, Inc. will focus on brand rather than simply store expansion. Management plans to shift from a store chain to a third stage of evolution, that of a global brand.

In branding, UNIQLO has employed various forms of media, from print and television ads to innovative online marketing tactics to innovative retail environments and packaging. The company commissioned an eclectic range of artists, designers, musicians, and actors, ranging from Sonic Youth's Kim Gordon to hip-hop celebrity Juelz Santana. On the Web, it released UNIQLO Mixplay, videos featuring break dancers sporting UNIQLO gear, and UNIQLOCK, a twenty-four-hour, color-changing clock, interspersed with Japanese models performing a variety of dances.

UNIQLO has also blossomed as an interactive information center, delivering and exchanging ideas with consumers. Shuda-san explained that its Soho store was envisioned as a center of Japanese culture. The company released a compilation CD featuring "cutting-edge Japanese music," and it employs various tactics to bring Japanese culture to New York such as having forty designers "design today's Tokyo" with a hundred or so limited-edition T-shirts and setting up listening booths in the store filled with CDs of little-known Japanese music selected by Japan-based DJ Tanaka.

(Continued)

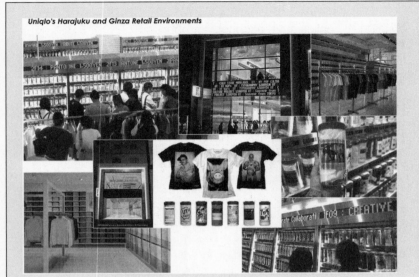

Uniqlo's Harajuku and Ginza Retail Environments

With a wide array of ambitious and constantly evolving marketing and promotion activities, the company listens carefully to customers. As part of its mission to develop a global brand, the R&D centers act as active listening posts that directly acquire information on the most up-to-date fashion trends, including fabrics, clothing functions, and customer needs and lifestyles, and then translate them into fashion. Each of these centers consists of five divisions: men's wear, women's wear, children's wear, bags and accessories, and undergarments. It works closely with its subcontractors as partners and provides them with cutting-edge technology through its "Tukami team," a group of twenty-two textile industry experts.

Most recently, responding to the relentless pressure and speed of "fast retailing," UNIQLO now plans to restructure once again. It aspires to become a third-generation SPA by combining the methodology of first-generation SPAs (high-volume sales of low-cost single items by uniting manufacturing and sales) with the business model of the second-generation SPAs (business strategy on fashions and trends).

UNIQLO's parent, Fast Retailing, has also become Asia's biggest clothing retailer, with its sights set on becoming a $1 billion selling brand with three hundred stores in the United States by 2011. Its online store accounts for approximately $8.8 million annually (in fiscal 2006), one of the largest volumes of any online shopping site in Japan. Rates of growth in the United States and the Asia-Pacific region have continued on an upward trend.

UNIQLO today is a top-10 energy brand in Japan and is building its energy abroad. It is the brand of choice for many consumers because it sells more than clothes. It continues to prosper by pushing its entire value chain to see farther. Whether it is research, design, product, manufacturing, marketing, or merchandising—everyone is empowered to watch, listen, react, and lead. The company pioneered the concept of "discount clothing turned popular with youth" against great odds. In doing so, it transformed the way consumers perceive fashion, culture, and in turn the brand.

EPILOGUE

A Brand May Be Famous, But Is It Creating Return for Shareholders?

> *Snap back to reality, oh there goes gravity*
>
> —EMINEM

We're the first to say there's much more to learn, so we hope you'll join the conversation at www.thebrandbubble.com. What we know thus far is enough to warn managers it's time to take stock of their brand. The consumer is sending worrying signals about the state of brands today. If we take action now, we can bring brand value and brand price back into alignment—and this can be done not by lowering the share price of brands but by raising the true worth of brands as experienced by the consumer.

Irresistible brands create sustainable brand differentiation. They permeate all aspects of the organization. They are full of measurable energy. They offer consistent and immersive brand experiences. And they create a platform of growth for brand value, or "brand immortality" as we learned from Booz & Company.

This is vital, as the consumer's (investor-driven) perceptions are now a determining factor in whether a brand is merely known or actually valuable. We now have a more unifying brand metric and a powerful predictor of a brand's future success. We can track its impact on future as well as immediate sales. We can organize around the brand to manage forward and be consumer-centric in all decision making.

We urge you and your organization to think about brands in a new way. In ConsumerLand, if you're not moving, you fall behind and die. Yet too often we manage brands through the rearview mirror. *We think of brand equity in terms of size, rather than velocity.* We put a tape measure around a brand, when what's required is a speedometer. While the ground beneath brands has irrevocably shifted, the methods for managing brands haven't changed for decades. This mind-set of resting on brand reputation has influenced the way we define success metrics and manage toward them. Brand management is more like "brand maintenance." It tries to control brands, creating consistency and predictability in a world that demands that businesses surprise, innovate, adapt, and respond.

Which brings us full circle back to our love of brands. While there is no shortage of advice about driving change and fostering product, service, and management innovation, we hope to have imparted the importance of *brand innovation* as both a fiduciary responsibility and also an ever-vital competitive weapon for business. Consumers are judging brands on their ability to deliver value tomorrow as well as today, so *redefining the future of brand management to both grow and protect shareholder value* is now a key imperative for business.

Today business must maximize consumer perceptions of value by continuously managing forward brand expectations with creativity, innovation, and new brand experiences. We must strip away the hype and deliver real value for our brands to be seen as worthy of consumer investment. Just as Warren Buffett exemplifies the wisdom of investing in value stocks, consumers are now recognizing the same intrinsic value in brands. Companies that organize around their consumer and bring their brand into their business will enhance future shareholder value by restoring and enhancing consumer value.

Y&R's BAV data revealed the patterns that led to identifying Energized Differentiation as the new force driving this shift. BAV also helps us see the reasons behind consumers' intolerance of complacent and uncreative brands. In a fractured, chaotic, and uncertain world, consumers are drawn to creativity because a brand with a creative attitude helps them hedge against the future. In effect, we've identified that consumers invest in highly creative brands. We have come to believe that most brands have customers, but brands with energy have followers. The idea isn't so outlandish. After all, a brand, regardless of its balance sheet value, is only ever worth something if consumers want to buy it . . . and buy it again.

NOTES

Chapter One

1. Calculation is from the 2007 IMF list based on GDP under purchasing power parity.
2. Based on a modeled BAV Index fund of the top fifty energy-gaining brands compared against the S&P 500. (Also see Figure 2.10.)
3. "Consumer Confidence Plunges," Thomson Reuters (Reuters.com), February 18, 2008.
4. Statistics from Harper's Index, *Harper's Magazine,* March 2008 and April 2008.
5. Datamonitor, "New Developments in Global Consumer Trends," April 2007. This report sources the 2006 Schneider Associates/ Stagnito Communications/IRI report, "Most Memorable New Product Launch Survey," which was released in February 2007 and conducted by comScore Networks during December 2006.
6. "The Decline of Brands," James Surowiecki, *Wired Magazine,* November 2004.
7. "What's the Difference? Not Much If You Ask Consumers," Mark Dolliver, *Adweek,* January 22, 2001.
8. "Brand Confusion," Jack Trout and Kevin J. Clancy, *Harvard Business Review,* March 2002, Vol. 80, Issue 3.
9. "Save America's Dying Brands," Kevin J. Clancy, *Marketing Management,* Sept./Oct. 2001, Vol. 10, Issue 3.
10. "If Brands Are Built Over Years, Why Are They Managed Over Quarters?" Leonard M. Lodish and Carl F. Mella, *Harvard Business Review,* July-Aug. 2007.
11. Datamonitor, April 2007.
12. "Follow Your Nose to Marketing Evolution," Martin Lindstrom, *Advertising Age,* May 23, 2005, Vol. 76, Issue 21, p. 136.
13. "Consumers Love to Hate Advertising: Clutter, Interruption and Irrelevance Spur Ad Avoidance," Peter Kim, Forrester report, November 27, 2006. Cited in a graph (which includes these statistics) in this report are the original Forrester's Consumer

Technographics October 2002 North American Retail & Media Study and Forrester's NACTAS Q2 2006 Survey.

14. "The Evolving Role of the CMO," David Court, *McKinsey Quarterly,* August 2007.

Chapter Two

1. "How Brand Attributes Drive Financial Performance," Robert Jacobson and Natalie Mizik, Marketing Science Institute, Working Paper Series, 2005.
2. Under the *efficient markets* hypothesis, stock price reflects both the current profitability of a firm and expectations of future earnings. The model is built on the hypothesis that brand affects stock return in two ways: First, the indirect effect, where changes in brand equity impact current profitability, that is to say, a stronger brand leads to more sales and, all other things being equal, higher earnings in the current period, which in turn generates changes in stock price. Second, the direct effect, where changes in brand equity influence expectations of future earnings, that is to say, a stronger brand today will probably be a stronger brand in the future and will drive more sales—this measurement of the strength of the brand had never before been as accurately reflected in current profitability measures.
3. For a complete list of brands included in each of the periods that comprise the Energy Fund analysis, see www.thebrandbubble.com.

Chapter Three

1. *Advertising Age,* "CMO Strategy," Spring 2007.
2. "In Baby Boomlet, Preschool Derby Is the Fiercest Yet," Susan Saulny, *New York Times,* March 3, 2006.
3. *The Average American: The Extraordinary Search for the Nation's Most Ordinary Citizen,* Kevin O'Keefe (New York: Public Affairs, 2005).
4. BIGresearch, "Simultaneous Media," Executive Briefing, 2007. Available online: www.bigresearch.com/news/big081006.htm.
5. *Everything Bad Is Good for You: How Today's Popular Culture Is Actually Making Us Smarter,* Steven Johnson (New York: Penguin Group, 2006).
6. "Trend-Watcher Sees Moral Transformation of Capitalism," Jane Lampman, *Christian Science Monitor,* October 3, 2005. Available online: www.csmonitor.com/2005/1003/p13s01-wmgn.html. Access date: May 31, 2008.
7. This current-term behavior is captured in BAV's Brand Stature metric, which comprises Esteem (favorability) and Knowledge (deep, lasting awareness and brand associations).

Chapter Five

1. "Wave.3," Universal McCann, March 2008. Available online: www.universalmccann.com/Assets/; click "26903747 2413 - Wave 3 complete document AW 3_20080418124523.pdf," dated Friday, April 18, 2008. Access date: June 2, 2008.
2. "Web 2.0: The Global Impact," Universal McCann, December 2006. Available online: www.universalmccann.com/Assets/; click "Web 2.0 The Global Impact 2006_20080108085312.pdf," dated Tuesday, January 8, 2008. Access date: June 2, 2008.
3. "Social Commerce Report 2007," E-consultancy and Baazarvoice, August 2007. Available online by special order: www.e-consultancy.com/publications/social-commerce-report-2007/. Access date: June 2, 2008.
4. ChoiceStream, January 9, 2007. Available online: www.choicestream.com/pdf/cs_press_surveyresults010807.pdf. Access date: June 2, 2008.
5. comScore, SEMPO data, 2007. Figures available online: 80 percent: www.fundraisingsuccessmag.com/story/story.bsp?var=story&sid=80837; 85 percent and 91 percent: www.zeroonezero.com/services/search-engine-marketing.html. Access date: June 2, 2008.

Chapter Six

1. Outlaw consulting, 2007. Available online for subscribers only: www.outlawconsulting.com/.
2. "Driving Radical Change," Josep Isern and Caroline Pung, *McKinsey Quarterly*, 2007, Number 4.
3. "Champions of the World,"*Forbes*, April 16, 2007.
4. "World's Most Innovative Companies by Region,"*Business Week*/Boston Consulting Group, *Business Week*, April 17, 2008. Available online: www.businessweek.com/table/08/0415_in_geographic.htm?popupWidth=770&popupHeight=660. Access date: June 2, 2008.
5. "Why Can't LEGO Click?" Charles Fishman, *Fast Company*, no. 50, August 2001.

Chapter Seven

1. While a factor analysis provides statistical correlations between imagery variables and factor dimensions, it is important to note that interpretation is not absolute; different solutions can be derived from the same data.
2. "Business Media" section, Stuart Elliott, *New York Times*, October 9, 2006.

Chapter Eight

1. "How Many Lightbulbs Does It Take to Change the World? One. And You're Looking at It," Charles Fishman, *Fast Company,* no. 108, September 2006.
2. "HD Marketing 2010: Sharpening the Conversation: The Team and Tools You Need to Market in an Increasingly 'Digitally Savvy' World," Adrea Rasumussen, Carolyn Ude, and Deward Landry, Booz & Company, 2007.
3. "If Brands Are Built Over Years, Why Are They Managed Over Quarters?" Leonard Lodish and Carl Mela, *Harvard Business Review,* July-August 2007,
4. Speech to the McGraw-Hill Companies, Anne Mulcahy, 2006.
5. Mulcahy, 2006.
6. "The Accidental CEO," Betsy Morris, *Fortune,* June 23, 2006.
7. "Leading Xerox Through the Perfect Storm," Anne Mulcahy, *Harvard Business Review,* January 26, 2005.
8. "Back from the Brink," William Bulkeley, *Wall Street Journal,* April 24, 2006.
9. Mulcahy, 2006.
10. "Xerox Overhauls Brand Image," Beth Snyder Bulik, *B to B,* January 7, 2008.
11. Bulik, 2008.

Chapter Nine

1. "Driving the Marketing Agenda: CEOs and CMOs Share the Same Vision—but How Do They Make It a Reality?" Rick Routhier, SpencerStuart, 2006. Available online: www.spencerstuart.co.uk/practices/consumer/publications/1072/. Access date: June 2, 2008.
2. For a variety of views of Mumbai Tiffin Box Suppliers operations, see www.mydabbawala.com/general/presentation.htm. Access date: April 11, 2008.

Chapter Ten

1. "More Consumers Are Watching TV Broadcasts Online," *Wireless News,* Coventry, October 21, 2007.
2. "Anytime Is Primetime Online for TV Shows," Solutions Research Group, February 5, 2008.
3. "Lessons from the Tarmac," Chuck Salter, *Fast Company,* no. 115, May 2007.

4. *Executive ESP*, Douglas Dean, John Mihalasky, L. Schroeder, and S. Ostander (Englewood N.J.: Prentice-Hall, 1974). Concept cited in "Deploying Your Intuition to Find Your Ideal Career," Katherine Hansen, n.d. Available online: www.quintcareers.com/using_ intuition_ideal_career.html. Access date: June 2, 2008.

5. "The UNIQLO Business," Annual Report, Fast Retailing, 2006. Available online: www.fastretailing.com/eng/ir/library/pdf/ annual2006_05.pdf. Access date: June 2, 2008.

Acknowledgments

We want to cite many dedicated Young & Rubicam and WPP Group partners for their ideas and insights. In London: Rich Brown, Richard Exon, Emily James, Ben Kay, Matt Steward, and Simon Sylvester. In Madrid: Rafael Esteve. In Mumbai: Mash Chauhan, Surya Prabhala, Sugata Rao, Kalpana Singh, and Nisha Singhania. In New York: Rachel Arnett, Julie Bazinet, Jessica Brown, Mitch Caplan, Rhonda Chahine, Jeff Cheal, Amanda Chin, Zoe Church, Jeremy Diamond, Aviva Ebstein, Stephen Fleming, Belle Frank, Jason Gaikowski, Leah Gritton, JaeHee Jung, Adam Kellogg, Sean King, Peter Law-Gisiko, Christy Liu, Michael Lundgren, Scott Lux, Hugh McGilligan, Maria McHugh, Daniel Morel, Cezary Pietrzak, Maureen Pine, Anne Rivers, Hayes Roth, Jim Scheele, Ric Scott, Ernie Simon, and Brian Truss. In Singapore: Ambar Brahmachary, and Tanuj Philip. In Tokyo: Sean Corcoran and Hironaga Yai.

We especially want to thank Emma Hrustic and Michael Sussman, our principal researchers and constant collaborators at every turn. Their input has been invaluable in shaping our findings. We thank Graham Hall for his ideas and optimism. And we greatly appreciate the case writing research and help of Niketa Gupte, Amber Mason, and Anuja Palkar.

We are also in great debt to the consultation of Peter Georgescu, chairman emeritus of Young & Rubicam, Robert Jacobson, professor of marketing, University of Washington Business School, Kevin Keller, EB Osborn Professor of Marketing, Tuck School of Business, Dartmouth College, and Natalie Mizik, associate professor of marketing, Columbia Business School.

We also want to thank our editor, Rick Benzel, and the editorial staff at Jossey-Bass, Rebecca Browning and Byron Schneider, and our production editor, Mary Garrett. And we are enormously grateful for the marketing leadership of Lee Aldridge, Mark Fortier, and Mindy Romero. We also want to thank James Levine and Elizabeth Fisher at Levine/Greenberg for their generous advice and support.

Finally, we want to express our gratitude to CEOs Peter Stringham and Hamish McLennan, who lead our group companies and share our love of brands and creativity.

THE AUTHORS

John Gerzema is Chief Insights Officer for Young & Rubicam Group. One of the earliest founders of account planning in American advertising agencies, John has designed brand strategies for clients for almost twenty-five years, guiding campaigns to international strategic and creative recognition that resulted in The One Show Best of Show award, numerous EFFIE's and several gold lions from The Cannes Advertising Festival. Prior to joining Y&R, Gerzema oversaw the international network for Fallon, and founded offices in Tokyo, Singapore, Hong Kong, and Sâo Paulo. He holds a master's degree in integrated marketing from the Medill School of Journalism at Northwestern University and a B.S. in marketing from The Ohio State University.

Ed Lebar is CEO of BrandAsset® Consulting Group. Ed manages BrandAsset® Consulting around the world. He has helped grow BrandAsset® Valuator into the largest brand model and database in the world, which now includes input from over 500,000 customers on 38,000 brands across 48 countries through 250 studies.

Before his career in marketing and advertising, Lebar was a professor of economics at CCNY and Finch College. He holds advanced degrees in economics from NYU and the University of Denver, and a B.A. from Syracuse University.

ABOUT YOUNG & RUBICAM GROUP

Young & Rubicam Group is a global network of preeminent companies specializing in advertising, public relations, public affairs, brand identity and design, consulting, direct and database marketing, digital and interactive marketing, multicultural marketing, and health care communications. YRG provides marketing communications solutions to more than 750 clients worldwide.

Each of its companies is a leader in its field. They include Y&R, Wunderman, Landor, Burson-Marsteller, Penn Schoen & Berland Associates, VML, Sudler & Hennessey, The Bravo Group, Cohn & Wolfe, Robinson, Lerer & Montgomery, RTC Relationship Marketing, Sicola Martin, Kang & Lee, The Banner Corporation, Brand-Asset Consulting, Blast Radius, BrandBuzz, and ZAAZ.

Young & Rubicam Group has more than 16,000 employees in over 550 offices in 90 countries around the world. Young & Rubicam Group is part of WPP.

INDEX